GAME PROGRAMMING GOLDEN RULES

MARTIN BROWNLOW

CHARLES RIVER MEDIA, INC.
Hingham, Massachusetts

Publisher: Jenifer Niles
Production: Publishers' Design and Production Services, Inc.
Cover Design: The Printed Image

CHARLES RIVER MEDIA, INC.
10 Downer Avenue
Hingham, Massachusetts 02043
781-740-0400
781-740-8816 (FAX)
info@charlesriver.com
www.charlesriver.com

This book is printed on acid-free paper.

Martin Brownlow. *Game Programming Golden Rules.*
ISBN: 1-58450-306-8

Library of Congress Cataloging-in-Publication Data
Brownlow, Martin.
Game programming golden rules / Martin Brownlow.
p. cm.
ISBN 1-58450-306-8 (pbk. with cd-rom : alk. paper) — ISBN 1-58450-306-8
1. Computer games—Programming. I. Title.
QA76.76.C672B76 2004
794.8'1711—dc22
2003028309
Printed in the United States of America
04 7 6 5 4 3 2 First Edition

CHARLES RIVER MEDIA titles are available for site license or bulk purchase by institutions, user groups, corporations, etc. For additional information, please contact the Special Sales Department at 781-740-0400.

Requests for replacement of a defective CD-ROM must be accompanied by the original disc, your mailing address, telephone number, date of purchase and purchase price. Please state the nature of the problem, and send the information to CHARLES RIVER MEDIA, INC., 10 Downer Avenue, Hingham, Massachusetts 02043. CRM's sole obligation to the purchaser is to replace the disc, based on defective materials or faulty workmanship, but not on the operation or functionality of the product.

For my wife Andie, who makes every day worth living.

Contents

Introduction

Writing computer games is hard. As game programmers, we are perpetually pushing the boundaries, and not just of the capabilities of the machines for which we are writing. Oftentimes, we also push the design limits of the compilers and linkers, stressing their architectures to the breaking point and beyond. Games today are huge affairs involving many different people. Whereas in the early days of computer games, a game could be completely created by a single person (including all art, sound, and programming), in modern times, it is not unusual to have 10 programmers on a single project. It is now becoming more common for programmers and artists to have specialties, such as sound programmer or background artist, and to be lost if asked to perform duties outside of these areas. Even with 10 programmers on a project, however, there is more than enough work to go around.

This book presents a series of nine Golden Rules—one for each chapter—that help to define a methodology for creating a modern game. Many of the rules involve empowering the designers and artists to put their own content directly into the game, bypassing the need for a programmer's involvement beyond the initial setup. This frees up the programmers' time to concentrate on creating the systems that make the game, rather than the uses these systems are put to. The order in which the rules are presented was carefully chosen so that each rule presents a topic that is then put to use in later rules.

The first rule, "Trust the Compiler... But Not Too Much," describes some of the features of C++ in detail. It shows how and when these features can be misused, and how it affects the code when this happens. In this way, it attempts to overcome some of the animosity and mistrust that many programmers hold toward C++.

The second rule, "Divide & Conquer," covers orders of complexity. Choosing an algorithm with a poor order of complexity can adversely affect your game in many ways, including nonlinear slowdowns as the number of objects in the game rises. Topics covered in this chapter include the binary search, binary trees, red-black trees, and binary space partitioning (BSP) trees.

The third rule, "Trust Your First Impressions," introduces the concept of hashing. Proper use of hashes can speed up comparison checks considerably. They can also be used to enable all of a game's data to be stored and indexed by arbitrary-length strings, increasing the user friendliness of the game's assets without complicating the code. This chapter also describes three structures that can be used to efficiently store and retrieve data by an associated hash: the hash list, hash table, and hash tree. These structures are used and referenced throughout the remainder of the book.

In rule four, "A Script Is Worth a Thousand Lines of Code," we take a close look at how to efficiently implement a scripting language for a game. This is the first chapter that truly allows us to offload some of the programmer's work onto the level designers, allowing them to perform their duties to the best of their abilities without involving a programmer. This rule also defines a parser that is used in later chapters to load and interpret data files.

Rule five, "Always Use the Right Tool for the Job," describes the data pipeline for a game in detail and presents an extendable program that can be used as a build tool. This program allows minimal data rebuilds—only files that have changed are rebuilt—and forms the basis for the data processing routines found in rule six. This rule also shows how to assemble the compiled data files into an efficient format for fast loading, and how to use compression to reduce disk space and further decrease the loading times for our data.

The companion to rule five is rule six, "Don't Use a Square Peg for a Round Hole." This rule shows how to process three common data types into the best format for the target platform: textures, fonts, and meshes. Three different plug-in DLLs are created for the build tool developed in rule five, one for each of these data types. Topics covered in this chapter are texture format conversion, using D3DX, creating a font texture from a TrueType font, vertex compression, and efficient triangle strip generation.

Rule seven, "Exploit Your Data," shows how to use finite state machines to reduce the complexity of the code while allowing the designers full control over things like game flow and the animation and behavior of the game's characters. This chapter introduces a scripting language that can be used to explicitly define a finite state machine for a variety of uses. The culmination of this chapter is the presentation of a simple fighting game that is controlled almost completely by a finite state machine defined in script.

The eighth rule, "Save Early, Save Often," covers a topic often ignored by programmers until it is too late: saving game state. This chapter presents an almost completely automated method for safely saving the current state of the game. This method is simple and robust, and will even notify the programmer when a structure has changed and needs its save definition updated.

Finally, rule nine, "Measure Twice, Cut Once," explains how to focus optimization efforts to the areas of the game that really need optimization. This chapter shows how to determine where the code needs optimization, and helps decide what types of optimizations are needed, based on the measured result. The chapter ends by showing how the measured improvements to the speed of the game based on the finished optimizations might differ from expectations.

1 Embracing C++

In This Chapter

- Rule #1: "Trust the Compiler . . . But Not Too Much"
- On Data Types
- Access Modifiers
- Storage Modifiers
- Virtual Functions
- The `new` Operator
- The Preprocessor

Modern computer games are huge affairs, involving dozens of people. It wasn't always like this. Back in the days when computers were relatively new, a single person could do all the art and programming that was required to produce a blockbuster game. Games back then were written in machine code in order to squeeze every last cycle of performance out of the machine.

In recent years, though, computers have gotten faster, and project sizes have ballooned, and it is now not uncommon to have half a dozen or a dozen programmers on a single project. It would be suicide to attempt to write a game in machine code now, and indeed nowadays, games are written in a high-level language like C++. However, many programmers have attitudes that are stuck back in the early days; although they write in C++, they refuse to take advantage of some of the modern language features that would make their jobs that much easier. More often than not, they cite the poor translation efforts of early compilers and the hidden cost of these features as justification for this.

Then there are the progressive programmers who use every language feature they can find, often without regard for the performance penalties associated with them. These are the programmers who load their code up with intertwining and serpentine template definitions, which only they can understand.

RULE #1: "TRUST THE COMPILER . . . BUT NOT TOO MUCH"

The first golden rule is all about using all of the available features of the high-level language, but only where their use will aid our productivity[1]. To do this effectively, we need to understand what the compiler must do to achieve the functionality of each of the features. We will also see that some of the features of C++ require the compiler to do some horrible things if used incorrectly; these features should be avoided or used with caution.

ON DATA TYPES

There are five predefined data types in the C language: `char`, `int`, `float`, `double`, and `void`. Additionally, there are four type modifiers that modify the size and behavior of these predefined types: `signed`, `unsigned`, `short`, and `long`.

Unfortunately, the sizes of the predefined data types are not defined in terms of bits or bytes; they are defined in terms of the minimum range of values that each type must hold. The exception to this rule is the `char` type—it always occupies 1 byte. Table 1.1 shows a list of types and the minimum range of values that they must hold. The last column in this table is the minimum number of bits required to give the proper range for each type.

TABLE 1.1 Standard C Data Types and Their Minimum Ranges

Data Type	*Minimum Range*	*Minimum Size in Bits*
`Char`	-128 to 127	8
`Unsigned char`	0 to 255	8
`Short int`	-32768 to 32767	16
`Unsigned short int`	0 to 65535	16
`Int`	-32768 to 32767	16
`Unsigned int`	0 to 65535	16
`Long int`	$\pm(2^{31} - 1)$	32
`Unsigned long int`	0 to $(2^{32} - 1)$	32
`Float`	6 digits of precision	32
`Double`	10 digits of precision	64
`Void`	cannot hold a value	Undefined

This leads us to an interesting problem: a program compiled for one platform, where an `int` contains 32 bits, might exhibit severe bugs when compiled for another machine, where an `int` only contains 16 bits. We could get around this by always defining our variables based on the range of values needed. However, even when a variable turns out to be larger than expected, this could still be a source of bugs, especially when using unsigned data types. Need convincing? Consider an unsigned, 16-bit integer holding a value of 0, and then subtract 1 from it; what is the result? Now try it for an unsigned, 32-bit integer.

Another problem when writing games is that of the data cache; we want our data to be as small as possible, but we also ideally want it to fall neatly onto the underlying cache-lines. To achieve this with any degree of reliability, we need exact control over the size of individual data elements. The first thing we should do, then, is define ourselves a new set of data types whose sizes are predictable. The exact definition of these types could, and should, vary depending on the combination of compiler and target machine, in order to maintain their correct sizes.

However, which types should we define? At the very least, we need to be able to define 8-, 16-, and 32-bit signed and unsigned integers. It would also behoove us to define a type for unicode characters, since more likely than not, we will be making internationally localized versions of our game.

ON THE CD

For a combination of a 32-bit PC target machine and the Microsoft® Visual C++® compiler, the following code should adequately define our set of types. This code is also included on the companion CD-ROM, in the file common\types.hpp. These data type definitions are used throughout all the example code, both in the book and on the companion CD-ROM.

```
typedef signed char    s8;
typedef unsigned char  u8;
typedef signed short   s16;
typedef unsigned short u16;
typedef signed int     s32;
typedef unsigned int   u32;
typedef float          f32;
typedef double         f64;
```

Pointers

Like the size of each of the default types, the size of a pointer also changes based on the target machine. Usually, a pointer takes the minimum amount of space required to uniquely define an address on the target platform. For example, on a 32-bit PC, pointers are usually 32 bits in length. Over the past few years, it has been acceptable to presume that the size of a pointer would be 4 bytes, but with the advent of the 64-bit machines, this is no longer a safe assumption.

Unlike with the default variable types, however, knowing the size of a pointer is important for a reason other than just structure alignment. In C and C++, all additions to, and subtractions from, pointers are performed in multiples of the size of the thing being pointed to (hereafter called an *element*). This multiplication is performed implicitly, so adding 1 to a pointer really increments the pointer by the size of one element, and adding 2 increments it by the size of two elements. This is directly analogous to the `[]` operator, which de-references a pointer in multiples of the element size.

This feature of C means that we have to jump through a few hoops in order to increment a pointer by an amount that is not a multiple of the element size. In practice, this means that we must cast the pointer to a different data type before performing the arithmetic, and then back again afterwards. The ideal destination data type of this cast would be one in which the required arithmetic could be performed without modification.

An example of when this would be useful is when parsing through a chunk-based file that has been loaded into memory. Each chunk header structure contains the chunk type and the number of bytes in the chunk, followed by the chunk data. The next chunk in the file immediately follows the chunk data for the previous chunk. To move between chunks, then, we need to be able to increment a pointer to a chunk by a given number of bytes.

The first method that springs to mind is to cast the pointer to an integer, where all arithmetic works as expected. However, since the size of a pointer can change across machines, this is not the best way to do what we want—we would have to change the type of integer that we cast to when compiling the code for different pointer sizes. For a machine with 32-bit pointers, we would cast to our new u32 type, but for a machine with 64-bit pointers, we would have to cast to an as-yet-undefined u64 type.

Luckily, there are other types that we can cast to where all arithmetic works as expected. If all pointer arithmetic is implicitly multiplied by the size of the pointed-to element, then we just have to choose a pointer type where the pointed-to element has a size of 1 byte. There are at least two such pointer types: u8* and s8*. By casting to another pointer type, we ensure that no data is lost, since both pointers are guaranteed to be the same size.

ON THE CD

Using templates, we can define a simple function to increment any type of pointer, as shown in the following code. This code is also included on the companion CD-ROM, in the file common\types.hpp.

```
template<class X>
inline X *IncPointer( X *ptr, s32 offset )
{
    return (X*)(((u8*)ptr)+offset);
}
```

ACCESS MODIFIERS

When optimizing a piece of code, the compiler has a large number of options. However, for the compiler to be free to make as many of the optimizations that it can, it needs to make certain assumptions. A simple example of this is a while loop in which the loop variable is never changed. This is shown in the following code:

```
void somefn()
{
    u32     i = 1;
    while( i!=0 )
    {
        // some code that does not change the value of i
    }
```

```
        printf("hello\n");
    }
```

A smart compiler would see that the value of the loop variable is never changed, and that therefore the loop is infinite. This would cause it to discard both the loop variable check (since it always succeeds) and any code after the loop (since it is now unreachable). However, what happens if the loop variable is changed outside of the compiler's knowledge? Many things could cause this to happen. One example is if the program that this code resides in is multithreaded; a second thread could modify the contents of the loop variable, causing the loop to end. Another possible example occurs if the variable is a reference to a hardware port, such as an internal clock. Any change in the hardware's state could be reflected in the value of this variable, but the optimized code would never check the value of it for changes.

So, why does the compiler optimize the code in this way? To answer this, we must look at the alternative situation, in which the compiler assumes that the value of every variable can be changed without its knowledge at any time. In this case, every time a variable is accessed in the source code, it must explicitly be accessed in the compiled code. Consider the following code:

```
class MONSTER
{
public:
    MONSTER *pTarget;
    s32      hitPoints;
    s32      damagePerHit;
    u32      numKills;
};

void Attack( MONSTER *attacker )
{
    // does the attacker have a valid target?
    if( attacker->pTarget==0 ||
        attacker->pTarget->hitPoints==0 )
        return;
```

```
        attacker->pTarget->hitPoints -= attacker->damagePerHit;
        if( attacker->pTarget->hitPoints <= 0 )
        {
            // attacker->pTarget is now dead
            attacker->pTarget->hitPoints = 0;
            attacker->numKills++;
        }
    }
```

Now, we would expect a well-behaved compiler to just read the value of `attacker->pTarget` once and use the result to speed up the subsequent accesses of it. However, when the compiler must assume that any variable can change without its knowledge it cannot do this, since the value of this variable might change between its initial reading and the subsequent uses of it. This has the effect of producing slow, bloated code, especially when there are multiple uses of large chains of indirection.

The `volatile` Modifier

In the vast majority of cases, though, variables do not change outside of the compiler's control. It makes sense, then, to have the programmer explicitly mark the cases where it can happen, and have the compiler treat these cases specially. This is done through the `volatile` access modifier keyword. By marking a variable as `volatile`, what we are really doing is telling the compiler that the value of this variable is liable to change due to external factors beyond its control. This forces the compiler to explicitly read the contents of the variable every time it is accessed. Care should be taken when using the `volatile` keyword, as it can severely limit the compiler's ability to produce optimized code.

The `const` Modifier

Unlike the `volatile` modifier, which tells the compiler what it cannot do, the `const` modifier tells the compiler what the *program* cannot do. By declaring a variable `const`, we are telling the compiler that our program cannot change the value of the variable. The compiler will enforce this by flagging any attempt to *directly* change the value of the variable as a compile-time error. Note that this does not necessarily stop the value of the variable from changing: for example, consider the following code:

```
void somefn()
{
    u8          myString[] = "This is a test string";
    const u8    *pString = myString;

    myString[0] = 't';
    pString[0]  = 't';
}
```

This code declares an array of ASCII characters on the stack, and creates a pointer to that array, whose destination is `const`. This means that the value of the pointer itself can be changed, but the value of anything it points to cannot. The next two lines are the important ones; in the first line, we explicitly change the first element of the array. This line will compile without error, as the array itself was never declared as `const`. The second of these lines, however, will produce an error; by de-referencing the pointer like this, we are attempting to change a value that has been declared constant.

The best way to think of the `const` modifier is as a contract between the programmer who initially created the code and any subsequent programmers who must use this code. Through the use of `const`, the original programmer promises that certain things will not be changed. This allows subsequent programmers to do things that they otherwise would not strictly be able to do. For example, suppose we had an implementation of a function that outputs a character string to the screen. Now, common sense tells us that this function will not modify the input string in any way. However, this behavior is not guaranteed without adding a `const` modifier to the function's input string parameter. Without this modifier, any client code could not assume that the contents of the string were unchanged after the function call.

Adding `const` to a variable definition changes the type of the variable; a variable declared as a `u32*` is a distinctly different type from one that has been declared as a `u32 const *`. The conversion of a variable *to* a `const` type (by adding one or more `const` modifiers) is performed automatically and invisibly by the compiler. However, once a `const` modifier has been added to a data type, the compiler cannot remove it. The only way to remove this modifier is through an explicit typecast operator, which can be dangerous and so should be avoided.

This simple rule has a profound effect on the use of `const`, an effect that deters many programmers from using it properly. Since this modifier cannot be implicitly removed, changing a variable to a constant type will change the required function prototype for any function to which it is passed as a parameter. This has a cascading effect down the stack, requiring a chain of function prototype changes. For this reason, it is best to start aggressively using `const` as soon as possible in the development cycle of a project.

`const` Classes

It is also possible to declare a structure or a class as `const`. When this occurs, all of the member variables of the class or structure automatically inherit the `const` modifier. This requires special attention, since calling any member function of the class instance would pass an implicit `this` parameter, which is *not* constant, breaking the rule that `const`-ness cannot be taken away by the compiler. For this reason, when a class instance is declared `const`, only member functions that are forced to obey that `const`-ness can be invoked for the instance. But how does the compiler know which member functions uphold the `const`-ness of the instance? We tell it; that's how.

The addition of a `const` modifier at the end of a member function declaration lets the compiler know that any class instance it is invoked on will remain unchanged. This has the effect of making the function's implicit `this` parameter `const`. Since all member variables accessed from within a member function are implicitly de-referenced through the `this` pointer, they too receive this `const`-ness. The compiler is then forced to uphold the rule that none of the member variables can be modified, maintaining the constant property of the instance.

The `mutable` Modifier

In some cases, our code will require the ability to change a member variable of a class instance that has been declared constant. This is useful for things like tracking performance data or API usage statistics; changing the values of these member variables in no way changes the behavior of the class. If these values are hidden or protected from outside scrutiny (for example, due to inheritance), then we can change them without violating the `const` contract—as far as the calling code is concerned, the class instance has not changed in the slightest.

In cases like this, we can use the `mutable` modifier. This modifier allows the value of the variable to be changed, even though it might have inherited a `const` modifier. Care should be taken when using this modifier not to break the `const` contract, because doing so might introduce subtle bugs in any client code, and the cause of these bugs might not be immediately apparent.

Modifier Placement

One of the most often misunderstood concepts when dealing with access modifiers is the correct placement of the modifier. What many programmers fail to realize is that, in the case of pointers, there are many different things that the modifier can apply to. For example, consider a simple pointer, say a `u8*`. When we declare this pointer `const`, what we are usually attempting to tell the compiler is that the value of anything pointed to by this pointer cannot change. However, this pointer has another property that can receive an access modifier: the value of the pointer itself. This only becomes more complex as additional levels of indirection are added; a pointer to a pointer (`u8**`) has three things that can be declared `const`.

We obviously need some rules that allow us to unambiguously specify to the compiler exactly which properties a modifier applies to. This is done through the placement of the modifier. By changing where in the variable declaration the modifier appears, we can change which property of the variable the modifier applies to. The rules for this are simple: the modifier applies to whatever is directly to the left of it. The following code should shed some light on this:

```
u8 *                ptr1;
u8 const *          ptr2;
u8 * const          ptr3;
u8 const * const ptr4;
```

Each line of the preceding code declares a pointer to an unsigned, 8-bit value. However, the access modifiers for each of these variables give each of these variables different properties. The first line declares `ptr1`, our control pointer. Since there are no access modifiers on this variable, both the value of the pointer and the value of anything it points to can be changed without restriction.

The second line declares `ptr2`, which has a `const` modifier applied to it. Following our rule, to find out what the modifier applies to we must look at the type immediately to the left of the modifier. For this declaration, the type immediately to the left of the modifier is `u8`, meaning that this element of the pointer receives the modifier. This translates into the value of anything pointed to by this variable being constant.

Next up is `ptr3`, which has its access modifier placed differently. This time, the type to the left of the `const` modifier is `u8*`, meaning that the value of the pointer itself cannot be changed. Finally, the declaration of `ptr4` declares two `const` modifiers. The first of these applies to the type `u8` and the second applies to the type `u8*`. This means that neither the value of the pointer nor the value of what is pointed to can be changed.

The only exception to this rule of modifier placement occurs when there is no type to the left of the modifier. In this case, the modifier applies to the type immediately to its right. This allows the commonly used form (`const u8 *`) to operate as expected.

Combining Access Modifiers

Now that we know how to unambiguously apply a modifier to a specific property of a variable, we can look at more complex examples that use multiple modifiers in a single definition. Although it seems contrary to common sense, the most common use of multiple access modifiers is when a variable is both `const` and `volatile`. In this situation, we are obligated to not change the value of the variable, but we are also told that the value of the variable might be changed outside of our control.

One of the most common examples of this is that of a hardware status port; this usually takes the form of an address in memory that is read-only. A good example of this is a hardware clock or cycle counter. We are allowed to read the value of the clock from this address, but we are prevented from writing to it. Additionally, the value stored at the clock's address is liable to change beyond our control.

When defining a variable that points to the hardware clock, we must take several things into account. The first is that the location of the hardware clock in memory will never change—this implies that our pointer's value must be constant. Next, we are not allowed to write to the hardware clock—the thing pointed to must be constant. Finally, the clock's value will change unpredictably (from the compiler's point of view)—the thing pointed to must be `volatile`. Using these considerations, we end up with the following definition for a variable that points to a 32-bit integer hardware clock at address 0x1234:

```
u32 const volatile * const pHWClock = 0x1234;
```

STORAGE MODIFIERS

In addition to access modifiers, C also has modifiers that affect how a variable is stored. These aptly named storage modifiers allow us to change the behavior of the compiler to better suit our needs for the affected variables.

The `static` Modifier

The first modifier we will look at is accessed through the `static` keyword. This modifier tells the compiler that there should only be a single instance of this variable. Use of the `static` modifier causes the compiler to allocate memory for the affected variable at the global scope, while keeping the variable visible at its defined scope only. Any accesses to this variable then go to the same place, and any values placed in the variable persist until changed, even across function calls. For example, the following function will only ever run the bulk of its body once:

```
u32 GetLanguage()
{
    static u32 languageID = 0;
```

```
    if( languageID==0 )
    {
        // find the correct language ID
        // this section may take some time, and so
        // should only be run once

        assert(languageID!=0);
    }
    return languageID;
}
```

Notice that although the variable `languageID` is defined at the local function scope, it is declared as static, making its value persistent. Declaring it at the local scope rather than the global scope effectively hides this variable so that no code outside of this function can see it or modify it.

The `static` modifier can also be used on a class's member variables and functions. The meaning of the modifier is unchanged—there will only ever be a single instance of each static variable created, regardless of how many instances of the class are created—however, using the modifier in this fashion has an important implication. Since there is only a single instance of each static variable per class, we no longer need a class instance to access them (provided they are declared public). Storage space for nonstatic member variables is reserved in the memory used by the instance, but storage for static member variables must be explicitly reserved. This is as simple as redeclaring the variable—including its complete scope (usually simply `classname::`)—outside of the class definition; we can also set its initial value at this point. An example of this is given at the end of this section.

Declaring a class member function static tells the compiler that there should only ever be a single instance of the member function. But what does this mean in plain English? Each class member function, when invoked, has an implicit `this` pointer that is used to de-reference all of the class members accessed in the function body. This effectively makes the behavior of each function different for each class instance that invokes it; the variables accessed change to be those local to the owning instance. This can be said to be creating a new instance of the member function for each instance of the class. By implication, then, a static member function, which is defined as having only a single instance, cannot access any instance-specific variables (since doing so would effectively create another instance of the function). In practice, the compiler enforces this by omitting the `this` pointer from the function implementation and any invocations of it, rendering any instance-specific variables inaccessible. Again, as with member variables, given the correct access privileges, no class instance is needed to access a static member function.

The following code shows a simple example of a class containing both static member functions and member variables:

```
class TestClass
{
public:
    static void staticFn();
    void        localFn();

protected:
    static u32  staticVar;
    u32         localVar;
};

void TestClass::staticFn()
{
    // the static function can access the static variable
    staticVar = 0;

    // but cannot access a local one (there is no this pointer)
    localVar = 0;   // this will cause a compile error
}
void TestClass::localFn()
{
    // the non-static function can access both static
    // and local variables
    staticVar = 0;
    localVar = 0;
}
```

```
// we must explicitly supply storage space for
// the static member variables
u32 TestClass::staticVar = 0;

void main()
{
    TestClass inst;

    // call the non-static member function - instance needed
    inst.localFn();

    // call the static member function - no instance needed
    TestClass::staticFn();
}
```

The `register` Modifier

When writing optimal code, it is often desirable to keep an intermediate value for a calculation in a hardware register, allowing fast access to it without touching memory. However, in C, all variables are stored in memory, and any accesses to them implicitly read from or write to this memory. The register modifier allows us to give a hint to the compiler that a variable should be kept in a hardware register where possible. However, it is only a hint, and the compiler often disregards this hint, especially when the code is not structured correctly. This happens more readily on platforms with limited register space, such as the x86. So, how do we structure our code in such a way that the compiler will take notice of our hints?

The most effective way to help the compiler out in this situation is by limiting the amount of code and number of variables that it has to consider at one time. This is done through manipulation of the compiler's scope: a variable is more likely to be kept in a register if its scope (the number of instructions it exists over) is limited. When a variable is declared, its scope encompasses the current code block and any code blocks contained within it, where a code block is defined as a section of code delimited by { and }. A code block can be declared at any point in the code, not just after a `for`, `if`, or `while` instruction. It is important to note, however, that whenever a code block is exited, any variables declared within it are destroyed and hence lose their value. Similarly, whenever a code block is entered, any variables declared within it are constructed, which can result in their constructors being called. Bearing all this in mind, it is possible to effectively limit the scope of a variable, making it more likely to be kept in a register.

A Class Is a Struct Is a Class

One of the common misconceptions among junior programmers is that a class is somehow superior to a struct. This causes them to always use structs for certain kinds of data, and classes for other types, and to get confused when another programmer makes the opposite choice. Here are some of the common misconceptions:

- A class can contain functions, but a struct cannot.
- A class can have private, protected, and public data members, but all struct data is public.
- A class can take advantage of inheritance, but a struct cannot.
- A class has some inherent invisible overheads that make it hard to represent binary data.
- A class must be generated using the `new` operator, but a struct can be `malloc`'d.

Obviously, all of these are false, or they would not be misconceptions. In fact, the differences between a class and a struct are so slight as to be almost negligible. The whole reason why these misconceptions are so widespread is because in C, a structure could not contain anything other than data; many programmers believe that this is still true in C++. Let's take a closer look at each of the preceding misconceptions.

A class can contain functions, but a struct cannot. This is both untrue and unfounded. Any struct can contain both member variables and member functions. Member functions inside a struct are defined in exactly the same way as they are for a class.

A class can have private, protected, and public data members, but all struct data is public. Although this is untrue, it does highlight an important difference between the two. When defining both a class and a struct, we can change the access rights for any member variables or functions by using one of the access modifiers (private, protected, or public). However, what are the access rights for a member declared before any access modifiers? In a class, the member would be automatically declared as private, but in a struct the member would be public. This is needed in order to maintain backward compatibility with C; if all the data members in a struct were automatically private, many C programs would fail to compile with a C++ compiler.

A class can take advantage of inheritance, but a struct cannot. Again, this is simply untrue. In fact, a class can be derived from a struct, or a struct from a class, without penalty.

A class has some inherent invisible overheads that make it hard to represent binary data. This misconception stems from the fact that some C++ features, notably virtual functions, require a virtual function table, or *vtable*[2], to be attached to every class instance. In most compilers, this vtable is prepended to the class, offsetting every data member by the size of a pointer (usually 4 bytes). However, if none of the offending features is used, no additional data will be attached to a given instance, and the binary representation of the class will be exactly as predicted. Incidentally, these same features, if used in a struct, will also cause a vtable to be added to its binary representation, with exactly the same results.

A class must be generated using the `new` operator, but a struct can be `malloc`'d. To understand how this misconception came to be, we must examine the differences between the `new` operator and the `malloc` function. The first thing that the `new` operator does is allocate an area of memory of the correct size. It then proceeds to fill out the vtable pointer (if needed) and call the constructor (if supplied) for each class that is being created, starting with the deepest (a class that is instanced within another class is defined as being deep in this context). We can see from this that in the case where the class being created and all its instanced member variables have both no vtable and no constructor (or a constructor that we do not want to call), the new operator is really not needed. Again, any struct that has either a constructor or a vtable should also be created with the `new` operator.

As you can see, the only appreciable difference between a class and a struct is that a class definition begins with private access rights by default, whereas a struct definition begins with public. Although the two constructs are almost the same, we must still use the correct type when using a forward reference to them: if we declare a forward reference to a named struct, when the compiler finally encounters the definition it must be a `struct`. Similarly, a class must be forward referenced as a `class`. For example, the following code will produce a compiler error, since `myStruct` is declared in the function prototype to be a `struct`, but is later defined as a `class`:

```
void someFn( struct myStruct *ptr )
{
}

class myStruct
{
public:
    myStruct()    {    }
};
```

VIRTUAL FUNCTIONS

One of the most useful features of C++ is inheritance, which is made possible for the most part by the use of virtual functions. When we declare a function as virtual, we are telling the compiler that the address for this function will be supplied at runtime. This forces the compiler to make every invocation of a virtual function read the address of the function from memory prior to jumping to it. Obviously, this adds some extra overhead to a function call, since the read from memory is not free. Additionally, we might encounter some excessive processor stalls as we try to jump to an address contained in a register; many processors have a greater latency on a value in a register that is used as an address than if that value were used in a calculation. However, the compiler, through interleaving the address lookup with some of the preceding instructions, easily counters this latency.

Many game programmers who are opposed to C++ cite virtual functions as one of its disadvantages. They believe that since the mechanism for the address indirection is implicit, and hence invisible to the programmer, it is more prone to misuse or overuse. In some respects they are correct; as we will see later, overuse of virtual functions can severely impact performance. Having said that, however, if these same programmers were to write an equivalent C program, in many situations they would be forced to explicitly use pointers to functions to garner the same results. These function pointers would have to be explicitly initialized and then checked each time before they are used (although these checks could be debug-only code). Needless to say, this is error-prone and dangerous. It would be better to just use virtual functions and let the compiler sort out their automatic initialization.

Virtual functions are implemented by the compiler through the use of an implicit virtual function lookup table, called a *vtable*. There is a single, static instance of a vtable for each distinct class that employs virtual functions (if a class does not specify any virtual functions, yet is derived in some way from a class that employs virtual functions, then it too needs a vtable). If a class specifies the use of virtual functions, the compiler silently and invisibly adds a pointer to the correct vtable to the class definition. Although the exact location of this vtable varies by compiler, many compilers prepend the class definition with the pointer. No matter how many layers of inheritance a class employs, it can only ever have a single vtable pointer. For example, consider the following two classes:

```
class parentClass
{
public:
    parentClass();
    virtual ~parentClass();
    virtual void doNothing();
    virtual void doSomething();
};
```

```
class childClass : public parentClass
{
public:
    childClass();
    ~childClass();
    void doSomething();
    virtual void doSomethingElse();
};
```

The first of these two classes, `parentClass`, contains three virtual functions (actually two virtual functions and a virtual destructor). Because of this, the compiler creates a vtable for the class, and invisibly prepends the class definition with a member variable for a pointer to this vtable. The vtable for `parentClass` contains three function pointers, one for each virtual function, and looks something like this:

Table Element	***Value***
[0]	parentClass::~parentClass
[1]	parentClass::doNothing
[2]	parentClass::doSomething

The second class, `childClass`, is derived from `parentClass` and so inherits all of the virtual functions from it, obliging it to supply its own vtable. The functions in this vtable will be indexed in the same order as for the parent class, allowing pointers to classes of type `childClass` to be cast to type `parentClass` and still behave correctly. Additionally, `childClass` defines an extra virtual function, which will be appended to the vtable after all of the inherited virtual functions. The vtable for `childClass` is shown in the following table. Note that where `childClass` does not explicitly implement a virtual function, the function supplied by `parentClass` is used instead.

Table Element	***Value***
[0]	ChildClass::~childClass
[1]	ParentClass::doNothing
[2]	ChildClass::doSomething
[3]	ChildClass::doSomethingElse

The vtable pointer for a class instance is automatically initialized by the compiler before the constructor for the class is called. This can lead to problems if the class instance is created in such a way that the constructor is never called; for example, by typecasting a pointer to an arbitrary chunk of allocated memory. There are two situations in which the compiler will invoke the constructor for a class: when a variable of that class type is created (e.g., a local variable), and when the `new` operator is used to create a new instance of the class. The `new` operator is described in more detail later in this chapter.

Although knowledge of the inner workings of the vtable concept is not required for successful use of virtual functions, it is very beneficial, as it allows you to understand why certain things are bad or will not work. For example, it is perfectly safe for a class that uses no virtual functions to `memset` itself to zero using `memset(this,0,sizeof(*this))`. However, if a class contains any virtual functions, this operation will prevent the class instance from functioning correctly, since it will also zero out the pointer to the class's vtable. Any operations that require the vtable to be accessed (any virtual function invocation) will then cause an exception due to either reading from an invalid memory location or jumping to an arbitrary address.

Calling a Specific Implementation of a Virtual Function

Sometimes it is necessary to call a specific version of a function that has been declared as virtual. The most common occurrence of this is when a child class wants to extend the behavior of one of its parent class's functions, but still needs to retain the parent class's behavior. Although we could do this by copying the code from the parent class's function into the child class's implementation of it, this is error prone, since any future changes to the parent class's function will be missing from the child class. A better way, then, would be for the child class to be able to call its parent class's member function explicitly, avoiding a vtable lookup. This is accomplished by simply fully qualifying the function name in the function call. For example, consider the following implementation of the `childClass::doSomething` function for the previous example:

```
void childClass::doSomething()
{
```

```
        // do extended functionality here

        // now we invoke the parent class' functionality
        parentClass::doSomething();

        // do any final extended functionality here
    }
```

When a virtual function is fully qualified in this manner, the compiler does not need to use the vtable to find the correct function implementation; we have told it exactly which function to use. This can be done at any level, not just inside a child class's implementation. In the following code, we create an instance of type `childClass` and store it in a pointer to a `parentClass`; then, we proceed to invoke some member functions:

```
    {
        childClass    temp;
        parentClass   *pTemp = &temp;

        // this calls childClass::doSomething explicitly
        temp.doSomething();

    // this also calls childClass::doSomething, via the vtable
        pTemp->doSomething();

        // however, this calls parentClass::doSomething explicitly
        pTemp->parentClass::doSomething();
    }
```

The first function invocation occurs explicitly (not via a vtable lookup); the function is fully qualified due to the fact that the type of the variable it is invoked on is fully known. The second invocation happens via the vtable because the exact type of the instance it is called from cannot be known (it could be a `parentClass` or a `childClass` at this point). In the third case, although the exact type of the instance is not known, the function to be called is fully qualified and so no vtable lookup is required.

The Inheritance Trap

Calling member functions explicitly in this way has one major drawback: you have to know in advance which class's member function you want to call so that you can use the fully qualified function name. The problem with this is that we are then left with a section of code that exists outside of the class hierarchy, and is oblivious to changes in that hierarchy. For example, suppose in the previous example we change the class hierarchy by inserting another class between `parentClass` and `childClass`. This new class is to be derived from `parentClass`, and `childClass` is then derived from the new class. The problem now is that `childClass`'s implementation of `doSomething()` explicitly invokes `parentClass`'s implementation of `doSomething()`, even though `childClass` is now derived from the new class. This does not produce a compile error, since `childClass` is still ultimately derived from `parentClass`, but it is still not the behavior that we would like.

Unfortunately, C++ does not provide a standard mechanism for getting around this; there is no way to invoke a function of the parent class without knowing the parent class's name. This leads to code that is not flexible, since there might be many places throughout the code where the parent class's name is repeated in order to explicitly invoke one of its member functions. Having said that, there are ways around this problem.

Some C++ compilers, notably Microsoft's Visual C++, define a local type for each derived class that resolves to the typename of its immediate parent class. In MSVC++, this type is called `__super` (with two underscores). We can then use this type any time we want to explicitly specify that the immediate parent should be used, without knowing its name. For example, an implementation of `childClass::doSomething()` would now look like this:

```
void childClass::doSomething()
{
    // do extended functionality here

    // now we invoke the parent class's functionality
    __super::doSomething();

    // do any final extended functionality here
```

```
}
```

This code works as expected, calling the immediate parent class's member function, regardless of which class childClass is actually derived from. However, this code can only be compiled by compilers that support the __super type. A more general-case way would be for us to emulate this keyword by explicitly defining a local type for each class. The class name that this type resolves to would still have to be changed if the parent class was changed, but at least it only needs to be changed in one place. The following code defines such a type:

```
class childClass : public parentClass
{
private:
    typedef parentClass super;

};
```

This can be neatly encapsulated in a macro, where we could even use the __super keyword when supported. The following code defines such a macro:

```
#ifdef _MSC_VER
    #define SUPER(classname)    typedef __super super;
#else
    #define SUPER(classname)    typedef classname super;
#endif
```

As each newly derived class is assigned this local super type, it shadows the definition of super from the parent class. By using a local type in this way, it is possible to access member functions of my parent class's parent class (provided that it has one) without knowing any class names by chaining together super qualifiers. For example, a single super:: qualifier refers to my parent class, while super::super:: refers to my parent class's parent class, and so on. If we ever use more qualifiers than there are levels of inheritance (or there is a class for which super is not defined), a compiler error will be generated, since it will not be able to resolve super into the proper class name.

It is important to realize that the class name that `super` resolves to is not dependent on the actual class of the object, but on the *perceived* class of the object. For example, in the function `parentClass::doSomething()`, the `this` pointer will have a type of `parentClass*`, even if the actual instance is of type `childClass`.

Virtual Function Overuse

By far the biggest trap that you can fall into while using virtual functions is that of overuse. When creating a new class that will have other classes derived from it, it is tempting to just declare all of its member functions virtual; that way, we never need to worry about whether the function is virtual when we override it in a derived class. The problem with this is that the compiler loses all ability to optimize any of the member function calls made on this class. Ordinarily, most compilers are intelligent enough to automatically inline small, oft-repeated functions, but when all of an object's functions are virtual, it cannot do this because at compile time it cannot tell which version of a function should be used.

For example, consider a simple game where all objects are derived from a base `Object` class. Each object can be a good guy (player), a bad guy (enemy), neutral (NPC), or inert (tree). When we need to see which side an object belongs to, we call one of four query member functions off of the `Object` class:

```
bool Object::IsGoodGuy();
bool Object::IsBadGuy();
bool Object::IsNeutral();
bool Object::IsInert();
```

By declaring these functions virtual and overriding them on a class-by-class basis, we end up with simple, single-line implementations of them. The following code shows examples of these functions for appropriately named classes called `Player`, `Tree`, and `BadGuy`:

```
bool Player::IsGoodGuy()    {   return true;    }
bool Player::IsBadGuy()     {   return false;   }
bool Player::IsNeutral()    {   return false;   }
```

```
bool Player::IsInert()       {   return false;   }

bool Tree::IsGoodGuy()       {   return false;   }
bool Tree::IsBadGuy()        {   return false;   }
bool Tree::IsNeutral()       {   return false;   }
bool Tree::IsInert()         {   return true;    }

bool BadGuy::IsGoodGuy()     {   return false;   }
bool BadGuy::IsBadGuy()      {   return true;    }
bool BadGuy::IsNeutral()     {   return false;   }
bool BadGuy::IsInert()       {   return false;   }
```

This completely solves the problem: moreover, it is unambiguous, easy to read, and easy to expand as we add new classes. However, as a solution for a game, it's dead wrong. As we detailed earlier, the compiler will not be able to optimize these functions at all; every invocation of them will involve an unavoidable function lookup. A much better solution would be to declare a series of flags in the base object class and correctly set them in the constructor for each derived class. The query functions then no longer need to be virtual, and indeed become a simple flag test, which the compiler will very probably automatically inline for us. The following code shows an example of this:

```
class Object
{
    // definition of class Object here
protected:
    bool    mb_goodGuy : 1;
    bool    mb_badGuy  : 1;
    bool    mb_neutral : 1;
    bool    mb_inert   : 1;

public:
    bool    IsGoodGuy()    {   return mb_goodGuy;    }
    bool    IsBadGuy()     {   return mb_badGuy;     }
    bool    IsNeutral()    {   return mb_neutral;    }
```

```
    bool    IsInert()       {   return mb_inert;       }
};

// class Player is derived from class Object
Player::Player() : Object()
{
    mb_goodGuy = true;
    mb_badGuy  mb_neutral = mb_insert  = false;
}
```

We can see from this that it is good practice to find ways outside the inheritance tree to implement simple member functions that are candidates for inlining. This allows the compiler to do the best job that it can do of optimization. Furthermore, it is generally good practice to not declare a member function as virtual until the time that it is first overridden. Doing this means that the compiler will never be forced to do a function lookup for a function that is never overridden. The downside to this is that we have to be aware when deriving a class from the base class which of the base class's member functions are *not* virtual, so that we can make them virtual if we need to. Failure to declare an overridden base class function as virtual will, more often than not, cause the newly supplied functionality to never be called.

THE `new` OPERATOR

The `new` operator, specific to C++, is used to create instances of classes and structures. Although it can be viewed as a simple replacement for `malloc`, the `new` operator actually performs a lot more work than simply allocating the required memory. It must also ensure alignment of the memory, in keeping with any alignment requirements of the created class, fill in any vtable pointers required by the class due to inheritance, and call the constructor for the created class. Unfortunately, no viable alternative method of performing these extra tasks exists; we are stuck with using the `new` operator. Isn't it lucky, then, that we can override it?

Overriding the `new` operator is a simple task, accomplished by defining a function with the correct prototype and name, whose body performs the required task. Luckily for us, any overloaded `new` operator is only responsible for allocating memory; the extra tasks described previously are performed invisibly by the compiler. The following code declares an overridden `new` operator that redirects the memory allocation through the familiar `malloc` function. This function can easily be changed to use any memory manager we desire:

```
void *operator new( u32 size )
{
    return malloc(size);
}
```

So, now we have overloaded the `new` operator to use our own memory manager, but we still need to free this allocated memory correctly; failure to do so will cause a memory leak. Luckily, we can overload the `delete` operator in exactly the same way:

```
void operator delete( void *ptr )

{
    free(ptr);
}
```

Although this is great for a release build of the game, most games feature an extended debug memory manager that tracks allocations by filename and line number; it would be nice if we could make our overloaded `new` operator do the same. Luckily, the C++ language allows us to create additional definitions of the `new` operator with differing parameter lists. The only restrictions are that the first parameter be the size of the allocation (this is implied in any invocation of the operator) and that there is a `delete` operator defined with a similar parameter list. The following code defines `new` and `delete` operators that will cooperate with a debug memory manager by providing filename and line number:

```
void *operator new( u32 size, const char *file, u32 line )
{
    return MyAllocator(size,file,line);
}
void operator delete( void *ptr, const char *file, u32 line )
{
    return MyDeallocator(ptr);
}
```

Notice that in the preceding code, the `delete` operator has the same parameter list as the `new` operator except for the first parameter. The `delete` operator is still invoked in the same way as normal; however, the compiler remembers which version of the `new` operator was used to create this memory and invokes the correct `delete` operator.

Sometimes it is necessary to create an instance of a class or structure in a specific place in memory. This often occurs when loading a data file that contains a binary image of one or more classes; if these classes contain any virtual functions (hence requiring a vtable), the only way to correctly set them up is to fool the compiler into initializing the vtable for us. The only way to do this is by using the `new` operator. Using our newfound ability to pass extra parameters into the `new` operator, we can supply our overloaded function with the address that we want it to return. This allows us to force the compiler to initialize the object's vtable (and call any appropriate constructor) without moving the object into an area of newly allocated memory. This type of operation is often called a placement `new`. The following code defines a placement `new` operator, and its accompanying `delete` operator. Notice that neither of these functions actually performs any operations; they are simply there to make the compiler do what we want it to do:

```
void *operator new( u32 size, void *ptr )
{
    return ptr;
}
void operator delete( void *ptr, void *unused )
{
}
```

THE PREPROCESSOR

A program called a *preprocessor* accompanies every C compiler. This program takes as input the required source file, and outputs a modified version of this source file that the C compiler then takes as its input. At the simplest level, the preprocessor is responsible for taking the input file and any files it includes and creating a single composite file that the C compiler can then process. It does this by examining the source file, looking for directives that tell it what to do. These preprocessor directives always begin with the # character. A good example of a preprocessor directive is `#include`, which inserts the named file into the output at the current location.

The preprocessor also allows us to define symbols; these symbols, when encountered in the source file, are replaced with whatever they are defined to be. This is done through use of the `#define` directive. For example, consider the following code:

```
#define OPTIONSFILE "c:\\options.dat"
FILE *fp = fopen(OPTIONSFILE,"rb");
```

When processing this code, the preprocessor first sees that there is a symbol defined, and stores this definition. Proceeding through the code, it finds an instance of the symbol, which it replaces with the correct definition. The result of the preprocessing step, and the code that the compiler sees, looks like this:

```
FILE *fp = fopen("c:\\options.dat","rb");
```

It is also possible to test the value of symbols, and whether they have been defined. The results of these tests can be used to cull large sections of code from the source file. This is often used to add additional code to a debug build, as in the following example, which performs the check for a `NULL` pointer only in a debug build:

```
void operator delete( void *ptr )
{
    #ifdef _DEBUG
```

```
        if( ptr==0 )
        {
            printf("Error: deleting a NULL object\n");
            return;
        }
    #endif
    free(ptr);
}
```

Macros

Another useful feature of the preprocessor is its ability to expand macros. The simplest way to describe a macro would be to say that it looks like a function but behaves like a preprocessor definition. It looks like a function because a macro is defined with a series of parameters; it behaves like a preprocessor definition because the entire text of the macro is pasted into the source file in place of the macro invocation.

A macro consists of three parts: a name, a parameter list (enclosed in parentheses), and a body. A macro's name can be any sequence of text that could be used as a variable name; although by convention a macro's name is usually defined in uppercase. Its parameter list consists of a comma-separated list of placeholder symbols representing each parameter; these placeholder symbols will be replaced with the actual parameter text wherever they occur in the body of the macro. Finally, the macro body is whatever is defined after the end of the parameter list, up until a valid new-line character (a macro's body can be defined over multiple lines by using a backslash character immediately before the new-line character).

When a macro is invoked, the preprocessor replaces the text that makes up the invocation with the complete text of the macro. Additionally, any occurrences of the placeholder symbols for each parameter in the macro body will be replaced by the actual text of the parameter used in the invocation. Although this sounds confusing, it really isn't: let's look at a simple example to clarify matters somewhat. The `min` function takes two parameters and returns the minimum value of them. If we wanted to define a macro to replace this, we could try something like this:

```
#define MIN(a,b)    (a<b)?a:b
```

Then, invoking that macro results in:

```
result = MIN(b,a);
```

Notice that we are free to use the variable names `a` and `b`, even though they are used as placeholder symbols in the macro definition; the preprocessor does not get confused. In fact, to emphasize this point, the variable names have been swapped in the preceding macro invocation. Once the preprocessor has expanded this macro, the result is:

```
result = (b<a)?b:a;
```

This works for any type for which the comparison is valid. We would have to author a great many overloaded functions that perform the same operation to achieve the same using regular coding techniques. So, why are macros so frowned upon among professional programmers?

Macro Pitfalls

The main problems with macros stem from the fact that they are completely handled by the preprocessor. As mentioned previously, the preprocessor simply replaces the macro invocation with the body text of the macro, replacing the parameter placeholders with the text supplied in the macro invocation's parameter list. It does this blindly, without altering the resultant code in any way. This can result in many unintended errors.

The most easily avoided errors occur when a macro invocation is included in an expression. This can lead the code produced to perform very differently from the intended function. For example, using the previously defined `MIN` macro in an expression can produce the following:

```
tempVar = MIN(input,100)*50;
```

```
tempVar = (input<100)?input:100*50;
```

This does not compile as we expect, because the multiplication operator has a higher precedence than the ternary operator, and so is performed first. The resulting code returns an incorrect value while `input` is less than 100, since the multiplication by 50 is not performed in this case. The solution to this problem is simple: by enclosing the macro body definition inside parentheses, we can ensure correct operator precedence. A more correct definition of the `MIN` macro then becomes:

```
#define MIN(a,b)    ((a<b)?a:b)
```

A similar problem occurs when a macro is invoked with an expression as a parameter. Unless care is taken in the macro definition to isolate each of the input parameters inside parentheses, the expanded parameters might fall foul of operator precedence rules. A good rule of thumb, then, is to always surround with parentheses any occurrence of a macro parameter in the macro body, in addition to the parentheses surrounding the entire macro body. Our `MIN` macro then becomes:

```
#define MIN(a,b)    (((a)<(b))?(a):(b))
```

The biggest problem with macros, however, occurs when using a complex expression (or function call) as a macro parameter. Since the macro parameters are blindly expanded into the output, any time a macro parameter is included more than once, it will be evaluated multiple times. For example, consider the following invocation of our `MIN` macro, and its resulting expansion:

```
tempVar = MIN(sin(angle),1.0f);
```

```
tempVar = (((sin(angle))<(1.0f))?(sin(angle)):(1.0f));
```

Obviously, this is not well written code, since the expensive `sin` operation is evaluated twice. At first glance, we might expect the compiler to do just one function call and save the result—after all, the value of `angle` is never changed here—however, this presumes that the `sin` function returns a consistent value for a given input value. In this case, it is a valid presumption, and an intelligent compiler should know enough about the `sin` function to make it. In general, though, the compiler is not free to make an assumption of this kind, and so the function, or expression, must be evaluated multiple times to ensure correct operation of the final program.

Useful Macros

Despite the aforementioned problems with macros, there are some situations where a macro is invaluable; in fact, some programming problems are best solved using macros. For example, consider the problem of finding the number of elements in an array. This is simply the size of the entire array divided by the size of a single element in the array. However, writing this expression each time we need to find the size of an array (e.g., in a `for` loop that iterates through the items in an array) is clumsy and error prone. It is a simple task to create a macro that safely does this for us:

```
#define countof(array)  (sizeof(array)/sizeof((array)[0]))
```

Another task best performed by a macro is finding the offset of a member variable within a class or structure. This can be done by finding the address of the member variable within an instance of the class and then subtracting the address of the class instance. Unfortunately, this method requires a valid class instance, and involves some math that the compiler will be hard-pressed to make disappear. We could make the math disappear, however, by ensuring that the address of the class instance is 0. Since nothing is actually read from the instance, this is safe to do, and can be achieved by casting a null pointer into a class instance pointer. The resulting macro looks like this:

```
#define offsetof(structName,memberName)\
    ((u32)(&((structName*)0)->memberName))
```

The preprocessor also supports a couple of useful directives that come into effect during macro expansion. The first of these, #, surrounds the term that comes immediately after it in quotes. This is useful for making a string out of a macro parameter, and can be used to make a handy error text lookup function. The following code is a simple example of such an error lookup function for a small portion of possible Direct3D errors:

```
#define D3DERROR(errorCode) case errorCode: return #errorCode;
const char *GetD3DerrorText( HRESULT error )
{
    switch(error)
    {
    D3DERROR(D3D_OK);
    D3DERROR(D3DERR_INVALIDCALL);
    D3DERROR(D3DERR_OUTOFVIDEOMEMORY);
    D3DERROR(D3DERR_DEVICELOST);

    default: return "Unknown error";
    }
}
```

This function takes as input an error code from Direct3D and returns a pointer to a string containing the text of the error code's definition. For example, given an error code of `D3DERR_INVALIDCALL`, the function will return `"D3DERR_INVALIDCALL"`.

Another useful preprocessor directive for use in macros is the ## directive. This directive concatenates the text to either side of it to form a single word. We can alter the preceding function to use the ## directive in the following manner, effectively stripping the `D3DERR_` from the front of the error messages:

```
#define D3DERROR(errorCode)\
    case D3DERR_##errorCode: return #errorCode;

const char *GetD3DerrorText( HRESULT error )
{
    switch(error)
    {
    D3DERROR(INVALIDCALL);
    D3DERROR(OUTOFVIDEOMEMORY);
    D3DERROR(DEVICELOST);
```

```
        case D3D_OK: return "No error";
        default:     return "Unknown error";
        }
    }
```

One of the more useful uses of macros is to invisibly change the parameters of a function in different build configurations. This can be used, for example, to pass filename and line number to a debug memory manager with each memory allocation. This must be done at the function invocation rather than inside the function in order to get the correct data (the filename and line number for every allocation would be the same otherwise). The following code shows an example of two macros of this type:

```
#ifdef _DEBUG_MEMORY
    #define MYALLOC(size)   MyAlloc(size,__FILE__,__LINE__)
    #define NEW()           new(__FILE__,__LINE__)
#else
    #define MYALLOC(size)   MyAlloc(size)
    #define NEW()           new
#endif
```

Finally, we come to possibly the most useful macro of all: `assert`. This macro is used to ensure that a given expression is true. In release builds, this macro expands to nothing, but in a debug build, the expression is checked and, if false, an error is generated, usually through a function call. Many implementations of the `assert` macro use the # directive to pass a text string of the condition tested to the failure function, as well as the filename and line number where the assertion occurred. The following code is a simple example of the `assert` macro:

```
// this is the function that will be called if
// and when an assert fails
extern void AssertionFailed( const char *condition,
                             const char *filename,
                             u32 lineNumber );
```

```
// the actual assert macro
#ifdef _DEBUG
    // in debug builds the assertion is checked
    #define assert(a)\
        if(!(a)) AssertionFailed(#a,__FILE__,__LINE__);

#else
    // in non-debug builds, the assertion is removed
    #define assert(a)
#endif
```

It is good practice to check every assumption made by your code with an `assert` macro before acting on that assumption. This is especially important before accessing a pointer that is presumed to be valid (i.e., non-`NULL`). These checks cost nothing in a nondebug build since the preprocessor removes them, but can quickly point out why your code is failing in a debug build. As such, the `assert` macro is an invaluable tool for writing error-free code.

Unfortunately, the `assert` macro is not a panacea; it brings with it its own rather nasty side effect: it is very important to *never* include active code inside an `assert`. In this case, active code is defined as code that performs an action; for example, modifying a variable or calling a function that causes a nonlocal variable to be altered. Including active code inside an assertion is very bad because the code will only ever be run in a debug build; in non-debug builds, the code will simply be removed. Errors of this type are often very subtle and nearly always extremely hard to find.

ENDNOTES

[1]As we will see, the term *productivity* applies to many different areas of programming, including authoring speed, ease of reading, and ease of debugging.

[2]For more information, see the section on virtual functions later in this chapter.

2 Orders of Complexity

In This Chapter

- Rule #2: "Divide & Conquer"
- Orders of Complexity
- Searching a Linear List, or Array
- Searching a Nonlinear List
- Binary Trees
- Self-Balancing Binary Trees
- Binary Space Partitioning (BSP) Trees

One of the most important concepts that it is necessary to understand to effectively create a game is that of time complexity. Choosing an algorithm with poor time complexity can balloon the processing time for your game objects at an exponential rate: two objects can take four, eight, or more times as long as a single object, and four objects can take 16 or 64 times as long, or even worse! Obviously, this is not a situation a game wants to find itself in. However, if implemented naively, many of the most common tasks that a game needs to do during a frame exhibit this kind of behavior. One of the worst offenders, and one that we will look closely at in this chapter, is collision. Each object needs to be checked to see if it collides with every other object in the scene; this implies that for a scene with n objects in it, there will need to be n^2 collision checks every single frame.

RULE #2: "DIVIDE & CONQUER"

The second golden rule, "Divide & Conquer," shows how we can remedy this situation by dividing the problem space into a hierarchy of subproblems. Doing this usually allows us to throw away large sections of the problem space without even considering its occupants, thereby reducing the number of operations needed. Before we can judge the efficacy of these improvements, though, we need a way to effectively measure the complexity of an algorithm.

ORDERS OF COMPLEXITY

A simple way of measuring the complexity of an algorithm is to count the operations required to solve it for a given size of problem space, n. The more operations that it takes for each member of the problem space, the more complex the problem. An algorithm that takes five operations per item is less complex than one that takes n operations[1] per item. However, what constitutes an operation? Surely, these changes depend on what machine we are running on and in what language the algorithm is implemented?

To answer this, we need to examine our measure of complexity more closely. What is the most significant factor about our measure? Let's look at three simple examples; in the first, our algorithm takes one operation per item, and in the second it takes five, but in the third, the algorithm needs *n* operations per item. Table 2.1 shows how many operations it takes to solve the algorithms for different values of *n*.

TABLE 2.1 Number of Operations for Different Complexities and Varying Problem Sizes, *n*

N	***Algorithm 1:* *1 operation per n***	***Algorithm 2:* *5 operations per n***	***Algorithm 3:* *n operations per n***
1	1	5	1
2	2	10	4
3	3	15	9
4	4	20	16
16	16	80	256
64	64	320	4096
256	256	1280	65536

As you can see in Table 2.1, although algorithm two is initially the most complex, it is soon outstripped by algorithm three, whose complexity rises quadratically. This leads us to our first conclusion: the true complexity of an algorithm is determined by the rate that the number of operations changes with the size of the problem space. To determine the rate of change, we must first calculate the equation for the rate by differentiating the complexity equation with respect to the number of operations. The complexity equation is given by Equation 2.1, where *y* is the number of operations needed and *n* is the number of items in the problem space:

$$y = (OperationPerItem) \times n. \tag{2.1}$$

This means that the algorithms in Table 2.1 can be represented by the complexity equations shown in Equations 2.2 through 2.4, respectively:

$$y = n, \tag{2.2}$$
$$y = 5n, \tag{2.3}$$
$$y = n^2. \tag{2.4}$$

Differentiating these three equations gives us the first-order rate of change for each of the algorithms. This is shown in Equations 2.5 through 2.7:

$$\frac{dy}{dn} = 1 \tag{2.5}$$

$$\frac{dy}{dn} = 5 \tag{2.6}$$

$$\frac{dy}{dn} = 2n \tag{2.7}$$

Notice that algorithms one and two have a constant rate of change, but algorithm three's rate is still dependent on the number of items in the problem space. If we differentiate Equation 2.7 again, this gives us the second-order rate of change for algorithm three, which is finally constant. Since the complexity of an algorithm is determined by the rate of change of the number of operations taken relative to the number of items in the problem space, algorithms one and two actually have the same complexity. This means that the complexity of an algorithm is not affected by its implementation (and so how many atomic operations are involved in each step of the algorithm, so long as this number is not dependent on the number of items in the problem space). This is generally true; however, as the constant multiplier rises it takes greater and greater values of n before the more complex algorithm takes longer than the simple one. For example, a complexity of $y=4000000n$ takes longer to complete than a complexity of $y=n^2$ for all values of n that are less than 2000 (the square root of 4,000,000).

A fourth algorithm, which takes n^2 operations per item in the problem space, is represented in Equation 2.8. We can see from this equation that even its second-order differential is variable; that is, its rate of change still depends on the number of items in the problem space:

$$y = n^3$$

$$\frac{dy}{dn} = 3n^2 \tag{2.8}$$

$$\frac{d_2y}{dn^2} = 6n.$$

Only when we differentiate this again do we get a constant rate. If each differentiation represents an order of magnitude of complexity, then algorithm four is an order of magnitude more complex than algorithm three, and two orders of magnitude more complex than algorithms one and two. Taking this a step further, we can say that the order of magnitude of the complexity for a given algorithm is approximately the number of times it must be differentiated before the result is a constant. This gives us an important result: only the most significant part of the complexity equation determines the final complexity.

For example, algorithm five takes n^2+n operations per item. After three differentiation steps, we find that the result is a constant. Therefore, although it apparently takes n more operations per item than algorithm four, the two algorithms are said to have the same order of complexity[2] (n^3). This represents the fact that although initially the term with the smaller power contributes equally to the overall number of operations, as n increases, the number of instructions it contributes to the total is quickly dwarfed by the larger term.

Notation

There is a very specific notation for communicating the order of complexity of an algorithm. As we saw earlier, as the size of the problem space increases, the less significant terms contribute less and less to the total complexity. Therefore, these can effectively be removed from the complexity rating, since over the long term their contributions to the complexity become negligible. So, the first thing to do when attempting to classify the order of complexity of an algorithm is to remove all but the most significant term from the complexity equation. This includes all constant multipliers and any additions to the major term. The remaining term is then enclosed in parentheses and preceded by a capital O (short for order):

$$y = 5n^2 + 7n. \tag{2.9}$$

For example, consider an algorithm whose complexity equation is represented by Equation 2.9. This equation's most significant term is $5n^2$. However, since the constant multiplier is comparatively insignificant, we can remove this without effect. We are now left with just the most significant term (n^2), which is then written as $O(n^2)$ and read as "order *n*-squared."

Visualizing Orders of Complexity

Figure 2.1 shows graphs of six increasing orders of complexity, with the number of items in the problem space along the *x*-axis and the number of operations taken along the *y*-axis. The first graph shows a complexity of $O(1)$, which is the best possible time complexity. An example of an algorithm exhibiting this level of complexity is an index-based lookup in an array. No matter the number of elements in the array, it takes exactly one operation to find an entry with a given index. Naturally, this order of complexity is the most sought after, but in practice it is almost impossible to achieve.

The second graph shows a complexity of $O(\log n)$. Notice that although this graph slopes upward with increasing values of n, the slope decreases as n increases. This means that as the number of items in the problem space increases, the average time taken per item actually decreases. A good example of an $O(\log n)$ algorithm is a binary search, which is described later in this chapter.

Next up is a complexity of $O(n)$. An algorithm that exhibits this complexity takes one operation for each item in the problem space. An example of an algorithm exhibiting this time complexity is a simple walk of a linked list, such as that used to iterate through each object during each frame of a game.

The fourth graph shows a complexity of $O(n \log n)$. An example of an algorithm that exhibits this complexity is the quicksort algorithm[3]. Although the average number of operations per item increases as the number of items increases, it does so at a decreasing rate. An algorithm with this time

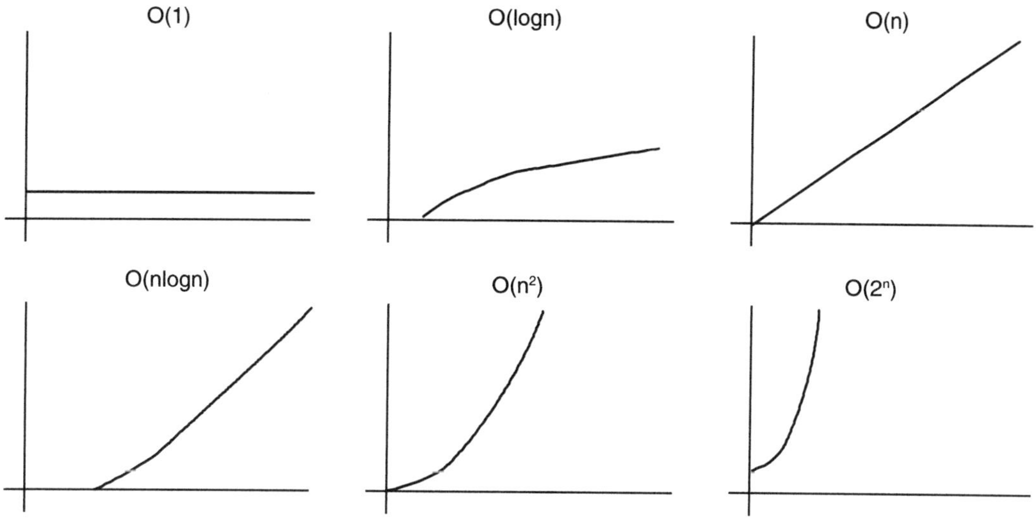

FIGURE 2.1 Visualizing orders of complexity.

complexity is probably the most complex that you would want to use in a real-time situation, unless the number of items is very tightly controlled.

The fifth graph shows a complexity of $O(n^2)$. An algorithm with this complexity takes more operations per item as the size of the problem space increases. This is a very bad time complexity for an algorithm that is used in a game, especially when the bounding values of *n* are not known in advance and tightly controlled. With just 16 items, an algorithm with this complexity takes 256 operations!

The final graph shows a complexity of $O(2^n)$. Notice that the number of operations taken increases extremely rapidly with the number of items. Algorithms that exhibit similar orders of complexity to this should be avoided wherever possible, and limited to offline operations where avoidance is not possible. With just 16 items, an algorithm with this complexity takes 65,536 operations!

SEARCHING A LINEAR LIST, OR ARRAY

One of the most common tasks that comes up while writing a game is searching for a specific piece of data in a large set. This task occurs a lot more than you might think; many tasks contain thinly disguised searches at their hearts. For example, in a collision system, the first thing that needs to be done is to identify which objects can potentially collide with each other. More often than not, this involves a search for objects that are in close proximity to each other. It is obvious, then, that we must attempt to make our searches as efficient as possible.

Let's look at the one of the simplest search algorithms (searching for an item of data in a linear list, or array, of items) and try to find its order of complexity. Once we have done this, we have a value that we can compare against other algorithms to tell if they are really an improvement. Possibly the simplest search is to compare each item in turn against the value we are searching for, until we find it or exhaust the list of items. Obviously, if the item we are looking for is at the front of the array, we will find it immediately. Conversely, if it is at the end of the array, we will have to traverse the entire array to find it. In the average case, though, for an array that is n items in length, it will take $n/2$ operations to find the item we are searching for.

Remember that any constant multiplier does not count toward the overall order of complexity. This means that the simplest search for a single item of data in a list of n elements has a complexity of $O(n)$. Put simply, the time taken by this algorithm to find a single item of data in an array is directly proportional to the number of items it contains. That seems pretty good, right? Surely we can't do better than this…

The Binary Search

Actually, we can, but not with the array of data as it stands. To see how we can improve this, we will look at an example from everyday life: finding an entry in a telephone book. Consider a telephone book with 300 pages, each with 4 columns containing 150 entries. That's a total of 180,000 entries. It would take you a very long time to find a specific entry in the book with the algorithm presented previously. Luckily, though, this is not the technique that we use when looking for a plumber in the directory; otherwise, in the event of a leak, all of our furniture would be ruined!

So, how do we find an entry in the telephone book? Well, the first thing we do is open the book somewhere in the middle and look at which letter is contained on the open page. Then, if the letter on the page is later in the alphabet than the one we are looking for, we turn back about halfway through the remaining pages. We can do this because we *know* conclusively that the item we are looking for cannot be any later in the book than the page we are currently looking at. Conversely, if the letter on the page is earlier in the alphabet, we turn forward about halfway.

When the new page is revealed, we again compare the letter displayed against the first letter of the word we are looking for, and turn in the required direction. Eventually, the letter contained on the page will be the first letter of our word, and we know that we're getting close, so we move to looking at the first two letters of our word, and continue as before. We keep doing this until we are sure that the word we are looking for is on the current page, and then we usually (and inexplicably) just search linearly through the items on the page until we find the correct one.

Obviously, this is much faster, but exactly how much faster is it? At each step of the algorithm, we compare the value midway through the current list against the value we are searching for. Depending on the result, we go on to process the appropriate half of the list, effectively discarding half the list as irrelevant, *without even looking at it.* So, for a list of eight items, the first step discards four of them, the second step discards a further two, leaving us with just two items. In all, it takes just three operations to find the correct item in a list of eight items. Since the list of items to be considered is halved at each iteration, this search is $O(\log n)$—a definite improvement over the previous $O(n)$.

To put this into perspective, for our 180,000-entry telephone book, this type of search, called a binary search, takes just *18* operations, even for entries located at the very end of the book. Compare this to the linear search, which takes an average of 90,000 operations, and a worst case of 180,000.

The reason why a binary search is possible is that we know something about the input array; we know it is sorted. Without this fact, we would not be able to discard half of the array at each step of the algorithm, and we are reduced to iterating through each item in turn. By sorting the array beforehand, we move the cost of the linear search into a preprocessing step whose result can be used multiple times.

The algorithm for a binary search is as follows:

1. Set the bottom index to be the index of the first element, and the top index to be the index of the last element of the array.

2. If the bottom index is greater than the top index, then stop; the item being searched for is not in the array.
3. Find the index of the item halfway between the top and bottom indices.
4. Compare the value of the item at this index with the value being searched for.
5. If the value of this item is the same as the one being searched for, then stop; this is the correct item.
6. If the value is greater than the one being searched for, then the item is in the bottom half of the list; set the top index equal to the middle index minus one and go back to step 2.
7. The item is in the top half of the list; set the bottom index equal to the middle index plus one and go back to step 2.

ON THE CD

A sample program that contrasts a binary search against a linear search can be found on the companion CD-ROM, in the folder chapter2/binsearch. This program takes the name of a text file as its single command-line argument. The file is loaded and a list of the words contained in it (including duplicates) is created. This list is then sorted using the C-runtime implementation of quicksort to produce the sorted list required by a binary search. Finally, the program chooses a few words at random and tries to locate them in the list, using both a linear search and a binary search, and the results are displayed and contrasted.

As you can see from experimentation with this program, there are very few cases where a linear search uses fewer iterations than a binary search does. Specifically, the searched-for item must be located within the first $\log_2 n$ items of the list for this to happen.

SEARCHING A NONLINEAR LIST

In a nonlinear list, each element might not be contiguous with the previous element in the list; that is, they might not abut each other in memory. Even if two elements are contiguous in memory, they might not be consecutive elements in the list; the first element might be contiguous with the fifth, or the third with the ninetieth. Each element in the list usually contains a pointer to the next and previous elements in the list, allowing navigation between elements. One of the most common forms of nonlinear list is the simple doubly linked list. However, as with an unsorted linear list, the only way to find a given item in this list is to visit each item in turn, testing against the wanted value, until either the item is found or the list is exhausted.

To get around this, we must apply some order to the list in a similar way to how sorting the linear list allowed a binary search to work. We must determine exactly what enables the binary search to do what it does as efficiently as it does, and find some way to incorporate that into our nonlinear list. Luckily, this is not too complicated; the key to the binary search's speed is that at each element it performs a comparison with the current element and chooses which half of the data set can then be discarded based on the result. Obviously, there's no way we're going to incorporate this into a simple linked list, where all we can do is move linearly either forward or backward through the elements. So, let's look a little more closely at a simple binary search example.

In this example, we have a simple linear list that contains seven elements—the letters A through G—and we want to find a specific character in that list, say the letter G. The first step of the binary search takes the central list element, D, and compares it against the character we are searching for. Now, clearly G is higher than D, so we discard the first half of the list, and then consider the central list element in the remaining region, F. Again, the character we are searching for is later in the alphabet, and so we discard the first half of the list, leaving a single character, which is our result.

We can perform a similar series of operations to find any item in this list. It soon becomes apparent, however, that any binary search will consider the list elements in a certain order; after the first comparison with the letter D, we always consider either the letter B or the letter F. Only these two letters are ever considered following the first comparison. This implies that in our binary-search compatible list, these two letters should both be linked to D. Similarly, after considering the letter B, we only ever consider A or C, and so these should both be linked to B.

BINARY TREES

It should be apparent that the sequence that we consider the letters in can be best represented as a binary tree—each letter forms a node in the tree, with its two branches leading to the two letters that can be considered next. The comparison of the search letter with the letter at each node determines whether the search ends at this node and, if not, which branch to subsequently take. Figure 2.2 shows how the binary search for our simple example can be represented as a binary tree.

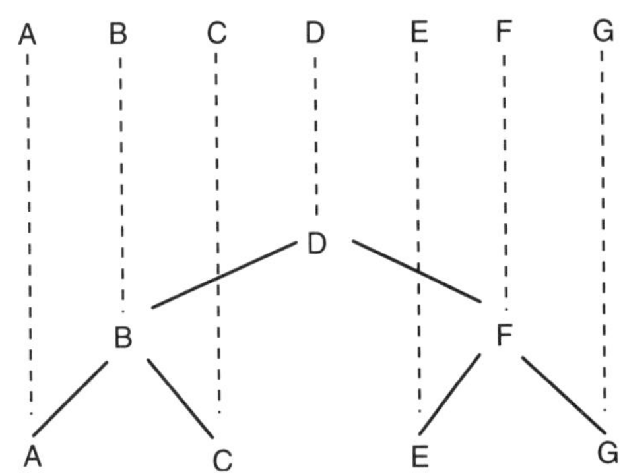

FIGURE 2.2 A binary search represented as a binary tree.

Each node in a binary tree has at least four properties that enable the tree to be navigated. The first two properties are the links that form the branches of the tree. Each node must contain these links, usually called the left and right links. The third property is the element that is stored at this node in the tree. Finally, each node contains a decision variable that enables us to choose which branch to take. In simple trees, including the tree depicted in Figure 2.2, the decision variable for each node and the element stored in the node are the same.

The following algorithm can be used to find a specific node in a binary tree:

1. Begin at the root node (`D` from Figure 2.2).
2. Is the search value the same as the element stored in the current node? If so, stop—we have found the searched-for item.
3. Compare the search value against the decision variable for this node.

4. If the search value is lower, the next node is down the left branch; otherwise, it is down the right branch.
5. If the next node is present, move to it and go to step 2.
6. Stop; the value we are searching for is not in the tree.

Provided that the binary tree is somewhat balanced, this algorithm will execute in O(log$n$) time. But what exactly makes a balanced binary tree? A tree can be said to be balanced when, for most of the nodes in the tree, there are as many elements down the left branch as there are down the right branch. A tree that is derived from a binary search, like that in Figure 2.2, is always balanced by virtue of the order that a binary search addresses its items. However, if a tree is unbalanced, like that shown in Figure 2.3, then the algorithm will exhibit its worst-case performance of O(n). This is because at this point the tree has devolved into a simple linked list.

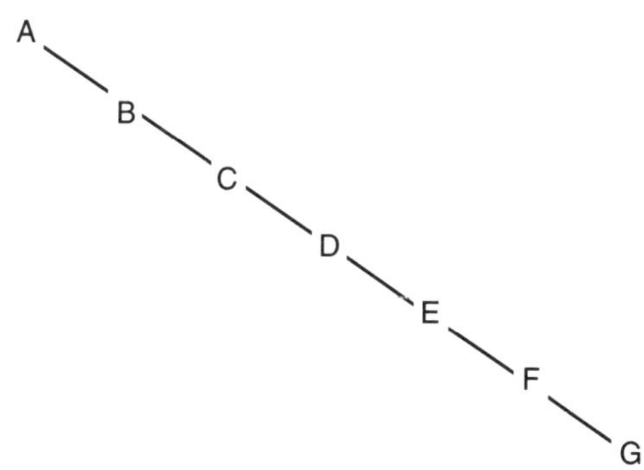

FIGURE 2.3 A perfectly unbalanced binary tree.

The problem, then, lies in creating a balanced tree in the first place. If we know all of the items that are to be stored in the tree ahead of time, then we can easily make these into a sorted list and recursively create the tree by doing the equivalent of a binary search. However, oftentimes we are called upon to make a balanced tree without having access to all of the items that are to be stored in the tree. In situations like this we are totally at the mercy of the order that the items are presented to us. In the best case, if the items are presented to us in the correct order, we can achieve a perfectly balanced tree with no effort. In the worst case, we get a perfectly unbalanced tree.

SELF-BALANCING BINARY TREES

Luckily for us, several algorithms exist that allow us to create a binary tree that balances itself as items are added to it. Obviously, since we are doing extra work to balance the tree as each new item is added, this comes at a cost, but the cost is surprisingly small for the majority of additions. Before we look at a self-balancing tree, though, we must first give ourselves the tools to enable the structure of a binary tree to be modified.

To safely change the structure (the order of the items) of a binary tree, we must understand the properties of the decision function. That is, the function that determines which branch of a node a given item must follow. There are two main classes of decision functions; those that are reversible and those that are not.

A reversible decision function says that if an element, B, should occupy parent element A's right branch, then if B were the parent, element A would occupy element B's left branch. Equation 2.10 illustrates this as a function that takes two arguments, A and B. The first argument to this function can be considered the value contained in the parent node, and the second argument is the value that we are trying to place in the tree:

$$f(A, B) = \neg f(B, A). \tag{2.10}$$

A nonreversible decision function is one in which Equation 2.10 does not hold. Functions of this type are somewhat akin to the logical implies function, where if element A implies element B, element B does not necessarily imply element A. For an example of a binary tree that uses this type of function, see the following section on BSP trees.

In the case of a reversible decision function, we are able to modify the order of the items in a tree using two simple operations. These operations both maintain the correctness of the tree by taking advantage of the reversible nature of the binary tree's decision function. Figure 2.4 shows two simple three element binary trees, one of which is unbalanced. In the unbalanced tree, the relationship of the three elements is such that $A<B$ and $B<C$, whereas in the balanced one, $B>A$ and $B<C$. Since we know that the decision function is reversible, we can see that these two trees can actually represent the same data.

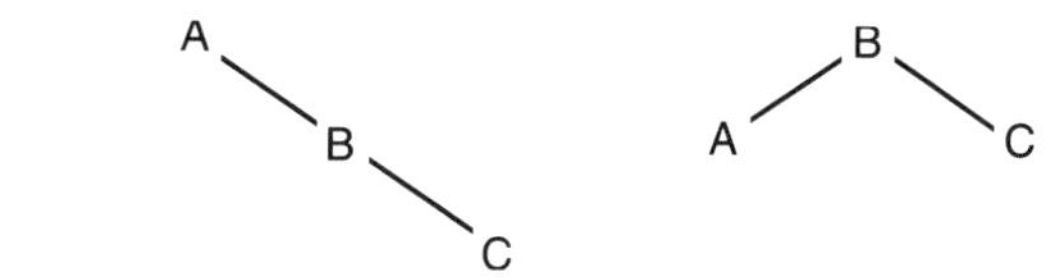

FIGURE 2.4 Two equivalent binary trees.

The operation that takes us between the unbalanced tree on the left and the balanced tree on the right is called a *rotation*, because we have effectively rotated the tree about node A. There are two types of rotation operation; clockwise and counterclockwise. Figure 2.5 shows a more complex tree, and the effect of rotating this more complex tree clockwise about node D.

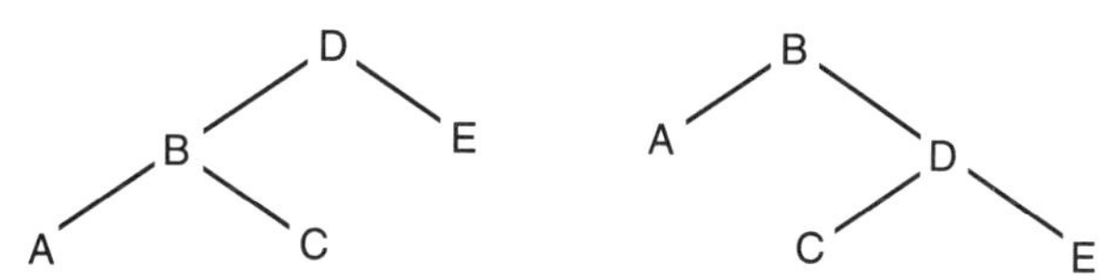

FIGURE 2.5 A more complex rotation.

As we can see from Figure 2.5, a general rotation about a node is a little more complex than that shown in Figure 2.4; we have to do more work to maintain the correct relationship between all of the tree's elements. Although at first glance, the rearrangement of the tree in Figure 2.5 looks quite extensive, only two nodes have had their children changed (not counting any parent of node D). These nodes, D and B, we will call the primary and secondary nodes, respectively. The algorithm for rotating a binary tree clockwise around a given primary node is then:

1. Move the secondary node's right branch to the primary node's left branch.
2. Move the primary node onto the secondary node's right branch.
3. Make sure the primary node's original parent points to the secondary node.

Step 1 of this algorithm ensures that the correct order of elements is maintained in the binary tree. Since, in Figure 2.5, node C is positioned ultimately down node D's left branch, in any derived tree it must either be positioned above node D (in which case node D must be placed down node C's right branch to maintain correctness) or to the left of node D.

Similarly, step 2 maintains the correct relationship between nodes B and D. Finally, step 3 maintains the integrity of the tree above the primary node. Without this step, our tree could not be properly navigated, since nothing would link to node B, and hence anything down node B's left branch.

A counterclockwise rotation can similarly be achieved by exchanging left for right in the clockwise rotation's algorithm.

Red-Black Trees

One of the most commonly used self-balancing binary trees is the red-black tree. A red-black tree adds an extra property, called *color*, to each node. Each node is assigned a color (red) as it is added to the tree. The tree is then modified to attempt to maintain the following properties:

- Every node is either red or black.
- Empty branches are presumed to lead to a black node.
- If a node is red, both of its children must be black.
- Every simple (always descending) path from a node to a leaf (empty branch) contains the same number of black nodes.

After a new, red node has been inserted, we must examine the resulting tree around the newly inserted node to see if we have broken any of the rules. We know a rule has been broken if the new node's parent is red; in this case, we have two red nodes in a row. The way we resolve this differs based on the color of the new node's *uncle* (that is, the new node's grandparent's *other* child). The following cases all presume that the uncle of the new node is down the right branch of its parent (and so the new node's parent is down the left branch of its parent). If the opposite is the case, then right and left, counterclockwise and clockwise must both be swapped.

In the following figures, the node that we are concentrating on is shown with a circular surround; all other nodes are shown with a square surround. Additionally, nodes that are designated red are unshaded, and nodes that are designated black are shaded.

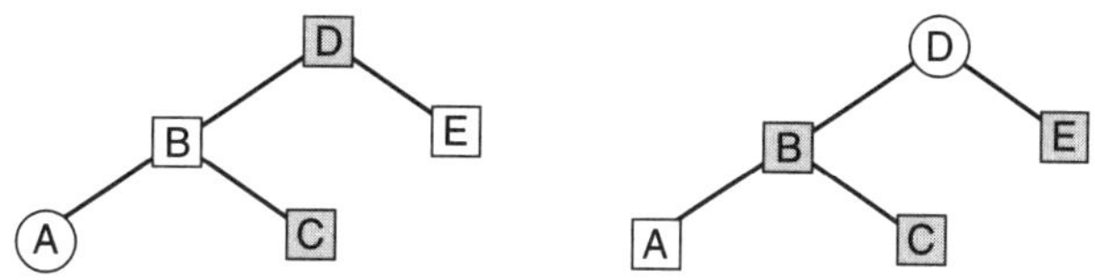

FIGURE 2.6 The new node, A, and its uncle, E, are both red.

Case 1: If the new node's uncle is also red, as shown in Figure 2.6, we must change the color of the new node's parent and uncle to black and its grandparent to red. This fixes our local color clash, but possibly introduces a new one at our grandparent's level; so we make the grandparent the new node and recheck the tree. Notice that this might produce a black-black sequence in the tree (nodes B and C in Figure 2.7). This sequence of nodes is not strictly prohibited by our red-black tree rules (only red-red sequences are prohibited), so this is perfectly acceptable.

If the new node's uncle is black, however, as shown in Figure 2.7, things become more complicated. Depending on the branch of its parent that the new node occupies, we must do one of two things.

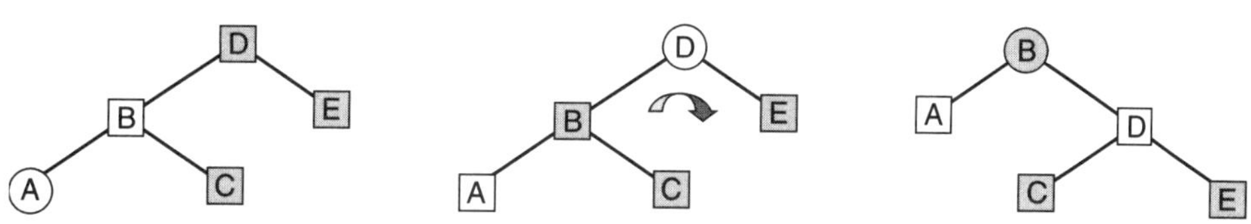

FIGURE 2.7 The new node, A, is a left child, and its uncle, E, is black.

Case 2: If the new node is down the left branch of its parent and its uncle is black, we must color the new node's parent black and its grandparent red before performing a clockwise rotation about the new node's grandparent.

The result of this operation is always such that the new node's parent is black; hence, no further corrective actions are necessary.

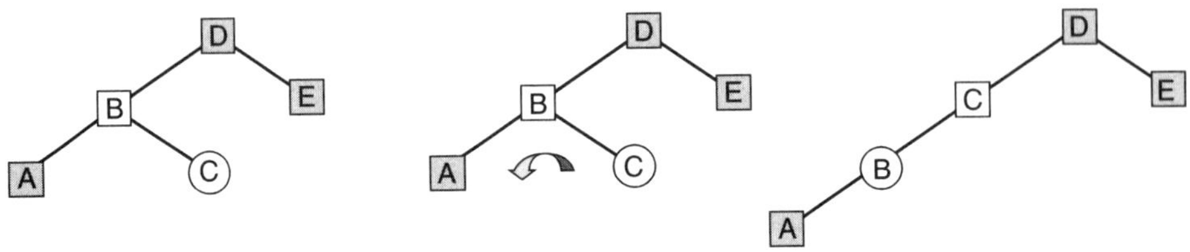

FIGURE 2.8 The new node, C, is a right child, and its uncle, E, is black.

Case 3: If the new node is the right child of its parent and its uncle is black, as shown in Figure 2.8, we must first perform a counterclockwise rotation about the new node's parent. The element that was the new node's parent is then considered the new node. As we can see from the diagram, we are now in the same situation as Figure 2.7, and so we now perform the operations described in case 2.

The preceding operations are repeated iteratively until the red-black tree violations caused by the insertion and any subsequent operations no longer apply. Once all violations have been resolved, the final step is to color the root node of the tree black. The resulting tree is then a valid red-black tree. A single insertion operation might cause a large number of recolor operations (up to the maximum depth of the tree), but only two rotation operations.

It should be noted at this point that a red-black tree navigates back up the tree to resolve color clashes; this implies that in addition to the new color property, we must also store a pointer to each node's parent.

Deletions from red-black trees are also possible, but these require more complex tree manipulations to maintain the validity of the red-black tree. Many common uses of red-black trees (e.g., sorting of translucent objects before drawing) do not require that we implement a deletion operation; we can simply reset the tree each frame. For this reason, we will omit a description of the deletion operation from this text.

BINARY SPACE PARTITIONING (BSP) TREES

As we stated at the beginning of this chapter, one of the most time-intensive tasks that a game must accomplish is that of collision. However, all of the algorithms that we have considered so far are inherently one-dimensional and so are useless to us for this purpose, since our collision space, ignoring time, is usually three-dimensional. However, the underlying concept of these algorithms—that of dividing the problem space in two at each node—is the key to speeding up collisions.

A BSP tree is a type of binary tree in which each node is represented by a plane that cuts the problem space in two (not necessarily in half). Each of these spaces (called *half-spaces*) is then further cut in two by any subsequent child nodes.

A BSP tree is particularly well suited to work with triangular meshes, since each triangle in the mesh forms a plane that can be used as a node. For each new node in a BSP tree, a triangle (and hence a plane) is chosen from among the remaining set of triangles. Every other triangle is then compared to this plane, with one of five possible results:

- The triangle is completely in front of the plane.
- The triangle is completely behind the plane.
- The triangle intersects the plane.
- The triangle lies on the plane, facing the same direction as the plane normal.
- The triangle lies on the plane, facing the opposite direction to the plane normal.

Triangles on either side of the plane are grouped together, while those that intersect the plane are first decomposed into subtriangles that lie on either side of the plane, and then added to the corresponding group. Triangles that lie on the plane are assigned to the current node, along with the triangle that originally supplied the node's dividing plane. Two child nodes are then created, one for each of the sides of the plane, using the appropriate group of triangles. This is repeated until there are no unassigned triangles left.

It should be noted here that a BSP tree uses a nonreversible decision function at each node. That is to say, just because node A is in front of node B does not mean that node B is behind node A. This is illustrated in Figure 2.9. Because of this, we cannot use any rotation operations on the nodes of a BSP tree.

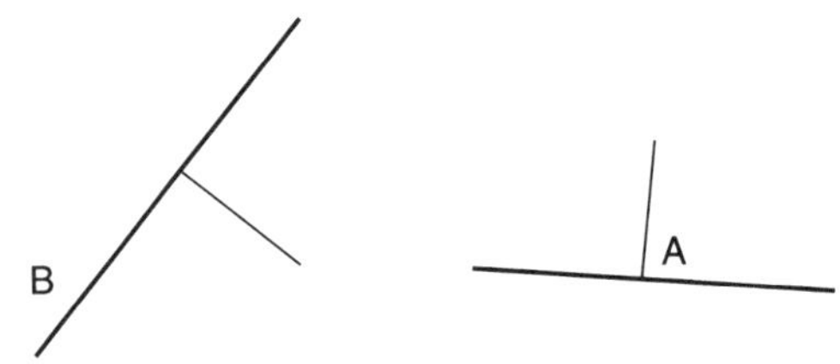

FIGURE 2.9 Plane A is in front of plane B, but plane B is not behind plane A.

The following code outlines one possible data structure for representing a BSP node:

```
class BSPNODE
{
public:
    BSPNODE *front;
    BSPNODE *back;
    PLANE   plane;
    FACE    *faces;
};
```

Although creating a BSP tree sounds relatively simple, in practice creating a viable, balanced tree is a very mathematically intensive task. For this reason, BSP trees are almost always precalculated in a game's data pipeline. To see why creating a viable BSP tree is so hard, let's look at what it entails. The first thing to consider is that for a given set of n triangles, there can be up to $n!$ different possible BSP trees. This worst case occurs for a completely convex shape with no coplanar polygons—at each node you can choose any of the remaining faces for the plane, and all remaining faces will fall on the same side of it, giving $n*(n-1)*(n-2)*...*2*1$ different possible trees. For a simple set of 12 triangles, this means that there are somewhere in the region of 479 million different BSP trees possible—if we had to try every one of these to find the best one, we'd be in trouble. Luckily, though, we don't need to find the single best BSP tree; in most cases, just a fairly balanced one will do, and for that we can take a few shortcuts.

Creating a Good Enough BSP Tree

As detailed previously, an amazingly large number of different possible BSP trees can represent a given set of triangles. This number is so large that it is inconceivable that we would find the single best BSP tree in a reasonable amount of time. However, by making intelligent choices locally at each node, we can find a BSP tree that is "good enough." This is done using what is called a *heuristic*, which is simply a function that returns a value that attempts to rate the quality of a certain choice. Before we can do this, though, we need to examine exactly what makes a good choice at each node.

The most important thing from our perspective is that the resulting tree be as balanced as possible. Failure to produce a balanced tree will skew our algorithm performance away from the optimal. To this end, we need to include a term in our heuristic that takes into account how balanced the resulting tree is likely to be. A simple way to do this would be to ensure that an equal number of faces fall on each side of the chosen plane. Translating this into a quantifiable term, we can say that the heuristic depends on the product of the number of faces that fall on each side of the plane. This will be greatest when the plane separates the remaining faces into two halves. It would behoove us to keep this value within a predictable range (usually 0–>1), so we should divide the resulting number by its maximum possible value. For a set of n triangles at a given node, the maximum result occurs when $n/2$ triangles fall on each side of the plane, making the maximum value of the product $n^2/4$. The value of the heuristic term for tree balance can then be represented by Equation 2.11

$$h_{balance} = \frac{n_{front} * n_{back} * 4}{\left(n_{front} + n_{back}\right)^2} \tag{2.11}$$

Another important desire for our tree is that we want it to contain as few nodes as possible. To this end, we need to incorporate into our heuristic a value that represents how many faces are removed by the chosen node. A face is said to be removed by a node when it is coplanar with the node's plane. Again, we want this term of the heuristic to fall within the range 0–>1, so we define this term as shown in Equation 2.12:

$$h_{coplanar} = \frac{n_{coplanar}}{n_{total}} \tag{2.12}$$

We also want to generate as few extra pieces of geometry as possible. Extra geometry is generated when the plane of the chosen face splits another face in two. Sometimes these splits are unavoidable, but we would prefer not to choose faces that generate them, as they increase the size of the data and the number of nodes in the BSP tree. Given that generating a larger number of splits should decrease the desirability of a given face, and keeping the heuristic term in the range of 0–>1, we get Equation 2.13:

$$h_{split} = 1 - \left(\frac{n_{split}}{n_{total}}\right) \tag{2.13}$$

Our final heuristic term takes into account the nature of the BSP tree's conception: each node splits the problem space in two. Now, a badly chosen face could split the problem space in such a way that one of the resulting half-spaces becomes a long, thin sliver of space. This is undesirable for us; ideally, we would like our half-spaces to be regular in shape. One of the ways to accomplish this is to compare the relative orientations of the chosen face and the two previously chosen nodes (the current node's parent and its grandparent). The ideal face would necessarily be at right angles to the two previously chosen nodes, preserving the regularity of the new half-spaces. Since each node's plane normal is unit length (by definition), we can use the dot product of two nodes' plane normals to determine their relative orientation; when the two nodes are at right angles to each other, the dot product will be 0. This gives us the final heuristic term shown in Equation 2.14. Notice that this term can never fall to 0; we never want this term to preclude a face from selection:

$$h_{regular} = \frac{\left(2 - abs\left(N_{current} \bullet N_{parent}\right)\right) * \left(2 - abs\left(N_{current} \bullet N_{grandparent}\right)\right)}{4} \quad (2.14)$$

Now that we have these four heuristic terms, it only remains to combine them into a single value for the overall score for a choosing specific face as the current node. This is more art than science, as it involves judging how important each of the four heuristic terms is to the final result and weighting them accordingly. A good starting point is given in Equation 2.15. Notice the large power that the split term is raised to (we really want to discourage splits) and the fact that the coplanar term only ever increases desirability for a face to be chosen:

$$h_{final} = h_{balance}^{1} * \left(1 + h_{coplanar}\right)^{1} * h_{split}^{4} * h_{regular}^{1} \quad (2.15)$$

Although Equation 2.15 is a good starting point, the actual values chosen should be based on empirical results from examples of final geometry. This allows the BSP generation algorithm to be tailored toward actual game geometry, producing better results.

Using the preceding heuristics, the following algorithm generates a "good enough" BSP tree:

1. Select the first face in the current face set.
2. Generate a heuristic for this face by testing every other face in the set against the currently selected face.
3. If this heuristic is the best so far, remember the currently selected face as best.
4. If there are more faces, select the next face and go back to step 2.
5. Create a node for the best face from step 3 and remove this face from the current face set.
6. Select the first face in the current face set.

7. If this face is in front of the current node, add it to the front face set and go to step 11.
8. If this face is behind the current node, add it to the behind face set and go to step 11.
9. If this face is coplanar with the current node, add it to the current node and go to step 11.
10. The current node splits this face. Create two or three new triangles that cover the selected face without crossing the current node's plane, and add them to the appropriate face set.
11. If there are more faces, select the next face and go back to step 7.
12. If there are faces in the front face set, recursively create a new node for the front branch using this algorithm.
13. If there are faces in the rear face set, recursively create a new node for the rear branch using this algorithm.

Improving BSP Tree Results

Although the previously described algorithm works well for most meshes, some meshes prove to be problematic. The problem lies with the fact the algorithm can only select existing faces as the source for the plane at each node. This problem is especially pronounced in convex meshes, where no matter which face we choose as the basis for the plane, all of the remaining faces are guaranteed to be behind it. In this case, the generated BSP tree will be perfectly unbalanced, and all of the complexity advantages of using a BSP tree will be lost.

Obviously, we need to be able to consider planes that are not present in the source mesh when creating the BSP tree in order to avoid this problem. Unfortunately, there are an infinite number of arbitrary planes, so we cannot just test every plane at random until we find a good one. Even making new planes from the existing data set (e.g., by taking two points from one face and a third point from a different face) results in many possible planes to test against. Any change to our BSP-tree generation algorithm that must somehow generate and test a viable plane is going to slow it down, just from the sheer number of planes that are possible. We could make it so the algorithm only tries to find a new plane when the heuristic score for the best face is below a certain threshold, but this will still produce unacceptable slow behavior for a convex mesh (where any given face will fall below this threshold).

Luckily, there is a better solution. Although a computer is not very good at picking out planes with a good heuristic score, the human eye is. It is a simple task for a human (even an artist) to look at a mesh and pick out a plane that neatly separates two groups of faces. Figure 2.10 shows a good example of a convex mesh—a sphere.

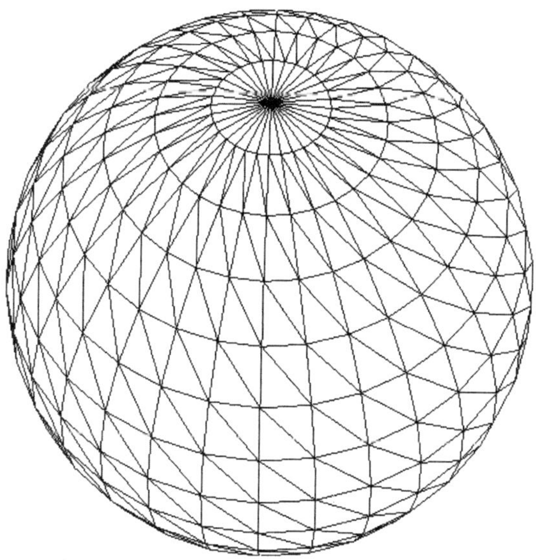

FIGURE 2.10 A convex mesh.

Even a quick glance at Figure 2.10 reveals several planes that could be created that would split the faces of the sphere neatly into two groups. We can help the BSP tree generation algorithm out by creating additional faces that can be used to generate these splitting planes. By assigning these faces a known material or property, we can mark them as dummy faces; that is, faces that only affect the generation of the BSP tree and do not make it into the final model. Figure 2.11 shows the same convex mesh with two dummy faces inserted.

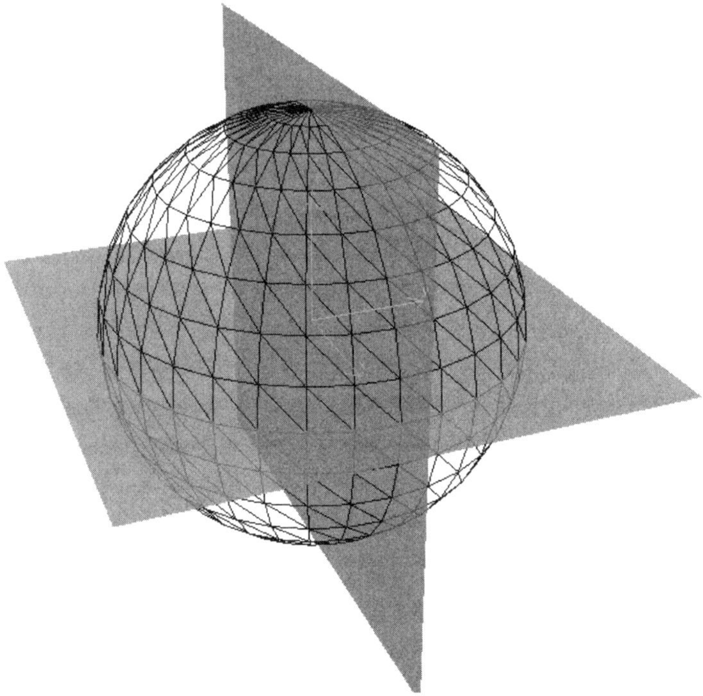

FIGURE 2.11 Adding dummy faces to aid in BSP tree creation.

We can then modify the heuristic given by Equation 2.15 for these dummy faces to give them a bonus for preferential selection over similar quality existing faces. We must also take precautions to not include the dummy faces in any of the heuristic calculations; after all, we don't care if a dummy face is split because it supplies no geometry to the final mesh. We also need to ensure that the dummy faces are passed down both sides of the chosen plane—the dummy faces are meant to represent infinite cutting planes and are effectively split by nearly every possible node. Finally, we need to make sure that the dummy faces do not persist too far down the tree—they should be removed as their relevance diminishes (e.g., when all remaining faces are either split by the dummy face or on a single side of it).

Figure 2.12 shows the two half-spaces generated by choosing the horizontal dummy face from the previous figure. Notice that the second dummy

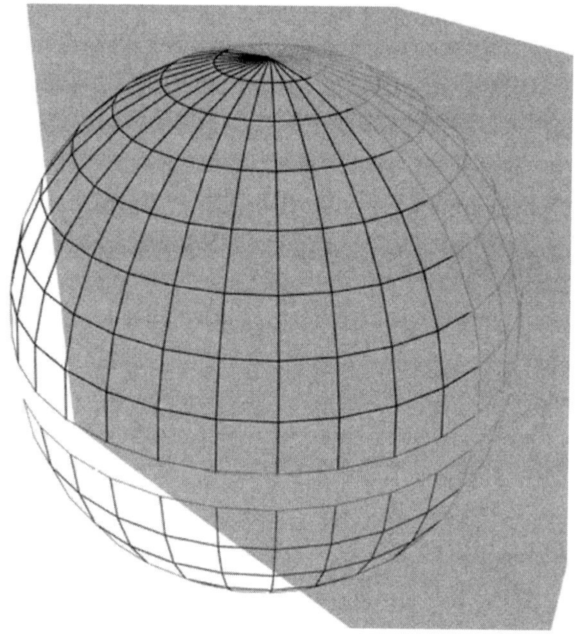

FIGURE 2.12 Half-spaces generated by choosing a dummy face.

face occurs in both of the resultant half-spaces. This allows both half-spaces to be further subdivided by the suggested face.

Using a BSP Tree

Before we can make any more improvements to our generated BSP tree, we must look at some of the uses to which it can be put. By understanding the requirements of each, we can better decide what shortcuts, if any, we can take during its construction.

There are two main uses for BSP trees in games: sorting and collision. When used for sorting, we require that the BSP tree provide us a sorted list of faces for a given position in the world. When used for collision, however, we need the BSP tree to supply a list of faces that the ray could collide with, in the order in which they could be collided with. These are two subtly different requirements, and result in two different algorithms.

Using a BSP Tree: Sorting

When using a BSP tree for sorting purposes, we generally have a single input: the viewpoint. To traverse the BSP tree, we start at the first (root) node and test the point against the plane that the node represents. The viewpoint is then either situated exactly on the plane or to one side of it. What does this tell us? Consider looking at a distant, tall wall that completely crosses your field of view. The wall conceals anything on the opposite side of it, and anything on the same side of the wall as you can obscure part of the wall.

In sorting terms, then, anything on the opposite side of the wall to the viewpoint sorts behind the wall, and anything on the same side sorts in front of it. So, by drawing everything on the same side of the node as the viewpoint first, then the faces that are coplanar with the node, then everything on the reverse side of the node, we end up drawing the scene from front to back. Drawing the scene back to front is as simple as starting with everything on the opposite side of the node. In the case where the viewpoint lies on the plane of the current node, it does not matter which side of the plane we begin with; both sides sort with equal priority.

The following algorithm recursively creates a front-to-back sorted list of faces from a given BSP tree:

1. Start at the root node of the BSP tree.
2. If the current node is empty, stop.
3. Find which side of the current node's plane the viewpoint is on.
4. If the viewpoint is in front of the current node's plane, choose the front branch of the current node as the next node; otherwise, choose the back branch.
5. Recursively go to step 2, making the next node the current node.
6. Add the faces for the current node to the sorted list.
7. If the viewpoint is in front of the current node's plane, choose the back branch of the current node as the next node; otherwise, choose the front branch.
8. Go to step 2. This does not need to be recursive.

This algorithm has a time complexity of $O(n)$, since it visits every node in the BSP tree exactly once. Its output is a perfectly sorted list of faces from any viewpoint. Contrast this with the best real-time sort algorithm, which has a best-case time complexity of O($n\log n$) and a worst case time complexity of O(n^2).

Notice that step 8 in the algorithm does not need to be done recursively. This is an optimization and is made possible by the fact that the algorithm ends immediately after this step. Any recursive call here would be redundant.

Using a BSP Tree: Point Collisions

The algorithm for using a BSP tree to resolve point collisions is slightly different. This is mainly because to correctly resolve any collisions of a point moving through a BSP tree, we require two inputs: the starting location of the point and its ending location. As when sorting, we start by finding out which side of the current node's plane the starting point lies on. Additionally, we calculate which side the ending point lies on. By examining these two values, we can determine whether the point's motion makes it cross the plane.

When both the start and the end points occupy the same side of the plane, the point's motion does not make it cross the plane. In this case, we only need to test against all of the faces on the same side of the plane, since the point could not possibly have hit anything on the opposite side of it.

If, however, the point does cross the plane, we must first test against all of the faces on the same side of the plane as the starting point. These are the faces that would be hit first, because the point must cross the plane to hit any of the other faces. Next, we test against all of the faces that lie on the plane. Finally, we test against all of the faces on the same side of the plane as the ending point. If during any of these tests, a face is hit by the point, this is guaranteed to be the first collision, by virtue of the way we walked the BSP tree.

The following algorithm will find the first collision of a point with the faces contained in a BSP tree:

1. Start at the root node of the BSP tree.
2. If the current node is empty, stop.
3. Find which side of the current node's plane the starting point lies on, and which side the ending point lies on.
4. Select the node on the same side of the plane as the starting point as the next node.

5. If the start and end points lie on the same side of the plane, go to step 2, making the next node the current node.
6. Recursively go to step 2, making the next node the current node.
7. If step 6 produced a collision, stop.
8. Find where the point crosses the current node's plane, and check the resulting point against all of the faces attached to the current node. If there is a collision, then stop; this is the first possible collision.
9. Select the node on the opposite side of the plane as the starting point as the current node.
10. Go to step 2. This does not need to be recursive.

Given a balanced BSP tree, this algorithm has a best-case time complexity of O(log*n*), but a worst-case time complexity of O(*n*). The best case is O(log*n*) because no faces are tested until a leaf node is found due to the way that the recursion operates, and so the algorithm cannot terminate until a leaf node is reached. The worst case occurs when the motion of the point crosses every plane in the BSP tree, colliding with none of the faces contained within. In this case, every node in the BSP tree is visited, and every face in the BSP tree is tested for collision.

Using a BSP Tree: Sphere Collisions

Interesting things begin to happen when we attempt to use the BSP tree to solve collisions where the colliding object has volume. In this section, we will look at the extra work we need to perform when the colliding object is spherical. This is the simplest case of a colliding object that possesses volume, and one that many games use.

When the colliding object has volume, we introduce cases where the object can straddle a node's plane. Effectively, we have moved the point at which the object is considered in front of the plane behind the plane. Similarly, the point at which the object is considered to be behind the plane has now been moved forward and lies in front of the plane. These two states now overlap; an object with volume can be both in front of the plane and behind the plane.

Figure 2.13 shows a spherical object that straddles a plane. The area where the object is considered to be simultaneously on both sides of the

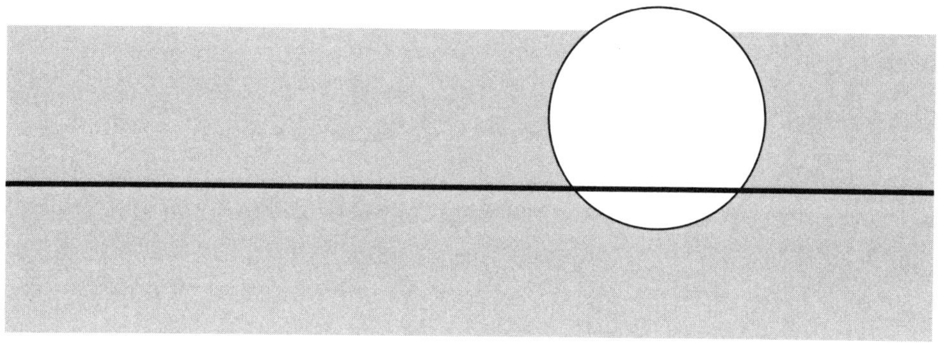

FIGURE 2.13 An object with volume can straddle a node's plane.

plane is shaded. We will call this area the *area of uncertainty*. While in the area of uncertainty, the object is able to collide with faces on either side of the plane and also with faces that lie on the plane. This breaks our previous algorithm, where the first collision that we found was guaranteed to be the first collision made by the object. Now, if we find that the object collides with a face in front of the plane while in the area of uncertainty, we must continue to check the rest of the faces it is possible to collide with to see if another collision occurs earlier.

This adds complexity to our algorithm, skewing its time complexity toward its worst case. This occurs because we must test against a greater number of nodes when a collision occurs in the area of uncertainty around a plane. However, the worst case is still only $O(n)$.

Avoiding Splits: Multiroot BSP Trees

Given the advent of modern, Z-buffered graphics hardware, and the penalties associated with dynamic polygon-level drawing, there is no longer a need for the BSP tree to be used for sorting purposes. Games rely instead on gross frustum culling to avoid drawing objects that are outside of the current view, and then on the Z-buffered drawing to maintain the correct sorting. When we also consider the fact that most of the collision needs of a game surround objects with volume (even bullets are often considered as spheres), we can see that we do not really need a BSP tree to be completely accurate. This allows us to take some liberties with its construction.

One of the worst aspects of constructing a BSP tree is dealing with faces that are split by the chosen node. Although our selection heuristics are tailored to avoid choosing faces that generate these splits, with most models they are unavoidable. To maintain an accurate BSP tree, any faces that are split must be degenerated into multiple faces that do not cross the plane. This adds geometry to the model (sometimes the best plane will split many faces at once) and is generally undesirable.

However, since we no longer require an accurate BSP tree, it is possible for us to take the faces that would be split and create a new BSP tree from just these faces. The resulting secondary BSP tree could then be attached to the node that caused the splits. Any tests against this node must necessarily also be done against the attached secondary BSP tree, since they both now occupy the same half-space.

Such a BSP tree is called a *multiroot* BSP tree, since each node in it could contain a secondary BSP tree with its own root. The advantage of this is obvious; less splits means less generated geometry, and less seams to provide collision problems. The downside is that for a node that contains a secondary BSP tree, the area of uncertainty is expanded to include the whole half-space. Luckily, although splits are often unavoidable, they are still uncommon, making the multiroot BSP tree a viable alternative to creating split faces.

ENDNOTES

[1]Remember that *n* is the size of the problem space, so what we are saying here is that the number of operations on each item needed to run the algorithm depends on the number of items in the problem.

[2]Remember that the original rating is per item, so the actual complexity equation for algorithm five is n^3+n^2.

[3]Quicksort actually only exhibits $O(n\log n)$ complexity in the average case; in the worst case (with an already sorted list), its time complexity rises to $O(n^2)$.

3 Hashes and Hash Functions

In This Chapter

- Rule #3: "Trust Your First Impressions"
- Hash Collisions
- The Birthday Paradox
- Creating a Hash
- Reducing Collision Frequency
- DNA Hashes
- Structures for Storing Data by Hash (Hash List, Table, and Tree)
- Localization of Text Assets
- Binding Names
- Dynamic Data and DNA Hashes
- Further Reading

Have you every caught a glimpse of someone out of the corner of your eye and thought you recognized that person? Did it turn out to be the person you expected it to be when you finally got a closer look at him? The brain classifies faces by the relative positions and shapes of different parts of the face. For example, you might think of your brother as having nose #1, eyes #17, and mouth #4, arranged just so, and your father as having nose #1, eyes #12, and mouth #4. At first glance they might appear similar, since the nose and the mouth are superficially the same, but on closer inspection you would be able to see that their eyes are very different and so you can tell them apart.

What does this have to do with game programming? We're glad you asked.

RULE #3: "TRUST YOUR FIRST IMPRESSIONS"

Oftentimes, a situation will occur where you need to compare two large or variable-length data structures as quickly as possible. A good example of this would be to find a given resource by name (a zero-terminated character string). In this example, you would need to search through all the loaded resources, comparing their names to the name that you are searching for until a match is found. Now, the string compare operation is not the fastest thing at the best of times, especially if it needs to be case insensitive. Can we find a better way? Can we adapt the way our brain works and apply it to this problem?

The answer, obviously, is yes. If we precompute in some way a number that is representative of each string, then all we need to do is compare the representative number for our string with the precomputed representative numbers for the strings in the resource database until we find a match. This is much faster than a complete string compare is. If the two numbers are different, then the strings are *definitely* different, but if the two numbers are the same, then the strings are only *possibly* the same. To find out for sure, we need to break down and do a full string compare, in the same way that you would need to take a closer look at someone who looked like one of your friends to determine that you were looking at a different person.

The process of making a representative number for a piece of data is called a *hash function*, and the result of this operation is called the *hash* of that data, and usually takes the form of a 32-bit number. The hash function usually works by chopping up, or hashing, the input data into small pieces and iteratively recombining them into a single value in such a way that a small change in the input data produces an unpredictable change in the hash for that data. A good hash function will map each possible value of the input data onto a unique hash value, spread over the entire possible range of values that the hash can take.

HASH COLLISIONS

The astute among you will by now have realized that a 32-bit hash contains significantly less data than a large data structure or variable-length string. This means that it is impossible to generate a unique hash for every possible input if the input contains more than 32 bits of data. When two different inputs result in the same hash, we say that a *hash collision* has occurred. In this case, if we just compare hashes to determine if two pieces of data are identical, then these two pieces of data will appear identical. This means that the result of a hash comparison has a distinctly different meaning when hash collisions are possible. As detailed earlier, the result of comparing two hashes tells us one of two things about the two input pieces of data: either they are *definitely* different, or they are *possibly* identical.

In the case where the hashes for two pieces of data are the same, a further check is needed to see whether the pieces of data are identical. This check unfortunately has to be a bit-wise comparison of the two pieces of data (but hey, you were going to do it anyway).

However, if we can guarantee that no hash collisions are possible, then comparing hashes is enough to determine if two pieces of data are the same. This has important consequences for how we store our data.

As an example, we will examine a system for storing and retrieving resource data. Each resource consists of two parts: an arbitrary length piece of data, and an arbitrary length character string for its name. The resources are indexed by the hash of their names. To request a resource from the system, you need to know its name. This is first converted to a hash, which is then used to find the correct resource. If two different resource names can have the same hash, then we will need to store the resource names so that we can identify the required resource. However, if there can never be a hash collision, then the resource names are never needed, since each resource can be uniquely identified by its hash.

However, a 32-bit hash means that there are 4,294,967,296 different possible hashes. Surely, collisions aren't that common, right? Wrong!

THE BIRTHDAY PARADOX

How many people would have to be in a room before the chances of two or more of them sharing the same birthday was better than 50 percent? The layperson would probably guess at around 182 (half the number of days in the year). In fact, you only need 22 people to be in a room before the probability of two or more of them sharing the same birthday is 50.59 percent. This is called the *birthday paradox*[1].

So, why is the actual value so different from the expected value, and how did we come up with these specific numbers? To answer that, we have to delve into the murky and often counterintuitive realm of probabilities for a little while.

We start by looking at the probability of any two people sharing the same birthday. As with a lot of probability problems, we turn it around and find the probability of any two people having different birthdays. Now, the first person can choose any birthday at all, leaving the second person with only 364 possible choices without getting the same day. The probability of any two people having different birthdays is shown in Equation 3.1.

$$\frac{365}{365} \times \frac{364}{365} = 0.9973 \tag{3.1}$$

So, the probability of them having different birthdays is 1 minus this, or 0.0027 (0.27 percent). Now, expanding our problem to three people, we find that again the first person can choose any day and the second person can choose 364 out of 365. Similarly, the third person can choose any of 363 remaining days. This can be written as shown in Equation 3.2:

$$\frac{365}{365} \times \frac{364}{365} \times \frac{363}{365} = 0.9918 \tag{3.2}$$

This means that the probability of any three people sharing the same birthday is 0.82 percent. Now we can expand this to any number of people, n, where $2 \le n \le 365$. The following is a small function to do just this:

```
double Birthday( unsigned int nPeople, unsigned int nDays )
{
    double          value = 1.0;
    unsigned int    n;

    if( nPeople<=1 )        return 0.0;
    if( nPeople>=nDays )    return 1.0;

    for( n=2;n<=nPeople;n++ )
    {
        value *= 1.0-((double)n)/((double)nDays);
    }
    return 1.0-value;
}
```

By calling this function with different values for the number of people, we can construct a graph of the distribution of probabilities as the number of people changes. Figure 3.1 shows this distribution, with the probability of clashing birthdays on the vertical axis and the number of people in the sample group on the horizontal axis. Looking at this graph, we can see that in order for there to be a 95-percent probability of at least two people having the same birthday, we need to only have a sample group of 46 people.

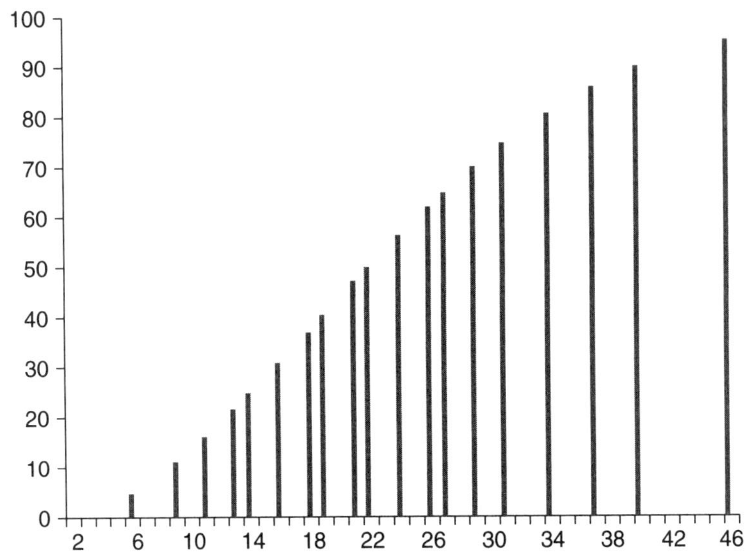

FIGURE 3.1 Probability of two or more people sharing a birthday, by number of people in the sample group.

ON THE CD

The values for this graph were obtained by using a variation of the Birthday function given earlier that calculates the probabilities for increasing sample sizes sequentially, and reports the required sample size for certain threshold probability values. The full source code for the application can be found on the companion CD-ROM in the Chapter3/Birthday folder, but the functional part looks like this:

```
void Birthday( double maxValue,
               double minReport=0.05,
               double dReport=0.05 )
{
    double  value = 1.0;
    double  numPeople = 1.0;
    double  ooMaxValue = 1.0/maxValue;
    double  report = 1.0f-dReport;
```

```
        while( value>minReport )
        {
            report = max(report,minReport);
            while( value > report )
            {
                numPeople += 1.0;
                value *= 1.0f - numPeople*ooMaxValue;
            }

            printf("%2.2f%% chance of a collision with %d samples\n",
                      100*(1.0-value),(int)numPeople);
            report -= dReport;
        }
    }
```

Now, this is all well and good, but what does it mean for our hash values? Well, using the previous program, we can calculate the probabilities of collisions for various sample sizes with a 32-bit hash—the results might surprise you. For a population of 4,294,967,296 (2^{32}) different values, it would only take 77,163 samples to have a 50-percent probability of a hash collision occurring, and only 160,415 samples for a 95-percent probability of a hash collision. The full output of the program for a population of 4,294,967,296 is:

```
C:\>birthday 4294967296
Birthday paradox demonstration

Calculating for 4294967296 samples
5.00% probability of a collision with 20991 samples
10.00% probability of a collision with 30084 samples
15.00% probability of a collision with 37363 samples
20.00% probability of a collision with 43781 samples
25.00% probability of a collision with 49711 samples
30.00% probability of a collision with 55352 samples
35.00% probability of a collision with 60831 samples
40.00% probability of a collision with 66241 samples
45.00% probability of a collision with 71661 samples
```

```
50.00% probability of a collision with 77163 samples
55.00% probability of a collision with 82820 samples
60.00% probability of a collision with 88718 samples
65.00% probability of a collision with 94962 samples
70.00% probability of a collision with 101695 samples
75.00% probability of a collision with 109124 samples
80.00% probability of a collision with 117579 samples
85.00% probability of a collision with 127656 samples
90.00% probability of a collision with 140637 samples
95.00% probability of a collision with 160415 samples
```

CREATING A HASH

There are innumerable ways to create a hash for a piece of data. Some are more popular than others; for example, the CRC-32 algorithm, widely used to check file integrity in compression programs such as Zip, makes an effective hash function. However, there are advantages to constructing your own, custom hash function and tailoring it to the data you are hashing; for example, when hashing a filename you might want to ignore a character's case and make `/` equivalent to `\`. This section covers custom techniques for generating hash functions.

Most hash functions work by iterating over each byte of the data in sequence, combining the byte at this location with the modified hash value. For each byte, y, something akin to Equation 3.3 is done to the cumulative hash value, x:

$$x' = f(x) + y. \tag{3.3}$$

A good function to use for $f(x)$ is the rotation operator. By rotating the previous hash for each byte in the input data, you ensure that every byte affects a very different set of bits in the final value from the previous and next bytes. Another side effect of this is that data that varies in length by a single byte will return a very different hash, even if the two data are identical except for the extra byte in one of them.

What is a good number of bits to rotate by? We want to choose a number that results in the entire 32-bit space of the hash value being filled as quickly as possible, so each new byte should write to as many virgin bits as possible. However, we also want to make sure that it takes the maximum number of iterations before any bit of the hash value returns to its previous location. This means that nice round values like 2, 4, and 8 are out because they take less than 32 iterations to cycle completely (16, 8, and 4, respectively). The best values to use are those that aren't a factor of 32, meaning they will take 32 iterations to cycle. We prefer to use 7 or 25 as the number of bits to rotate by. These values each take the maximum number of iterations to cycle and fill the complete range of the hash value quickly, with only 1 bit of overlap for each new byte.

We should take a moment here to lament the fact that the C programming language does not include an operator for integer rotation. Therefore, we must either resort to assembly language, or use two logical shift operators and then OR the results together in the hope that the compiler will recognize that we want to rotate the value. For now, we will represent the rotation operator as a function call whose implementation we can fill in later. An example of a hash function for an arbitrary structure with a rotation of 7 bits is given here:

```
template <class X>
inline HASH MakeHash( const X *data )
{
    HASH                ret = 0;
    unsigned int        i;
    const unsigned char *ptr;

    for( i=0,ptr=(const unsigned char*)data; i<sizeof(X); ++i )
    {
        ret = RotateLeft(ret,7) + *(ptr++);
    }
    return ret;
}
```

In the case of a null-terminated character string, we must modify the function to only stop when the incoming data byte is zero. As stated previously, it might also be desirable to modify the incoming bytes to make the hash value case-insensitive, to replace one character with another, or to ignore specific sequences of characters. The following function will create a hash from a null-terminated filename string, ignoring case and replacing `/` with `\`.

```
HASH MakeFilenameHash( const char *pString )
{
    HASH ret = 0;
    char c;

    while( c=*(pString++) )
    {
        if( c>='A' && c<='Z' )
            c ^= 32;
        else if( c=='/' )
            c = '\\';
        ret = RotateLeft(ret,7) + c;
    }
    return ret;
}
```

REDUCING COLLISION FREQUENCY

We've already covered in some detail the fact that hash collisions complicate things, and that they are so much more common than you would think. Life would be so much easier if we could be sure that we weren't going to get any. Well, now for some good news—for the most part, you *can* be sure that you aren't going to get any collisions!

Games usually have a very well defined palette of valid values for each piece of data that needs a hash created for it. This means that we can test *in advance* each piece of data to see if its hash collides with any other piece of data in the same scope. This is where using a custom hash function really pays off—if a collision occurs, we can simply change the hash function for that data type and start again. Unless you are really unlucky (or have a very large palette for a given data type), this will happen only once or twice throughout the entire development period of the game. In these rare cases, the burden of changing the hash function is more than balanced by the speed gain from not having any hash collisions to worry about.

For the rare set of data whose palette cannot be defined in advance (e.g., any player-entered strings), we can resort to lookups that properly handle collisions.

ON THE CD

Included on the companion CD-ROM, in the Chapter3/filenamehash folder, is the source code for a tool that recursively catalogs all of the filenames in a given path, and records the number of hash collisions generated. The code uses a data structure called a hash tree, which is detailed later in this chapter. As an exercise, you should try to change the hash function in this project and see if you can reduce the number of collisions for all the filenames on your C:\ drive.

DNA HASHES

One interesting use of hashes is to have each section of the hash mean something. Each bit in the hash would then be similar to a gene, and the entire hash could be thought of as a short sequence of DNA. This technique is extremely useful for caching procedural (or at least predictable) data that can be fully described in a few (less than 33) bits.

For example, say your game has a series of vertex shaders to process its geometry in different ways. Each vertex shader could be fully described by a series of limited-scope parameters defining, say, how many lights should affect each vertex and whether fog would be applied. If we were to collapse these parameters into the minimum number of bits that they could fit in, and concatenate them together into a single value, we would have a value that could be used as a hash, and yet fully and uniquely describes the vertex shader's function. The vertex shaders could then be stored and indexed by this hash. Changing how geometry is rendered is then simply a matter of changing a couple of the genes in the DNA hash for the vertex shader, and then looking up the address of the new shader.

STRUCTURES FOR STORING DATA BY HASH

Although hashes reduce the amount of work needed to compare two pieces of data, finding the correct piece of data in a data set is still an $O(n)$ operation; that is, the time taken to find a given piece of data rises linearly with the number of pieces of data in the data set. Luckily, there are some structures we can use that reduce the order of complexity of finding a given piece of data.

The structures we will be looking at are, in order, the hash list, the hash table, and the hash tree. Each of these structures uses some of the spatial subdivision methods introduced in the previous chapter, and each has different strengths and weaknesses. All of the structures can be modified to handle hash collisions, some more easily than others.

It should be noted at this point that if hash collisions are not possible, then the hash of a piece of data is enough to find it in the list or remove it from the list. However, when collisions can occur, a sample of the data itself is needed so that we can compare it to each collision case to be sure that we find the correct piece of data.

We will look at several aspects of each of the structures:

- The performance of finding an item by hash
- The performance of adding a new item
- The performance of removing an item
- The modifications needed to correctly handle hash collisions

Because we are writing a game and so are interested in speed, all of our hash structures will contain a pointer to the data associated with the hash; we will not attempt to copy the data into the structures as some more academic implementations might try to do. This means that the onus of creating and destroying the data and keeping it in scope is on the underlying application, not the hash structures.

And so without further ado, let's look at the first structure for storing data by hash.

The Hash List

A hash list is merely a list of structures, sorted by hash. Each structure contains the hash of a piece of data and a pointer to the data itself. The implementation we will examine represents the list as a linear array of structures. A simple diagram of a hash list is shown in Figure 3.2.

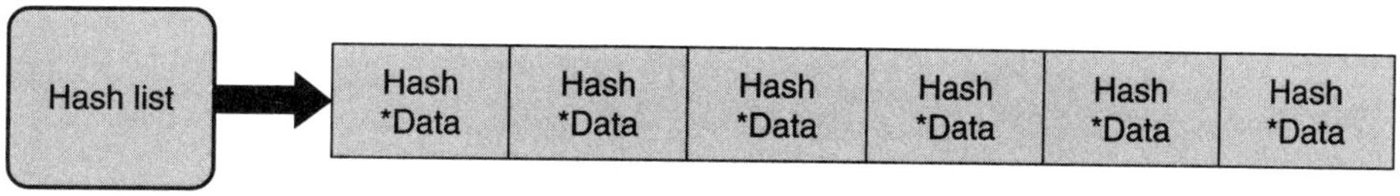

FIGURE 3.2 Block diagram of a hash list.

Because the list of structures is sorted by hash, finding a piece of data by hash can be done using a binary search, which has $O(\log n)$ complexity.

Adding or removing an item, however, potentially entails copying around large portions of the list to make room for the new element. For this reason, additions and removals are both $O(n)$ operations. A potential optimization that can be done is to not sort the list while elements are being added, instead waiting until all additions are completed before using an optimal sort routine, such as *quicksort*, to sort all of the additions. This optimization changes the complexity of any additions to $O(1)$ at the expense of adding an $O(n\log n)$ sort when all additions are complete. One thing to note here is that if the list is already sorted after all of the additions, then the quicksort algorithm reverts to its worst-case, $O(n^2)$ complexity. Another potential downside is that the list will be in an invalid, unsorted state while additions are being made, meaning that any removals or searches will not work as expected.

ON THE CD

A sample implementation of a hash list is included on the companion CD-ROM, in the common/hash folder. This implementation contains two classes: `StaticHashList` *and* `HashList`. *The* `StaticHashList` *class does not allow any operation other than searching, but the* `HashList` *class extends it to be a full implementation of a hash list. Internally, both classes store their lists in the same way, as a linear array of* `HashListItem` *classes.*

```
class HashListItem
{
public:
```

```
    HASH hashValue;
    void *data;
};
```

The member function `StaticHashList::FindByHash` is common to both classes and simply uses a binary search to find the given hash in the linear list of structures returning the data pointer associated with this item. Care must be taken that there are no `null` data items in the list, since it is impossible to tell a `null` item from a missing item using this function.

The member function `StaticHashList::FindByIndex` returns the data pointer for the item at the given index. If the index is past the end of the list, then the function returns `null`. This function can be used to easily iterate through the list.

The member function `HashList::AddByHash` associates the given data pointer with the given hash and adds it to the hash list in the correct place. This function often requires that other list entries be shuffled or that the memory for the list be extended to make room for the new item. Similarly, the `HashList::RemoveByHash` function finds the given hash in the list and removes it from the list, shuffling other list entries around as needed.

Unfortunately, the hash list structure does not handle hash collisions gracefully or easily. Possibly the simplest way would be to just add new `HashListItem` entries with the same hash to the list. These will all be placed next to each other by virtue of the list being sorted. However, extra work is needed when finding an item since the binary search will return an item at an arbitrary position among the duplicate items.

Another commonly used method is to actually increment the hash value of the data to be added until a hash collision no longer occurs, or the data pointer for the item at the current hash value is `null`, meaning it has been removed. The search routine would then find the original piece of data with the offending hash, and would have to check all the data items whose hashes have consecutive values, until there is a break. The lion's share of the extra work for this method is deferred until the removal operation. Since any breaks in a consecutive string of hashes now mean something, we can only truly remove an item if either the previous item or the next item has a hash that is not consecutive. In the cases where we cannot truly remove the data, we need to set its data pointer to `null` to indicate that it has been removed.

When a data item is truly removed, we must also remove any neighboring items with `null` data pointers, since these would now be on the end of a consecutive string of hashes. Care must be taken at either end of the list, as the hash value might overflow when incremented or decremented.

The following algorithm can be used to add an item to the hash list when collisions are enabled using the incremental hash collision method described in the previous paragraph:

1. Use a binary search to find where to place this hash.
2. If the data here has a different hash value from the one we are trying to add, then insert the new item here and stop.
3. If the data here is the same as the data that we are trying to add, then it is already in the list, so stop.
4. If the data here has a `null` data pointer, then overwrite with the new item and stop.
5. Increment the hash for the item we are trying to add.
6. Move to the next index in the list and go back to step 2.

To remove an item from a hash list that uses the incremental hash collision method, the following algorithm can be used:

1. Use a binary search to find the correct place for this hash.
2. If the data here has a different hash value from the one we are trying to add, then stop; the data we are looking for is not in the list.
3. If the data here is not the same as the data we are trying to remove, then increment the hash of the data we are trying to remove and go to step 2.
4. If the next data item has a hash that is equal to the current item's hash plus 1, then set the data pointer at the current position to `null` and stop.
5. Remember the position of the current item.
6. If the previous item's data pointer is `null` and the previous item's hash equals the current item's hash minus 1, then move to the previous item and repeat step 6.
7. Remove all items between the current position and the position remembered in step 5.

An alternative method would be to hang a linked list of data items that share the same hash off of each `HashListItem` entry. This method would require extra code to manage the pool of memory for recording the linked list entries. Although this method is effective, it is counterintuitive, since it makes the `HashList` class use two different methods of storing its lists (a linear array and a linked list).

The Hash Table

A hash table uses an array of *buckets* to store its items. Each bucket is actually a hash list, as described earlier. Each piece of data to be added is placed in a bucket based on its hash value modulo the number of buckets. By splitting up the work in this way, the complexity of each operation on the hash table is reduced, but only by a constant amount. A simple diagram of the hash table is shown in Figure 3.3.

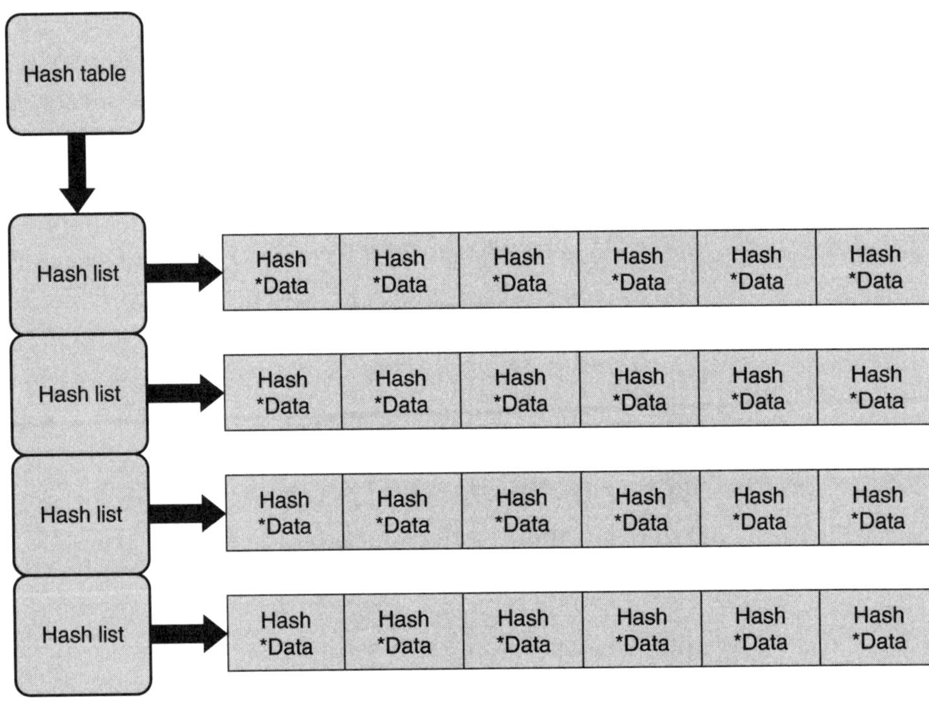

FIGURE 3.3 Block diagram of a hash table.

Usually, the typical number of items in a hash table is known beforehand, and an appropriate number of buckets is chosen. Too many buckets, and there might as well not be a table, since each bucket will contain a minimal number of items; too few buckets, and the complexity of the operations will not be reduced at all. For example, a 20-bucket hash table will be very effective for 400 items, since 20 is a respectable fraction of 400. However, the same 20-bucket hash table won't be much help at all if it is to contain 400,000 items.

The theoretical time complexity of each of the operations for a hash table is the same as the equivalent operation for a hash list (after all, it is just a collection of hash lists). However, if the items are spread pretty evenly among the buckets, then the time complexity is effectively reduced by a constant factor. This won't really help when the number of items is raised by an order of magnitude, or if all of the items end up in the same bucket, but for a well managed data set, a hash table can be a win.

ON THE CD

A sample implementation of a hash table is included on the companion CD-ROM, in the common/hash folder. This implementation uses an array of `HashList` *classes as its buckets.*

The Hash Tree

The final data structure that we will examine for storing data by hash is the hash tree. A hash tree is actually a binary tree of `HashTreeItem` structures. At each level in the tree, the decision to take the right or left branch is made based on the value of a specific bit in the hash value being searched for. At the top level, bit 0 is used; at the second level, bit 1 is used, and so on. Each node in the tree also contains a pointer to a piece of data, and the hash of that data. This means that the location of a node in the tree determines the first few bits of the hash of any piece of data that can reside in the node. The number of bits that are determined by position in the tree is equal to the depth of the node. A simple diagram of a hash tree is shown in Figure 3.4.

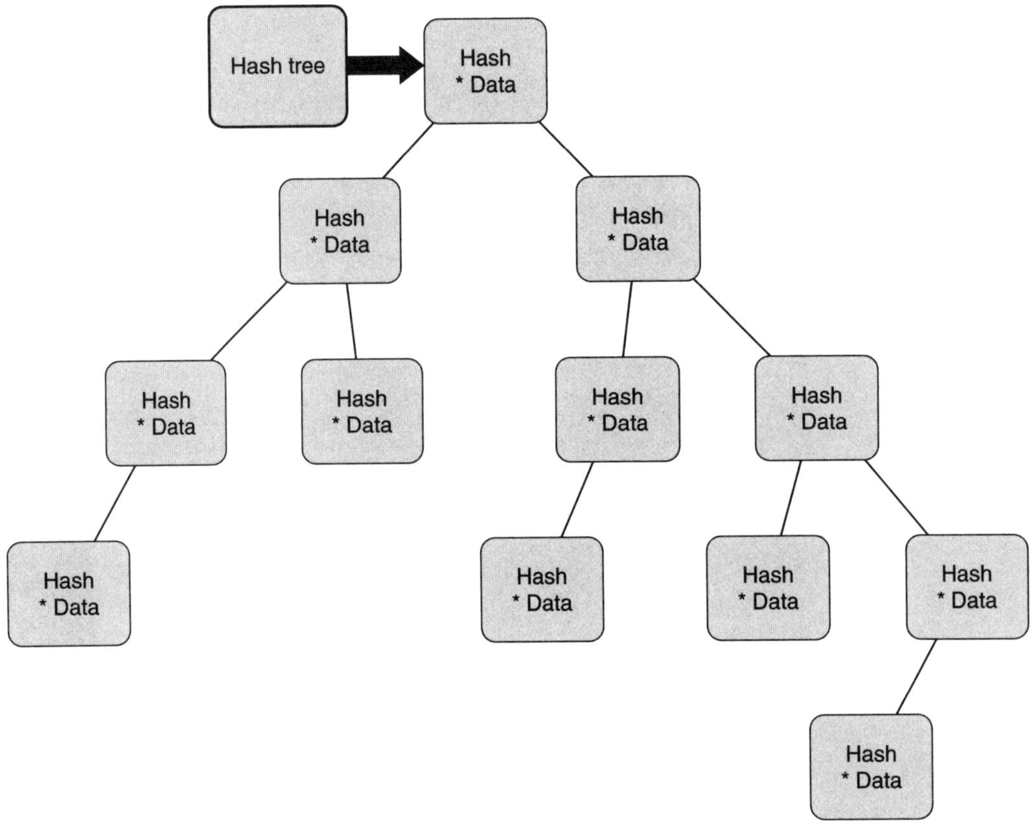

FIGURE 3.4 Block diagram of a hash tree.

The `HashTreeItem` class contains pointers to the left and right nodes at the next tree level, a pointer to the data item in this node, and the hash of the data item in this node. It looks like this:

```
class HashTreeItem
{
public:
    HashTreeItem *left;
    HashTreeItem *right;
    HASH         hashValue;
    void         *data;
};
```

To find an item in a hash tree, you must iteratively walk down the binary tree, choosing branches based on the corresponding bit of the hash being searched for. A simple algorithm for the search is given here:

1. Begin at the root of the tree.
2. If the current node does not exist, then the search has failed.
3. If the current node's hash is the same as the hash being searched for, the search has finished.
4. Check the bit of the input hash corresponding to the current tree level.
5. If the bit is 0, move down the left branch; otherwise, go down the right branch.
6. Go back to step 2.

This algorithm, by virtue of being a search of a binary tree, is $O(\log n)$, meaning that it takes an amount of time proportional to the log of the number of items in the tree.

Similarly, to add an item to the hash tree, we must first find where it should go using the previous algorithm. Once we have found the correct place (an empty leaf), we need to insert a new `HashTreeItem` class into the tree as a child of the last node visited. This also is an $O(\log n)$ operation. The final resting place of a piece of data with a given hash is dependent on the state of the tree when it is added; the fuller the tree, the deeper the data will reside, since it takes longer to find an empty leaf with the correct bit pattern.

Removal of an item from the tree is a more complex operation. When a node is removed, all of its child nodes need to be rearranged to keep the tree syntactically correct. Since all of its child nodes could equally reside in its current position, we can basically just move the child nodes up the tree. The only problem occurs when a node has two valid children; the decision of which branch the child occupies is based on the value of a bit in its hash that is dependent on its depth in the tree. This means that moving the node and its children up the tree as is will change the bit that the decision is made on, and so render the results invalid. An algorithm to achieve correct removal of a node, while preserving the correctness of the tree is given next. Note that this algorithm shuffles the data contained in the nodes around, and so avoids unlinking any nodes except for the final node that should be removed.

1. Start at the node to be removed.
2. Choose the left node as the next node if it exists; otherwise, choose the right node.
3. If the next node does not exist, move the current node into the free list and finish.
4. Copy the next node data and hash into the current node.
5. Move to the next node and go back to step 2.

By examination, we can see that the time complexity of this algorithm depends on how deep in the tree the item to be removed is, but that it should never be worse than $O(\log n)$ for a balanced tree. To better visualize how this algorithm works, take the example given in Figure 3.5. The figure depicts a partial tree containing five nodes, labeled A through E, and shows two steps involved in the removal of node A.

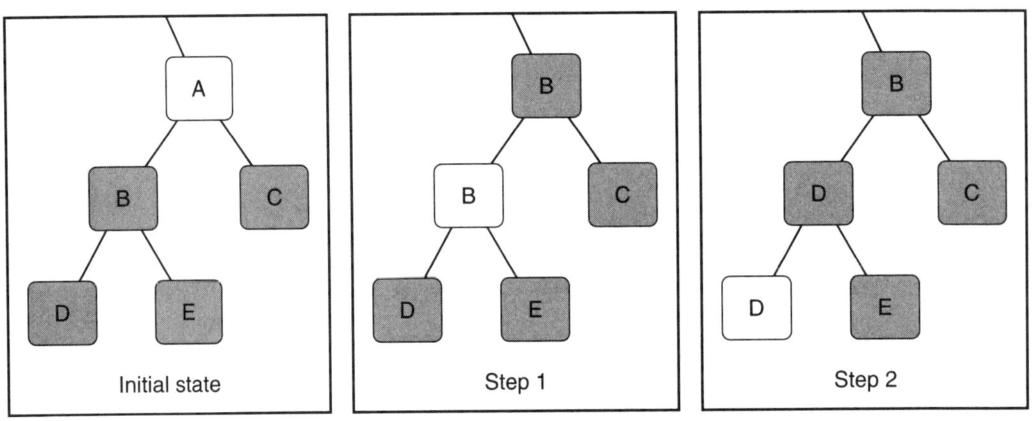

FIGURE 3.5 Removal of a hash tree node.

The initial state shows node A in a brighter color, indicating that this is our current node, or node to be removed. In step 1, according to our algorithm, we moved the contents of node B into what was node A, leaving the original node B intact, and changed the current node to the old node B. A similar operation for step 2 leaves the data from node D occupying the node that was originally B, and what was node D is now the current node. The final step is to remove the current node, since it is now an empty, isolated leaf node.

ON THE CD

A sample implementation of a hash tree is included on the companion CD-ROM, in the common/hash folder. This implementation contains two classes: `StaticHashTree` *and* `HashTree`. *The* `StaticHashTree` *class does not allow any operation other than searching, but the* `HashTree` *class extends it to be a full implementation of a hash tree. The* `HashTree` *class maintains a linked list of free* `HashTreeItem` *classes that are passed out as needed. The free items can be either dynamically allocated or added by an external source at any time.*

One of the most intriguing features of a hash tree is that the performance can be skewed based on the frequency of the queries for each item. By adding the most frequently requested items first, they will occur near the top of the tree and so will be found much earlier than they would otherwise. Cunning use of this feature can greatly increase the performance of any section of code that accesses the tree.

Out of all of the structures for storing hashes presented in this chapter, the hash tree is by far the easiest to extend to support collisions. Simply adding an extra element to the `HashTreeItem` class allows you to chain a linked list of data with the same hash off of each node in the tree. Since collisions are usually pretty rare, we can even afford the overhead of using a complete `HashTreeItem` for each item in the collision list.

LOCALIZATION OF TEXT ASSETS

ON THE CD

This simple program can be found on the companion CD-ROM, in the Chapter3/localization folder. It attempts to duplicate the conditions that exist in a localized game by storing all the character strings in the game in a big list. Then, when something needs to be displayed, the correct text for the current language is found in the list.

The program requires two text files to initialize. The first text file (keys.txt) is always the same and contains the identifiers for each string in the list, with one identifier per line. The second text file is dependent on the language being used. It contains the actual text to be displayed for each identifier, in the same order as they are listed in the first file. Again, the separate items of text are delimited by new lines. During initialization, these two files are simultaneously read a line at a time. The line from the keys file is used to create a hash, which the line from the language-dependent file is then stored under in the hash list. After the hash list has been created, the keys file can be removed from memory, as the keys are no longer needed.

The `FindLocalizedText` function attempts to find the localized version of the text stored under the given key. If the text is found, it is returned. If the text is not found, then the key is returned. This allows us to avoid a check for a `null` pointer every time something needs to be displayed.

BINDING NAMES

Any game that incorporates some degree of scripting will at some point need to be able to take an arbitrary text name and create a specific type of object. This gives script commands the ability to create any type of object whose name is recognized, giving the designers more freedom. The binding of an object's name to the correct class seems trivial, but if done incorrectly can lead to bloated and slow code. For example, the simplest way to achieve this binding would be to use a series of cascading `if` statements, as the following code illustrates:

```
Object *CreateObject( const char *name )
{
    Object *ret = 0;

    // make sure name is valid
    assert(name!=0);

    if( strcmpi(name,"Player")==0 )
        ret = new PLAYER;

    else if( strcmpi(name,"Alien")==0 )
        ret = new ALIEN;
```

```
        else if( strcmpi(name,"Bullet")==0 )
            ret = new BULLET;

        // make sure something was created...
        assert(ret);

        // do any standard setup tasks here

        return ret;
}
```

This code is already looking pretty bloated, and we only have a total of three objects! It is not uncommon for a game to have over 100 different types of objects, and for a single object to have multiple bindings (names). In such a situation, where our object creation function has 100 bindings that are tested sequentially, the speed at which different types of objects can be created varies wildly depending on how far down the list they are. In the previous example, creating a bullet involves three string compares, whereas creating a player takes only one. Obviously, this is not optimal, as we will be creating many more bullets during the course of a game than we will players.

We could ameliorate this somewhat by rearranging the order of the string compares, but this still is not ideal; what if your game has 10 different types of bullet? If all of the bullets occur with equal frequency, then in the average case it will take five string compares to create a bullet each time one is fired.

But why use string compares at all? If we could convert the given name into a number, we could then simply implement a `switch` statement to create an object of the requested type. Furthermore, if we could guarantee that the possible values of the resulting numbers were sequential, the `switch` statement would compile into a jump table that runs in linear time: *O(1)*. The first part of this is simple; we can convert an arbitrary string into a number by applying a hash function to it. We can even choose a hash function so that these hash values will be case-insensitive. However, we cannot guarantee that the hash values will be sequential. Or can we?

The structures presented in this chapter (hash list, hash table, and hash tree) associate a piece of arbitrary data with a number (ostensibly the data's hash). However, the number does not necessarily need to be derived from the data. We saw this in the localization of text assets example, where the localized text (the data) was stored under the hash for a different piece of text (the "key" text). We can use the same principal here by creating a hash tree that associates the hash of the object name with one of a sequence of class IDs (best represented by an `enum`). Using this method, our `CreateObject` function is now broken down into three distinct steps:

1. Take the hash of the object name.
2. Look this up in the hash tree to find the object identifier.
3. Use a large `switch` statement to create an object of the required type.

For this to work, we must first define a unique class ID for each type of object that we can create, and then construct the hash tree that binds these IDs to the hashes of the required object names. The code for this must only be executed once, at the start of the program, and looks something like this:

```
typedef enum
{
    OBJID_UNDEFINED = 0,
    OBJID_PLAYER,
    OBJID_ALIEN,
    OBJID_BULLET,
    OBJID_MAX

} OBJECTID;

static HashTreeItem objidHashItems[OBJID_MAX];
static HashTree     objidHashTree;

void InitObjectIDs()
{
    // initialize the hash tree
    objidHashTree.Clear();
    objidHashTree.AddFreeItems( objidHashItems,
```

```
                                    countof(objidHashItems));

    objidHashTree.AddByHash( MakeFilenameHash("Player"),
                             OBJID_PLAYER );
    objidHashTree.AddByHash( MakeFilenameHash("Alien"),
                             OBJID_ALIEN );
    objidHashTree.AddByHash( MakeFilenameHash("Bullet"),
                             OBJID_BULLET );
}
```

Although this looks cumbersome, we can use macros to make it a little more readable and easy to maintain. Two simple macros, `TREEINIT` and `DEFINEOBJECT`, improve things immensely, as the following code shows:

```
#define TREEINIT(tree,items)\
    tree.Clear();\
    tree.AddFreeItems(items,countof(items));

#define DEFINEOBJECT(name,class)\
    objidHashTree.AddByHash(MakeFilenameHash(name),\
                            (void*)OBJID_##class);

void InitObjectIDs()
{
    TREEINIT(objidHashTree, objidHashItems);
    DEFINEOBJECT("Player",PLAYER);
    DEFINEOBJECT("Alien", ALIEN);
    DEFINEOBJECT("Bullet",BULLET);
}
```

Note that the order in which the object IDs are added to the tree is important; the earlier the object is added to the tree, the faster the object is found. This implies that more commonly created objects should be defined first, hence causing them to be found in less operations. We can see from the previous example that we have things completely reversed; the `PLAYER` object that is only created once per game is defined first, and the `BULLET` object that is probably created several times a second is last. Simply rearranging the order in which the object types are added to the hash tree, so that the most commonly created objects are added first, improves the overall efficiency of our object creation routine for free!

Now that we have created the hash tree that binds the hash of the object names to an ID unique to each class, we can recreate our `CreateObject` function using the previously described three steps. As before, we can use macros to tidy the code somewhat, resulting in the following code:

```
#define CREATEOBJECT(class)\
    case OBJID_##class:\
        ret = new class;\
        break;

Object *CreateObject( const char *name )
{
    HASH     hash
    OBJECTID id;
    Object   *ret;

    // step 1: take the hash of the object name
    hash = MakeFilenameHash(name);

    // step 2: look up the class ID in the hash tree
    id = (OBJECTID)objidHashTree.FindByHash(hash);

    // step 3: large switch statement by class ID
    switch(id)
    {
    CREATEOBJECT(PLAYER);
    CREATEOBJECT(ALIEN);
    CREATEOBJECT(BULLET);
    default:
        assert(0);
    }
    return ret;
}
```

This code has an $O(1)$ behavior in the best case (for the first item added to the tree), and an $O(\log n)$ behavior for the worst (for the item located deepest in the tree), where n is the number of different types of classes. Comparing this to the code that we started this section with, that has an $O(n)$ behavior, we can see that we have made a great improvement, even in our worst case!

DYNAMIC DATA AND DNA HASHES

There are many situations where the data that a game needs to use must be tailored to the target machine. This is most profoundly true when the target machine is a PC; there are so many different possible configurations of PCs that to create a data set that will work well with every configuration is almost impossible. In many cases, though, it is possible to store one of the intermediate steps of the data, and then use this to recreate the final data just in time for its use. In this way, we can tailor the final step of the data creation to the exact configuration of the target machine.

Vertex Shaders

With the advent of vertex shaders, graphics programming became at once simpler and yet more complex. It was simpler because you could use vertex shaders to do anything that you wanted with the input data, but it became more complex due to the sheer number of vertex shaders needed in any large project. For example, with the old fixed-function graphics pipeline, it was simple to change the number and type of lights that you had in a scene. However, using vertex shaders, we either have to keep the number of lights and their types constant (by introducing dummy lights with no effect), or make a different vertex shader for every possible combination of number and type of lights. In practice, the first of these solutions is impractical; even if we efficiently introduced dummy lights, the graphics processor is still going to spend the same amount of time calculating the effect from these lights on a very large number of vertices. This leads to the vertices taking longer to process than they otherwise would, potentially slowing the graphics engine[2].

So, we are left with having a large number of vertex shaders. To determine how many we would need, let's look at a simple case. In this simple case, we will allow up to four lights to be active at any given time. Each light can be either inactive, a point light, or a directional light, and can also produce specular reflections, or not. This gives us a total of five possible settings for each of four lights, a total of 625 different possible vertex shaders.

Now suppose that we want to allow our game to use skinning (where multiple matrices affect each vertex to produce the final transformed position) with between zero and three bones per vertex. Again, we could simply hardcode our vertex shader to always use three skinning bones, but this both increases vertex traffic (each vertex would always need to specify bone indices and weight for three bones) and vertex processing time. This leaves us with the option of adding another setting for the vertex shader, with four possible values. This increases the total possible number of vertex shaders to 2500.

So far we've only looked at processing the position and color of the input vertices. One other element that we must address is that of texture coordinates. The fixed-function pipeline allows us to map any of the input texture coordinates to any texture stage, or to procedurally generate texture coordinates for a given stage by use of a texture matrix. If we allow a maximum of four input sets of texture coordinates, and three values that we can transform via the texture matrix, we end up with a total of eight possible mappings for each output channel, as show in Table 3.1.

TABLE 3.1 Possible Mappings for an Output Texture Coordinate

Value	*Meaning*
0	Output coordinates not used (disable)
1	Transform position by matrix
2	Transform normal by matrix
3	Transform reflection by matrix
4	Use input set 0
5	Use input set 1
6	Use input set 2
7	Use input set 3

To reduce the number of possible combinations, we will associate a single texture matrix with each output texture stage. If we did not do this, we increase the number of possible mappings for each output set of texture coordinates, since we would then need to specify a matrix index for each channel. Therefore, to incorporate four output sets of texture coordinates, we increase the number of possible vertex shaders by a multiple of 8^4, giving us over 10 million possible vertex shaders.

As you can see, the number of possible vertex shaders quickly becomes overwhelmingly large. Before we introduced the texture coordinate mapping, we could feasibly get away with creating all 2500 different vertex shaders (although even at 1KB each, that's still 2.5MB of memory given to vertex shaders). However, with over 10 million different vertex shaders, it is infeasible to generate every one. Even if we limit the vertex shaders that we create to the ones that are most likely to be used, what happens when the artists create a model that uses a vertex shader that has not been created? During development, a programmer could simply create the required vertex shader, but after the game has been released, any additional content would either be limited to using the vertex shaders that shipped with the final game, or have to patch the game to include additional shaders.

Luckily, though, the source code for these vertex shaders can be constructed through careful concatenation of several distinct sections of text. For example, a directional light always uses the same section of code, no matter whether it's the first light or the fourth. We can even use the same register names and let the vertex shader assembler optimize it for us. All we need to know is which pieces of code to use and in which order. We can encode this information into the way that we identify the vertex shader by using a DNA hash.

A DNA Hash for Vertex Shaders

As we described earlier in this chapter, a DNA hash is usually a 32-bit value that is made up of a concatenation of smaller sequences of bits. Each of these smaller sequences has a distinct meaning, and can be considered the equivalent of a gene in our vertex shaders' description. Limiting ourselves to a maximum of four lights, three bones, and four output texture stages,

Table 3.2 shows a possible structure for a DNA hash that can represent any of our vertex shaders.

TABLE 3.2 A Possible DNA Hash for a Vertex Shader

Bits	***# Values***	***Meaning***
0–2	5	Light 0 definition
3–5	5	Light 1 definition
6–8	5	Light 2 definition
9–11	5	Light 3 definition
12–13	4	Number of bones
14–16	8	Output texture coordinate 0
17–19	8	Output texture coordinate 1
20–22	8	Output texture coordinate 2
23–25	8	Output texture coordinate 3
26	2	Vertex data is packed
27	2	Vertices have diffuse color
28	2	Vertices have normal vectors
29	2	Vertices have binormal vectors
30	2	Fog enabled
31	2	Specular enabled
	655,360,000	Total # of possible values

Table 3.2 also includes some extra settings for the vertex shader: whether the vertex data is packed (see Chapter 6, "Processing Assets"); whether the input vertices have a per-vertex diffuse color, normal, binormal, and tangent vectors; and whether fog and specular values should be generated. The final row of the table shows a tally of the total number of possible (and legal) vertex shaders that it is possible to describe given the structure of our DNA hash. Although this number is huge, in practice only a small fraction of the possible vertex shaders will actually be used.

The key here is that a given DNA hash provides all of the information necessary to reconstruct the source code for the appropriate vertex shader.

This source code can then be assembled to provide the final vertex shader that is used by the hardware. We can then store these assembled vertex shaders in a hash tree (which gives us *O(logn)* additions and searches), indexed by their DNA hashes. This allows us to generate any of the vertex shaders that we need as they are needed, and guarantees that only the vertex shaders that are actually used get created.

Although this might seem prohibitively slow, remember that each vertex shader will only ever be assembled once; after that, it will be found in the hash tree and so can be reused as needed. We can also speed this process up by examining the models that are used by a level as they are loaded and creating the vertex shaders that are most likely to be used by each model before the level is started. In this way, we can reduce the processing cost of displaying the first frame, when every vertex shader used would otherwise have to be compiled.

Pixel Shaders and Materials

Pixel shaders and materials can be handled in a similar way to vertex shaders. The main difference here is that not all PC video cards support pixel shaders, and different cards support different numbers of simultaneous textures and texture operations. We could rely on DirectX to emulate vertex shaders where they were not supported, but no such emulation exists for pixel shaders. Either the graphics card supports them, or we don't use them.

This adds a little wrinkle that we must address in our implementation of materials: for every material that we want to process, we must create a representation of it that works for the current platform and the current game settings. If the current game settings change (e.g., if the player deselects the "bumpmapping" option in the Graphics menu), then all affected materials will need to have their representations changed to reflect this. The effect of this is that although the model still asks for a bump-mapped material, it will in fact be given a non-bump-mapped version that approximates the look of the material.

The DNA hash for a material is constructed in a similar way as for a vertex shader. However, generally only a few material types are used by a given game. This allows us to assign a value for each material type rather than specifying the complete texture combiner setup. In addition to the material type, we also require extra members to be present in the DNA hash for things like turning color channels, z-testing, z-writing, and fogging on and off. A possible structure for the DNA hash of a material is shown in Table 3.3.

TABLE 3.3 A Possible DNA Hash for a Material

Bits	*# Values*	*Meaning*
0–7	256	Material type
8	2	Fogging on/off
9	2	Z-test on/off
10	2	Z-write on/off
11–13	8	RGB channel write on/off
14	2	Alpha-write on/off
15	2	Alpha test on/off
16	2	Stencil on/off
	131,072	Total # of possible values

Depending on the abstraction level of the materials, more or less bits than those shown in Table 3.3 might need to be assigned to represent different aspects of the operation. For example, the choice of material types (defined in bits 0–7) might implicitly determine whether the stencil buffer is used, rendering the stencil bit in the DNA hash meaningless. However, the DNA hash might need to specify the stencil buffer settings more fully than simply on or off. However the DNA hash is finally defined, though, it is a good idea to keep individual settings for things like the stencil or alpha test value out of the hash to reduce the possible number of material types. If these individual settings are needed, then a way should be constructed to allow them to be externally referenced; after all, it does not really matter what value the stencil buffer is set to write, as long as it is set to write one at the appropriate time.

Decoding a Material's DNA Hash

Now that we know how to define a material's DNA hash, we must work on a way to decode that hash into a material that will work for the current game configuration. The simplest way to do this is to create a structure that represents all of the values of the pixel pipeline that can be changed by a material. Each material will then fill out one (or more) of these structures and store it in a hash tree, indexed by its DNA hash. When it comes time to set up the pixel pipeline for the given material, the material is first looked up in the hash tree and, if not found, is created. The material's structure is then compared against a structure representing the current state of the graphics pipeline, and any mismatched states are sent to the hardware. In this way, we also send minimal state changes to the hardware.

In cases where a material cannot be drawn as described due to the limitations of either the hardware or the current graphics options, compromises must be made. In many cases, we will still be able to draw the material correctly, but it will take multiple render passes. As an example, let's look at a material that uses three textures: A, B, and M. Textures A and B are textures representing two different surface types, and texture M is a grayscale texture whose intensity controls the mixture between textures A and B. Figure 3.6 shows an example of this kind of material.

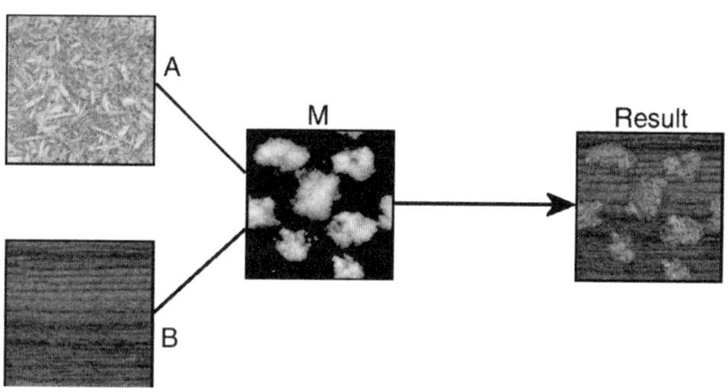

FIGURE 3.6 An example material using three textures.

On a graphics card that supports pixel shaders, this is very easily accomplished using a single pixel shader. If the graphics card does not support pixel shaders, but supports three simultaneous textures and a linear interpolation texture operation, the material can be easily encoded in three texture stages. Equation 3.4 shows the equation for the final color provided by the material:

$$R = (A * M) + (B * M') \tag{3.4}$$

This is all well and good, but if the graphics card only supports two simultaneous textures, we are in trouble. In this case, we must split the operation into two different render passes. In the first pass, we multiply textures A and M, writing the result to the frame. In the second pass, we multiply texture B with the complement of texture M, adding the result to the result previously written to the frame. Equation 3.5 shows how the two-pass method provides the same result as Equation 3.4:

$$\begin{aligned} T &= (A * M) \\ R &= T + (B * M'). \end{aligned} \tag{3.5}$$

Things become slightly more complicated when fog is involved. In the standard graphics pipeline, fogging is done immediately before the final color is written to the frame buffer. This changes the equation for the resulting color from our material to that shown in Equation 3.6. In this equation, f denotes the fog factor (how dense the fog is at the given pixel), while F denotes the fog color:

$$\begin{aligned} R &= (((A * M) + (B * M')) * f') + (f * F) \\ R &= (A * M * f') + (B * M' * f') + (f * F). \end{aligned} \tag{3.6}$$

Equation 3.7 shows the result that is obtained by leaving fog enabled for both passes of our two-pass implementation of the material. This is clearly not the same as Equation 3.6, since the fog color has been added to the result twice:

$$\begin{aligned} T &= (A * M * f') + (f * F) \\ R &= T + (B * M' * f') + (f * F). \end{aligned} \tag{3.7}$$

To get around this, we must eliminate the second fog color addition from one of our passes. We cannot simply turn fog off for the second pass, since then the second texture's color would not be modulated by the fog factor. The easiest way to accomplish this is to change the fog color for the second pass to black. Then, although the fog color is still used in the equation, its value is 0 and so it contributes no extra color to the result.

The final thing that we must consider here is how textures are declared to the graphics card: in this three-texture example, what do we do for a graphics card that only supports two textures? The simplest way that gives most flexibility is to use a virtual representation of the graphics card that supports the maximum number of textures required. When a texture is assigned by the game, it is not immediately sent to the graphics hardware. Instead, it is recorded in the appropriate virtual texture slot. Then, each material structure records how each of the virtual texture slots map to each of the texture stages on the graphics card. In this way, we keep our idealized picture of the graphics pipeline, with all textures intact, yet allow materials to pick and choose which of these textures to load, and in which order.

As can be seen from this simple example, creating a multipass material that approximates a more complex single-pass material can be a complex task. By using a hash tree to store the dynamic data created to represent the implementation of each material, we combine the flexibility to support multiple levels of target machine with the speed of using preprocessed material types. Decisions about how to best display a material need to be made just once, when the material is first processed (and additionally if the user changes any graphics options), saving processing time for subsequent uses of the material.

FURTHER READING

For more information on hashing, see the following text:

[Knuth98] Knuth, Donald, *The Art of Computer Programming, Volume 3, Sorting and Searching,* Second Edition, Addison Wesley, 1998.

ENDNOTES

[1]The birthday paradox is not really a paradox, merely a variation between the value we expect and the value that is born out through calculation. Perhaps it should be called the birthday *misapprehension*?

[2]Whether the graphics actually slow down depends on how long each polygon takes the pixel pipeline to draw; large polygons with complex materials take longer, giving the vertex processor more time to process the next vertex.

4 Scripting

In This Chapter

- Rule #4: "A Script Is Worth a Thousand Lines of Code"
- Drawing the Line
- Desired Features
- Leveraging the C Compiler
- Creating a Custom Scripting Language
- Further Reading

In the early days of video games, the prevailing style of game that was created was what we shall call the "Rinse & Repeat" genre. In this genre, simple game mechanics are repeated over and over, getting faster and harder, until the player is forced to lose because his reactions just aren't that fast. Look at any early video game and you will see that it falls into this category: *Space Invaders*, *Galaxians*, *Joust*, *Robotron® 2084*, *Tetris®*—the list goes on.

Although this genre of games is challenging and provably successful, a modern game made in this formula would almost certainly not be successful (or at least, not approved by a publisher). Modern game players, with few exceptions, demand more from a new game than this. They want to be involved, enthralled, and challenged. Modern games must to some degree emulate movies in order to be successful, but they must still be interactive.

This interactivity comes at a price, though; no longer can we rely on simple behaviors, rinsed and repeated, to capture the gamer's attention. We must now incorporate complex reactions to the player's presence and action. These reactions are often unique throughout the game—each only occurs once, at a given place in a given level.

This interactivity comes at a price: each unique reaction must be authored by someone. The task of authoring each reaction includes checking all of the conditions for it to be initiated, putting all of the assets (such as voice-overs) in place, and writing the code that performs the series of actions comprising the reaction. If each of these unique events were implemented in C code, our final project would be greatly increased in size and complexity and we would have designers camped behind our desks saying things like, "No, no, no! He should wave at the player before doing that."

RULE #4: "A SCRIPT IS WORTH A THOUSAND LINES OF CODE"

The answer, then, is to create a system where the actions specific to each level or character can be loaded at runtime (to preserve memory) and authored by someone other than a programmer. It is this second requirement that forces us to take special steps; not every designer is comfortable with learning C in order to create the events and behaviors required for a level. We can get around this by defining a simpler language that the designers can use to string together the behaviors they require.

DRAWING THE LINE

Before we can hope to create a designer-usable scripting system, we must decide exactly what duties the script will perform: where will we draw the line between scripted behaviors and the game engine? If we examine the game's systems, we can divide them into four categories: the game engine, object processing, object behaviors, and scripts.

The game engine comprises all the things that make the game run: the graphics, sound, loading from disk, creating and destroying objects, and so on. This is often supplied by a third party. Object processing consists of the code used to process the objects that make up the game world. This code is responsible for processing each object in turn, performing any default actions that cannot be changed (e.g., animation), and executing any scripts that are attached to the object. An object behavior is a small piece of code, often a single function, that performs a distinct operation on an object. These behaviors form the basis of the commands in the scripting language; each object behavior usually maps directly to a script command.

Finally, we can define the responsibilities of the scripting language. The scripting language must define a series of object behaviors that will be applied to a game object to perform a desired result. When new atomic behaviors are needed that cannot be expressed as a combination of existing behaviors, a programmer must become involved to author the new behaviors.

DESIRED FEATURES

Several features are desirable in a scripting language. Although some of these features can be omitted or worked around, an effective scripting language should support as many as possible. The following list shows these desired features:

Scripts should be easy to understand and create. Since our goal is to hand off the task of creating the scripts to the level designers, the scripting language that we use should be as simple to use as possible.

Scripts should be dynamically loaded. When scripts are dynamically loaded, the memory requirements for the game shrink, since the scripts for a level can be loaded with the level data instead of being resident in memory all of the time. An added advantage of this is that the game becomes expandable after shipping.

Scripts should never be able to crash the game. Our goal is to hand off creating the specific behaviors required for the characters in our game to the designers. If the game could crash due to a script action, the designers would constantly be coming back to the programmers to find out what they did wrong, since they would not have access to the tools required to investigate the problem.

Scripts should be inherently multitasking. A game world often consists of over 100 game objects, each of which can be executing multiple scripts. Without multitasking, each script would need to be split into bite-sized chunks that could be run completely each frame for each object. This would needlessly complicate the process of creating a script. It would also run into problems when a script contains an infinite loop—without multitasking, the game would hang, violating the requirement that a script should not be able to crash the game.

Scripts should have a debugger. Try as we might, at some point a script is going to work incorrectly. Sometimes the behavior of the object that the script is attached to will make the problem with the script obvious, but most of the time it won't be obvious at all. The designers need to have access to some sort of script debugger that allows them to single step through the scripts and to see any error messages produced.

Scripts should be extendable. It should be simple for a programmer to create additional base behaviors for the designer to incorporate into their scripts.

Someone authoring scripts should not be able to break the game build. It should not be necessary for someone authoring scripts to have access to any files that are critical to build the game. This includes all source files and project files. Any access into the game code should be strictly controlled through a tightly defined interface.

In the remainder of this chapter, we will examine two different methods of implementing a scripting language that the designers can use to make scripted behaviors for their game. In the first of these methods, we will look at using macros to make a scripting language that the C compiler can parse and compile for us. In the second, we will construct a custom text file parser to read the script files and a compiler to turn the parsed file into a raw data stream that we can then interpret.

LEVERAGING THE C COMPILER

The simplest way to create a scripting language that a designer can use is to leverage the C compiler. By defining a series of macros and function calls, we can sufficiently hide the complexities of the underlying code to make it usable by a novice designer. This method allows us to use the C compiler to generate all of the resulting script code, and the debugger to debug it, easing the initial burden on the programmers. As we will see in the following section, however, this initially promising method of scripting has several major drawbacks, not the least of which is that the probability of a designer successfully debugging a script full of macros is very low.

The first thing that we want to hide from the designers is the passing of function parameters that they do not need to know about. The most obvious example of this occurs in the definition of a script function, which takes at least one parameter representing the current scripting parameters. We can easily do this by using a couple of simple macros. The following code defines these macros:

```
#define SCRIPTBEGIN(scriptname)\
    void scriptname( SCRIPTOBJECT *pScript )\
    {
```

```
#define SCRIPTEND(scriptname)\
    } // scriptname
```

Notice that we also hide the braces that surround the function body. Although this is not strictly necessary, it might help us later if we decide to add debugging code to these macros. For example, we can redefine these macros slightly in a debug build to dump text on entry to and exit from each script function, as the following code illustrates:

```
#define SCRIPTBEGIN(scriptname)\
    void scriptname( SCRIPTOBJECT *pScript )\
    {   printf("Entering script function " #scriptname "\n");

#define SCRIPTEND(scriptname)\
        printf("Leaving script function " #scriptname "\n");\
    } // scriptname
```

Now that we have defined a script, we need to define some commands to make the script do some work. Although the actual commands available will vary by the needs of your game, we will define two commands for use during our examples. The first, SELECTOBJECT, selects the named object for use in subsequent commands, and the second, MOVETOSELECTION, instructs the character to walk to the currently selected object. Our script then becomes:

```
SCRIPTBEGIN(GoToSwitch)

    SELECTOBJECT("Switch")
    MOVETOSELECTION()

SCRIPTEND(GoToSwitch)
```

Notice that these commands contain no reference to the current context to confuse the designer. The underlying code, however, needs to be able to access this context. For this reason, these commands are once again implemented via macros. The following macros show an example implementation for these two functions:

```
#define SELECTOBJECT(objname)\
    pScript->SelectObjectByName(objname);

#define MOVETOSELECTION()\
    pScript->MoveTo(pScript->m_selectedObject);
```

This script as it stands is hardly useful. Although, given the correct implementation of the script functions, the character will move to the selected object, it will do nothing when it arrives there. Unfortunately, as we will see, extending this script to perform an action on arrival is not as trivial as it would seem.

Multitasking

One of the requirements for our scripting language is that it should be amenable to multitasking. That is, multiple scripts should be able to run at the same time. Ideally, we should be able to implement a script command such as `WAITFORNSECONDS` that can be used to insert a pause in the scripted actions. However, the limitations imposed on us by virtue of using the C compiler stop us from doing this.

Since each script function is implemented as a C function, when we invoke the script, we effectively call the corresponding function. This pushes the return address and any function parameters on the stack. We can only stop executing this script (or pause it) when these values are popped back off the stack, returning us to the section of code that ran the script. Unfortunately, any script commands that we can implement that pause the script for any length of time will also need to be implemented as function calls, pushing additional values on the stack. The only way to pop everything off of the stack to return control to our main program is to let the script function finish.

This means that each script function can last at most a single frame, since they cannot be interrupted or paused. To create a script that spans multiple frames and can be multitasked, we must break the script function into multiple functions. Then, at the end of a script function we need to identify the script function that is to run next, and how many frames gap there should be before running it.

We also need to determine what happens if no script is identified as being the next one to run. We have two choices here: we can repeat the current script on the next frame, or we can stop executing scripts. If we choose to repeat the current script, then we need to explicitly tell the script when we don't want this to occur, whereas if we choose to stop executing scripts, we always need to specify a new script to run. In the interests of brevity for the designer, it would be best to choose to repeat the current script unless otherwise specified.

Now we just need to determine the frequency with which to execute a given script, and the number of frames to delay before we execute it the first time. This can be done in a single command, which we will call `SETNEXTSCRIPT`. We will make this command take three parameters: the number of frames to delay before executing the named script, the number of frames between each execution of the script, and the name of the script. We also need to add a command to stop executing the current script. We will call this command `STOP`.

The following code implements these script commands as macros. Notice that the `STOP` command is implemented using the same function as the `SETNEXTSCRIPT` command. The `STOP` command also uses braces to surround the multiple commands that comprise it. This enables the `STOP` command to be used safely as a single command following an `if`, `for`, or `while` statement.

```
#define SETNEXTSCRIPT(delay,freq,name)\
    pScript->SetNextScript(delay,freq,#name);

#define STOP()\
    {\
        pScript->SetNextScript(0,0,0);\
        return;\
    }
```

The following code extends the previously defined `GoToSwitch` script to perform an action when the object is reached:

```
SCRIPTBEGIN(GoToSwitch)

    SELECTOBJECT("Switch")
    MOVETOSELECTION()
    SETNEXTSCRIPT(1,1,ActivateSwitch)

SCRIPTEND(GoToSwitch)

SCRIPTBEGIN(ActivateSwitch)

    IFATSELECTION(5)
    {
        ACTIVATESELECTION()
        STOP()
    }

SCRIPTEND()
```

Examining the preceding code, we see that the `GoToSwitch` script is pretty much the same as before, except for the addition of the `SETNEXTSCRIPT` command that identifies the next script to run to be `ActivateSwitch`, and that it should be run in one frame and then every frame after that. The `ActivateSwitch` script first checks to see if the current object is within five units of the selected object. If so, it activates the selected object and then stops executing the script; otherwise, the script ends its execution in the current frame and is re-executed next frame.

As you can see, this is exceedingly clumsy for designers to use. It also makes it hard to make a library of simple scripts that can be called from within other scripts. Any scripts in such a library must execute completely in a single frame, because when the script function ends, control will return to the previous script function on the stack.

Alternative Multitasking Methods

There are other ways to implement multitasking, but they are very dangerous, very slow, or just impractical. An example of a dangerous method is described in [GEMS2] "Micro-Threads for Game Object AI" by Bruce Dawson. This method involves emulating an operating system's multitasking by cleverly manipulating the stack to change the return address for a given function. This function, which could be called `Yield`, then needs to be called voluntarily each time a script wants to stop executing for the current frame. Inside the `Yield` function, the scripting system changes the contents of the stack so that when it returns, it arrives in the next object's script. Although this method is effective, it is compiler- and platform-dependent, since each platform/compiler combination could pass function parameters and return addresses differently.

An example of a method that is both slow and somewhat dangerous would be to use the operating system's built-in task switching. This involves creating a unique thread for each script object, allowing each script to be continually processed, and neatly stopping any infinite loops from locking up the game. However, this advantage is heavily outweighed by the risks and overheads involved in setting up this system. The risks involved come from the fact that the place in the frame that the scripts are executed cannot be easily predicted; this can lead to scripts being run for an object while other things are happening to it, and all the nastiness that this can entail. The overheads come from creating an operating-system thread for each new script object that is created. Creating a thread is not a simple task, and can take quite a long time in game terms. If scripts are created with any frequency at all, this could be a major problem.

Dynamically Loading C-Based Scripts

To make our scripts load dynamically, we must make a few changes to the language as defined so far. The easiest way to enable dynamic loading of compiled code is through the use of dynamic link libraries (DLLs), if the target platform is lucky enough to support them. Even if the target platform does not natively support DLLs, however, it is still possible to emulate them.

A DLL is a file that consists of compiled code that can be loaded and used dynamically by another program. Loading a DLL is a little more complex than loading a file, however, since the code in the DLL and the code in the loading program know nothing about each other. To successfully use the code located inside a DLL, the loading program must locate the addresses of the functions and variables inside the DLL that it wants to gain access to.

When creating a DLL, a programmer explicitly specifies which symbols (function and variable names) must be exported. For each exported symbol, the compiler creates an entry in a table inside the DLL consisting of the symbol name and its address. A program that loads the DLL can then retrieve the addresses of these symbols within the DLL and hence is able to use the exported functions and variables.

To do this, we need to know in advance the names of each function or variable within the DLL that we want to access. This presents us with a problem, since the whole point of using DLLs is to add new script functions whose names we don't necessarily know in advance. We can get around this, and at the same time simplify the process of loading a script DLL, by declaring just a single function with a specific name to be exported from the DLL. This function, when invoked, must then supply the calling program with the names and addresses of all of the functions it implements. In this way, we reduce our DLL loading code to a couple of lines of simple code.

The following code shows an example of loading a DLL and locating a named function inside it. The code first loads the DLL specified in the parameter list, then locates the address of a function called `RegisterScript`, and finally executes this function:

```
typedef void (*RegisterFn)( SCRIPTMGR *pScriptMgr );

HMODULE SCRIPTMGR::LoadDll( const char *filename )
{
    HMODULE     hDll;
    RegisterFn  pRegisterFn;

    // load the named DLL
```

```
    hDll = LoadLibrary(filename);
    if( hDll )
    {
        // find the RegisterScript function address
            pRegisterFn = (RegisterFn)GetProcAddress(hDll,
                                        "RegisterScript");
            if( pRegisterFn )
            {
                // call the RegisterScript function
                pRegisterFn(this);
                result = true;
            }
            else
            {
                // failed to find the RegisterScript function
                // unload the DLL
                FreeLibrary(hDll);
                hDll = 0;
            }
    }
    return hDll;
}
```

On the DLL side of the code, we must define a function called `RegisterScript` that takes as a parameter a pointer to a `SCRIPTMGR` class. This function must then use the supplied `SCRIPTMGR` class to furnish the calling program with addresses for all of the script functions that this DLL supplies, and their names. In this way, we can add several script functions from a single DLL without knowing their names in advance.

To register a DLL-based script function with the `SCRIPTMGR` class, the DLL code must call a member function of the `SCRIPTMGR` class. However, since the implementation of this function is located within the program that loaded the DLL, we do not know its address from within the DLL. We must somehow supply the DLL with an address for each of the `SCRIPTMGR` member functions that it needs to use. The easiest way to get a pointer to a member function in C++ is to define that function as virtual. This causes a vtable to be created containing a pointer to that function and any other virtual functions. We can then freely (and invisibly) access that function pointer merely by invoking the member function in the usual manner. Using virtual functions in this manner is a good way to exchange function pointers and limit the number of linkage points between a program and its DLLs.

The sole responsibility of the `RegisterScript` function in each script DLL is to report back to the main program the name of every script function, and a pointer to each one. This allows the game to link a named script with the code that implements it, independent of which DLL it is located in. Again, we do not want the designers to have to worry about this more than they have to, so we will use macros to simplify the process. We need to define macros to define the `RegisterScript` function and to register a single script function with the calling program. The following macros accomplish this:

```
#define BEGIN_SCRIPTLIST()\
    extern "C" __declspec(dllexport)\
        void RegisterScript( SCRIPTMGR * );\
    void RegisterScript( SCRIPTMGR *pMgr )\
    {

#define LISTSCRIPT(scriptname)\
        void scriptname( SCRIPTOBJECT* );\
        pMgr->RegisterScript(#scriptname,scriptname);

#define END_SCRIPTLIST()\
    }
```

Notice that the macro that declares the `RegisterScript` function first declares it as an externally declared C function. This forces the compiler to refrain from mangling the function name, allowing us to look up the name as is. Omitting this will result in a mangled name appearing in the DLL's symbol list, and will cause the symbol lookup to fail.

The macro also declares the `RegisterScript` function as an exported symbol through use of the `__declspec(dllexport)` command. This causes the symbol for the attached function to be exported into the DLL for later linkage.

Now that we have defined the macros that can be used to create the `RegisterScript` function, the following code would be used to declare the two scripts we authored earlier:

```
START_SCRIPTLIST()

    LISTSCRIPT(GoToSwitch)
    LISTSCRIPT(ActivateSwitch)

END_SCRIPTLIST()
```

As we stated at the beginning of this section, it is possible to emulate DLLs on a platform that does not natively support them. As we have seen, this is simply a matter of establishing the address of a single function within the loaded code. This can be done in several ways; for example, storing a pointer to this function at a known offset within the loaded code, or ensuring in some way that the function itself occurs at a known offset. All of this assumes, of course, that we have previously performed the necessary steps to relocate the loaded code correctly.

Measuring Up

So, how does this method of implementing scripts measure up against our requirements?

Scripts should be easy to understand and create. Although we have tried to make the scripts as easy as possible to understand, breaking up script functions is needlessly complicated. Additionally, although scripts are themselves simple to create, the act of creating a new DLL containing scripts is a little involved.

Scripts should be dynamically loaded. DLLs handle this nicely—if the target platform supports DLLs.

Scripts should never be able to crash the game. Since we are using plain C for our scripts, the designers are free to include arbitrary C commands in the script.

Scripts should be inherently multitasking. Although this can be achieved, it is awkward to do so.

Scripts should have a debugger. One of the high points of using C as a scripting language is that we get to use the same debugger as the rest of the program. Unfortunately, the heavy use of macros makes the debugger harder to use, and the use of dynamically loaded DLLs can cause problems with breakpoints.

Scripts should be extendable. Since all functions are accessed through the vtable of the `SCRIPTOBJECT`, simply adding a new virtual function to the `SCRIPTOBJECT` definition makes it usable in the scripting language. Unfortunately, if at any point the order of the functions in the `SCRIPTOBJECT` vtable changes, all of the script DLLs must be recompiled.

Someone authoring scripts should not be able to break the game build. The use of DLLs effectively isolates the script code from the game code. The designers do not need access to the majority of the game code to generate and compile new script DLLs.

Overall, the use of C as a scripting language meets most of our requirements. However, care must be taken to ensure that the script DLLs do not become out of date relative to the source code, and that the designers do not start to include potentially dangerous pure C code in their script files.

CREATING A CUSTOM SCRIPTING LANGUAGE

The alternative to using a combination of macros and C as a scripting language is to define a completely original language. This language would be compiled offline into a stream of raw data that can then be interpreted at runtime by our game. To accomplish this, we need to create three new components.

The first of these components is a text file parser. This component must load a file written in the scripting language and parse it using the syntax rules of our scripting language into a tree of symbols that can then be compiled.

The second component is the compiler. This takes the output of the parser and turns the symbol tree into a stream of raw data. These two components combine to form the scripting compiler tool, which is an offline tool used to process the scripts for use by the game.

The final component is the interpreter. This component is part of the game, and must interpret the stream of raw data produced by the compiler and perform the commands specified in this data stream.

Creating a Text File Parser

The job of a text file parser is a simple one: it must read the text file and decompose it into a linked series of tokens (generally speaking, a token can be thought of as a word). Each of these tokens is assigned a type based on its location relative to the previous tokens and the contents of the token, according to the *syntax* of the language we are parsing for. The syntax of a language is the set of rules that govern the placement of its symbols in meaningful statements.

The parser also arranges the tokens it creates into a tree structure according to the syntax. Each first-level node in this tree represents an individual statement, and every token that forms part of a given statement is then a descendant node. This allows us to easily navigate between individual statements when compiling the parsed tokens, making it easy to recover from errors. We can even jump over entire statements that can be omitted. A good example of statements that can be omitted is given in Chapter 5, "The Resource Pipeline," where we use the PLATFORM command to insert a platform-specific series of commands. During a preprocessing step, these statements are stripped from the syntax tree based on the result of the PLATFORM command.

The main advantage of creating our own parser is that we then have a parsing module that can be easily used in multiple projects. Later chapters in this book make heavy use of the parser that we are going to be creating here. For example, Chapter 5's DataCon build tool and Chapter 7's finite state machine compiler both use the parser defined here to load their text-based inputs.

Defining a Syntax

Before we can begin writing our parser, we must determine the syntax of our scripting language. Without this, the parser would not be able to extract sequences of symbols from the input file and classify them. For ease of use and readability, we will choose to selectively borrow parts of the standard C syntax. Since we are developing a scripting language and not a general-purpose programming language, we are free to cut out some of the more complicated features of the C syntax and hence simplify the parser.

The things that we will take from C include the general function call syntax and the ability to define blocks of code. We do not require the ability to form mathematical expressions, as the same things can often be done with a string of commands, and omitting them simplifies our parser significantly. In short, then, every statement in our language takes the form of a C-style function call. This allows us to easily create a simple parser and keeps the language easy to understand for the designers.

The first thing that we must determine is how to differentiate between different symbol types. This allows us to correctly associate type information with each symbol that we extract, and also gives us the ability to detect errors in syntax (when a symbol of an unexpected type appears in the input stream). We will define three different types of symbols: names, strings, and numbers.

A name symbol begins with either an underscore or a letter (upper- or lowercase is irrelevant). The symbol ends when a character is encountered that is not a letter, number, or underscore character. Strings begin with a quote character, either " or ', and end only when a second, matching quote character is encountered. Finally, numbers begin with either a number, a plus sign, or a minus sign, and end when a character is encountered that is not a number, a decimal point, or the characters *e* and *E*. There are some additional restrictions placed on numbers; the decimal point can only occur once, as can the characters *e* and *E*.

In addition to these three types, we also want to allow the designers to insert comments into their scripts to help them if they have to return to a script. A comment begins with two consecutive forward slash characters, //, and continues until a new-line character is encountered. Comments are not strictly symbols, since our parser discards them as they are encountered. A comment can occur anywhere within the script, even between a command and its parameter list, without causing problems. Table 4.1 summarizes the definitions for each of our symbol types.

TABLE 4.1 Definitions of the Symbol Types

Symbol Type	*Valid First Characters*	*Valid Characters*	*End Characters*
Name	_, a–z, A–Z	_, a–z, A–Z, 0–9	
String Type 1	"	Any	"
String Type 2	'	Any	'
Number	+, –, 0–9	0–9, ., e, E	
Comment	//	Any	New-line

Now that we have defined the individual symbols, we must define how these are combined to create a command. A command in our scripting language consists of a name symbol followed by a parameter list enclosed in parentheses. The occurrence of an open parenthesis character, (, following a name symbol transforms the name symbol into a command. An open parenthesis character at any other time (except within a string or a comment) will generate a syntax error. The parameter list for a command consists of zero or more symbols (of any type), separated by commas. To keep things simple for our parser, commands cannot appear in a parameter list; only names, strings, and numbers are valid.

Following the end of the parameter list for a command, there are two possible alternatives. The first, and simplest, alternative happens when we encounter a semicolon. This ends the current command. The second alternative allows a second command to occur after the first; in this case, the second command is executed conditionally, based on the result of the first. Only certain commands can handle this (e.g., commands that check for certain situations); however, remember that the parser knows nothing about the meaning of the commands themselves, and so these errors cannot be detected at parse time. Commands can be strung together in this way to an arbitrary depth, but become increasingly unlikely to execute as the conditions pile up.

In any place in the script that a command is expected, an open brace character, {, can be used instead. This causes all of the commands until the matching closing brace character, }, to be considered a single command. This allows us to execute multiple statements conditionally, based on the result of a previous command. For example, if there is a command called `IF` and a variable called `health`, then the following example would show two pieces of script that perform the same function:

```
IF( health, lessthan, 50 )
    CHANGESCRIPT("RUNAWAY");

IF( health, lessthan, 50 )
{
    CHANGESCRIPT("RUNAWAY");
}
```

In the second of these statements, we could add additional script commands inside the braces to execute more command based on the result of the `IF`. It should be noted that a closing brace must occur inside a block that was started with an open brace character. For example, the following code would cause an error, since the closing brace is not in the correct position (it is conditional upon the result of the `IF` command):

```
IF( health, lessthan, 50 )
}
```

Parsing the File

Now that we have the syntax of our language defined, it is possible for us to create a program to parse a file of the correct format. The parser must first load the file and then extract symbols from the file, creating a tree of symbols that represents the syntax of the file. Each statement consists of a command, a parameter list, and one or more conditionally executed commands. The parsed tokens can then be represented by the following partial class definition:

```
class PARSETOKEN
{
public:
    enum SYMBOLTYPE
    {
        NAME,
        COMMAND,
        STRING,
        NUMBER
    };

protected:
    PARSETOKEN *nextToken;       // next token in this branch
    PARSETOKEN *parameterList;   // only valid for a COMMAND
    PARSETOKEN *conditional;     // only valid for a COMMAND
    SYMBOLTYPE symbolType;
    const char *symbolText;

    const char *inFilename;
    u32        atLineNo;
};
```

This partial definition of a PARSETOKEN class shows how the syntax tree is formed. This is further illustrated in Figure 4.1. Each token contains a pointer to the next token in its branch (for a parameter list, this is the next parameter, but for a command, this is the next nonconditional command). Each token also contains two branch pointers that are valid only for commands; the first points to its parameter list while the second points to any conditional commands that are attached to this command. Figure 4.1 represents the syntax tree for the following script segment:

```
IF( health, lessthan, 50 )
{
    CHANGESCRIPT("RUNAWAY");
}
PAUSE(5);
```

In Figure 4.1, the pointers contained in each token are represented by the lines connecting the tokens. The `nextToken` pointer is represented by either a horizontal or vertical connection. The `parameterList` pointer is represented by a connection going down and to the left. Finally, the `conditional` pointer is represented by a connection going down and to the right. The shape of the surround for each token represents the token type; an ellipse is for a command, a rectangle for a name, a rounded rectangle for a string, and a pentagon for a number.

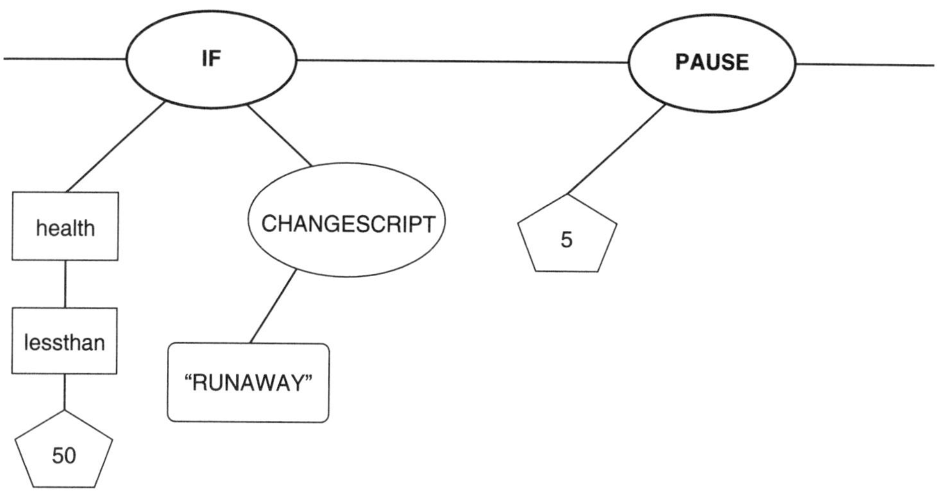

FIGURE 4.1 A simple syntax tree.

An important concept for our parser is that of the previous token. This token is simply the last token created that is still open for input in the current scope. Before each new token is created, it must check the previous token to see if the new token is valid at the current position. The only time that a new token can be created when a previous token is still open is when the previous token is a COMMAND, and the new token is a NAME. This case occurs legally only when a conditional command occurs in the input stream.

A Parsing Example

To create the syntax tree shown in Figure 4.1, the parser begins by looking at the first character in the input stream; in this case, the character `I`. This character uniquely defines the start of a name symbol, and so the parser continues until it finds a character that is not valid in a name symbol; in this case, `(`. The previous token is currently NULL, so it then simply creates a PARSETOKEN class of type NAME with the symbol that it just extracted: `IF`.

Next, the parser looks at the next character in the stream, `(`. This character is the start of a parameter list, so it looks at the previous token to check that it is a NAME. If it is not a name, then a syntax error has occurred and is reported as such. However, in this case, our previous token is of the expected type, so no error occurs. Providing the previous symbol is a NAME, the parser then changes it to a COMMAND and proceeds to read the parameter list. Before doing so, however, it pushes the COMMAND token on the stack and sets the previous token to NULL.

The first symbol that it finds is also a NAME (`health`), and so it creates a token for this after seeing that the previous token is NULL. The next character is a comma, which terminates the previous token and sets it to NULL. If the previous token was already NULL, this would mean that the comma didn't have anything preceding it and so would be an error. The next symbol that it finds is a NAME (`lessthan`), for which a token is created. After a comma, the next symbol is a NUMBER (`50`). Finally, the parser encounters a closing parenthesis symbol, `)`, which ends the current parameter list.

At this point, the stored COMMAND token is pulled from the stack and set to be the previous token again, and the parameter list that we read is stored in its `parameterList` pointer. The parser then continues reading characters from the input stream. The next valid character it encounters is the opening curly brace, `{`, which can occur in place of a single command. Examining the previous token, it sees that it is a command, and so the brace character is valid. Pushing the previous token on the stack, it then begins to parse a new block of commands.

The first token that it encounters is a NAME (CHANGESCRIPT), which is transformed into a COMMAND by the following open parenthesis character. Reading its parameter list yields a single STRING token ("RUNAWAY"). After assigning this command's parameterList pointer, the next token encountered is a semicolon, which ends the current command and sets the previous token to NULL. Looking at the next valid character, the parser encounters the closing brace. This ends the current command block, popping the previous COMMAND from the stack and assigning the new block to its conditional pointer. This also ends the COMMAND, setting the previous token to NULL.

Finally, the parser finds a NAME token (PAUSE) that is converted into a COMMAND by the following open parenthesis character. Reading its parameter list results in a single NUMBER token (5). After the parameter list, the parser encounters a final semicolon to end the current COMMAND.

Implementing the Parser

In addition to the previously defined PARSETOKEN class, we will create two additional classes: PARSER and PARSEDFILE. The PARSER class is responsible for loading the file, parsing it, and creating the relevant tokens. The PARSEDFILE class is responsible for holding the syntax tree of tokens and maintaining any memory allocated for the parsed file. The PARSER class creates an instance of the PARSEDFILE class during the parsing of a file. The following code shows a brief outline of the functionality of the two classes:

```
class PARSER
{
public:
    PARSER();
    ~PARSER();
    bool ParseFile( const char *filename, PARSEDFILE **result );
};

class PARSEDFILE
{
    friend class PARSER;
```

```
protected:
    PARSEDFILE( const char *filename, u32 memsize );


public:
    virtual ~PARSEDFILE();
    virtual PARSETOKEN *GetFirstToken();
    virtual const char *GetFilename();
};
```

Notice that the PARSEDFILE class members are declared as virtual. This allows the implementations of these functions to exist inside a DLL without us having to worry about locating them, as described earlier in this chapter. In this way, we enable the parser to be easily reusable. We will also use this method to provide query functions for the PARSETOKEN class.

ON THE CD

A full implementation of the PARSER, PARSEDFILE, *and* PARSETOKEN *classes is included on the companion CD-ROM, in the folder common/parser. This implementation is used often throughout the code in the rest of the book so a familiarity with it is recommended.*

Defining the Language

Now that we know how to parse the scripting language into a format that can be easily manipulated, we need to define some of the commands that the designers will be using and their effects. The first thing that the designers must do is to name the script and define the bounds of its code. This can be done through a single command, which we will call SCRIPT. The SCRIPT command takes a single parameter that must be of type STRING and which defines the name of the script being defined. By using a STRING, we can allow designers to use spaces and other such characters in the names of their scripts. This command must be followed immediately by the definition of the script. The following code gives an example of using this command to define an empty piece of script:

```
SCRIPT("Example1")
{
```

```
        // any commands in this section are assigned to
        // the script called "Example1"
    }
```

Although this command is part of our scripting language, it is different from the other scripting commands that we will add in that it is only valid outside a script. All of the other scripting commands that we will create are only valid inside the block that follows this command. In this way, we can integrate scripts within text files that define other resources, as we shall see in the following chapters.

Earlier in this chapter, we saw how using C as a scripting language made it awkward to implement a command that paused the script for a given number of frames. Since our scripting language is now interpreted, we face no such problems, and so we can define the following commands to pause the script for the given time periods:

```
BREAK();
PAUSE( <numFrames> );
PAUSEFRAMES( <numFrames> );
PAUSESECONDS( <numSeconds> );
```

The BREAK command causes the script to stop processing in the current frame and to continue in the next frame. The PAUSE and PAUSEFRAMES commands pause the script for the given number of frames. Although the number of frames specified can be a floating-point number, it will be converted to an integer during compilation since fractional frames are meaningless. A command of PAUSE(1) is equivalent to the simpler command BREAK(). Finally, the PAUSESECONDS command pauses the script for the given number of seconds. This number can and should be specified as a floating-point number.

We have encountered two other commands so far in our examples that we should define here: IF and CHANGESCRIPT. The IF command takes three parameters; the first and third are both either a NAME or a NUMBER that defines the quantities being compared, and the second is a NAME that defines the comparison. Some examples of valid comparisons are EQUALS, LESSTHAN, NOTEQUAL, and so on. If the first or third parameters are of type `NAME`, then the value is taken from a variable of the same name.

The `CHANGESCRIPT` command takes a single `STRING` parameter that is the name of the new script to run. The parameter must be of type `STRING`, since this is how we defined the script name in the `SCRIPT` command. We can also define a sister command to this, `CALLSCRIPT`, which runs the given script and then returns to the current script.

The complete definition of the scripting language for a game depends on the needs of the game in question, and so is beyond the scope of this chapter. The few commands described here should be enough to point the way to creating a unique scripting language that meets your game's needs.

Compiling a Script File

Once our script has been parsed, we must compile it into the raw data stream that the game expects. It is at this point that the semantics of the scripting language are applied. This includes checking the types of all command parameters against the expected types and making sure that conditional commands only occur after commands that expect them.

Before we can compile the parsed file, however, we must define the format of the raw data stream. The first thing that we must decide is the format of each individual command. Every command requires two things: an identifier representing the command and the total length of the command and all of its parameters and conditional commands—in effect the offset to the next command in the stream. Since 256 commands might not be enough (one possible reason for this will be covered later), we will use 16 bits for the command identifier. We will use another 16 bits for the length of the command, making each command a minimum of 4 bytes long. If we are careful throughout all of the parameters for each command, we can preserve this alignment, giving us some performance benefits due to aligned data reads.

After deciding the format of the data stream, we must now begin to create our command opcodes. These should be created sequentially as needed, and should never be changed once created (as this would invalidate any currently compiled scripts that use the affected opcodes). Although an `enum` is a good way to accomplish this, we would require a typecast in any comparisons to ensure that the `enum` was 16 bits in size. Because of this inconvenience, we will simply use `#define` to create our opcodes.

The first command we will look at compiling is the `BREAK()` command, which takes no parameters and can have no conditional commands. After identifying a `BREAK` command token, we must first check that both the parameter list and the conditional list for the `BREAK` token are empty. If they are not empty, then an error must be reported. Otherwise, we can go ahead and insert the opcode for this command into the data stream. After the opcode, we must insert into the data stream the total length of this command, which is 4 bytes. An example of the result of compiling a `BREAK()` command is given in Table 4.2.

TABLE 4.2 An Example of Compiling the BREAK Command

BREAK();			
Offset	***# Bytes***	***Value***	***Comment***
0	2	OPCODE_BREAK	BREAK command
2	2	4	Length of this command

The next command we will compile is the `PAUSE()` command. This command takes a single parameter, which can be either an integer (NUMBER) or a variable name (NAME). To correctly compile this, we need to create two different opcodes, one for the command with an integer parameter and another for the command with a variable name parameter. By examining the type of the single parameter, we can then select the correct opcode and insert it into the data stream, along with the total length of the resulting command. If the parameter is a NUMBER, we simply convert it to an integer and insert the result into the data stream (taking up 4 bytes). If the parameter is a NAME, we take the hash of the name (see Chapter 3, "Hashes and Hash Functions") and insert that into the data stream, also taking up 4 bytes. Of course, before doing any of this, we must first check to see that the command has a single parameter and that there are no conditional commands attached to it; either of these cases should result in an error being reported. Tables 4.3 and 4.4 show the results of compiling two different versions of the PAUSE command.

The PAUSEFRAMES and PAUSESECONDS commands can be compiled in the same way (in fact, the PAUSEFRAMES command should produce the same opcodes as the PAUSE command).

TABLE 4.3 An Example of Compiling the PAUSE Command with an Integer Argument

PAUSE(5);

Offset	***# Bytes***	***Value***	***Comment***
0	2	OPCODE_PAUSEINT	PAUSE command, integer argument
2	2	8	Length of this command
4	4	5	# of frames to pause for

TABLE 4.4 An Example of Compiling the PAUSE Command with a Variable Argument

PAUSE(health);

Offset	***# Bytes***	***Value***	***Comment***
0	2	OPCODE_PAUSEVAR	PAUSE command, variable argument
2	2	8	Length of this command
4	4	HASH(health)	Hash of the variable name

Table 4.5 shows an example of compiling the CHANGESCRIPT command. This command takes a single STRING argument, and can have no conditional commands. The resulting output in the data stream is always 8 bytes long. The CALLSCRIPT command can be compiled in exactly the same way, just with a different opcode.

TABLE 4.5 An Example of Compiling the CHANGESCRIPT Command

CHANGESCRIPT("RUNAWAY");

Offset	*# Bytes*	*Value*	*Comment*
0	2	OPCODE_CHANGESCRIPT	CHANGESCRIPT command
2	2	8	Length of this command
4	4	HASH(RUNAWAY)	Hash of the new script name

The most complex of the commands that we have so far defined is the conditional IF command. This command takes three parameters: a variable or integer, a comparison function NAME, and another variable or integer. Although the comparison function can be stored in the data stream as a hash of the comparison function name, this is not amenable to being used in a simple `switch` statement in the interpreter. Because of this we will convert the comparison function name into a predefined value representing the appropriate comparison. Since the value of the `#define` for the comparison function does not fill 4 bytes, we can also store the types of the first and third parameters in the spare bytes, reducing the number of opcodes needed. The final empty byte here is filled with the offset from the start of the IF statement of the first conditional command.

Once we have completed compilation of the 4 bytes for the comparison function and the parameter types, we can insert the parameters into the data stream. As with the PAUSE command, a NUMBER parameter is converted to an integer and then inserted into the data stream, while a NAME parameter has its hash inserted into the data stream. After compiling the IF command and its parameters, we must compile its conditional commands. Only then can we fill in the total length of the IF statement, completing its compilation. Table 4.6 shows an example of compiling an IF statement that has a single conditional command.

TABLE 4.6 An Example of Compiling an IF Command with a Single Conditional Command

IF(health, lessthan, 50)

Offset	# Bytes	Value	Comment
0	2	OPCODE_IF	IF command
2	2	24	Length of this command
4	1	COMPAR_LESSTHAN	Comparator definition
5	1	PARAMTYPE_VAR	Variable parameter to follow
6	1	PARAMTYPE_INT	Integer parameter to follow
7	1	16	Start of conditional commands
8	4	HASH(health)	Hash of the variable name
12	4	50	Integer parameter

PAUSE(5);

Offset	# Bytes	Value	Comment
16	2	OPCODE_PAUSEINT	PAUSE command, integer argument
18	2	8	Length of this command
20	4	5	# of frames to pause for

Using these examples as templates, it should be possible to easily compile any commands that you create. It is even possible to create commands that take variable numbers of parameters, with either the unspecified parameters being assigned set values or the number of parameters changing the opcode and behavior of the command. Remember, though, that the semantic checking for the language must be encapsulated within the code that compiles each individual command.

Interpreting a Script Data Stream

The final piece of our scripting puzzle is the interpretation of the compiled script. This is the only code that needs to be located within the game, and as such needs to run as quickly as possible. To aid this, we included certain things, such as the length of each command, in the compiled data stream.

The script interpreter is basically just a large switch statement focused on the opcode at the present position in the data stream. Unknown opcodes should be ignored. After each command has been fully processed, the position in the data stream should be advanced by the reported length of the command. Care should be taken to ensure that this is both a multiple of 4 bytes and less than the distance to the end of the current script definition. This simple check improves script stability and helps prevent hackers from breaking the game with corrupted scripts.

Care should also be taken to ensure that each frame a script can only execute a certain number of commands. Once a script reaches this limit, the interpreter should artificially stop execution until the next frame. This allows the script system to limit its maximum load and also handle an infinite script loop without hanging the game.

Measuring Up

So, how does our original scripting language as defined measure up against our initial requirements?

Scripts should be easy to understand and create. Since we defined our scripting language to be simple, we have definitely met the first part of this requirement. The fact that script files are simply plain-text files neatly addresses the second part of the requirement also.

Scripts should be dynamically loaded. Our scripts are compiled as data, and so they can be associated with the data for a level, a character, or anything else for that matter. Dynamically loading them is now a trivial task.

Scripts should never be able to crash the game. All of the responsibility for this requirement rests in the hands of the interpreter. As long as all of the opcodes for our language are correctly handled (even the ones not yet defined) and all their arguments checked properly, it should be impossible to crash the game from within a script. Any crashes that do occur are due to either a programmer not handling all cases for an opcode correctly, or a piece of corrupt data occurring in the compiled script.

Scripts should be inherently multitasking. As we saw earlier, pausing a script for a given length of time is now a simple task. Additionally, we can limit the number of commands that a script can execute in a single frame. This effectively performs a preemptive multitask, and allows our game to both balance its scripting load and effectively handle infinite loops in script without jamming.

Scripts should have a debugger. This is the one weakness with our scripting language as it stands. Although it is possible to create a script debugger, it will take a lot of additional work and must be constantly updated as new commands are added. An alternative is to use the C debugger, but a designer cannot be expected to do this. Indeed, many programmers will find it difficult to debug a script using the C debugger.

Scripts should be extendable. Adding a new command is as simple as assigning it an opcode and compiling it in the compiler, then handling it in the interpreter. As long as the number of opcodes doesn't break any limit due to the number of bits assigned to it, and we don't change the order of the opcodes, old scripts should not have to be recompiled each time a new command is added.

Someone authoring scripts should not be able to break the game build. Using a custom scripting language stored in plain-text files is the ideal solution to this requirement, since someone creating a script does not need to have access to any of the game's source code.

With the exception of the debugger requirement, we can see that creating an original scripting language is the ideal way to implement scripts in games. In addition to meeting almost all of our scripting needs, we get the added benefit of being able to use the parser developed for the scripting language to parse all of our data files.

FURTHER READING

[GEMS2] Deloura, Mark, *Game Programming Gems 2*, Charles River Media, 2001.

5 The Resource Pipeline

In This Chapter

- Rule #5: "Always Use the Right Tool for the Job"
- The Intermediate Philosophy
- Platform Differences
- Data Groups
- A File Format for Grouping Assets
- Asynchronous Loading
- File Compression
- A Resource Pipeline Model
- The DataCon Build Assistant
- Further Reading

Data comes in many forms—images, models, sounds—but it's very seldom that it comes in the exact form that it's needed in; the data is a square peg for your game's round hole. However, unlike in kindergarten, we can cheat; nothing is stopping us from whipping out a plane and some sandpaper and smoothing the edges off that peg. And that's exactly what we're going to do.

This means that at some point, you're going to have to load that data and change it so that it works for the targeted machine. A naïve approach would be to postpone this change until the last possible moment; for example, loading all textures directly into the game as jpeg files. However, although this might aid in speeding development (artists like nothing better than to drop something straight into the game as is), in the long run it is a very poor idea. Some of the disadvantages of this method are obvious (increased load times due to having to process the data), some are less so (the final memory footprint for a given asset set is not easily determined), and some are downright elusive (multiple memory allocations for each stage of the asset conversion cause fragmentation). Obviously, this is not an acceptable situation for a project to be in for any length of time.

RULE #5: "ALWAYS USE THE RIGHT TOOL FOR THE JOB"

A better approach, then, is to process all of the data before it is presented to the game. This means that the data conversion is no longer time-critical, as it now only needs to be done once, allowing more extensive changes to be made to it. The amount of processing required, and the configuration the data ends up in is dependent on both the type and original format of the data and the capabilities of the target system. In this rule, we will examine methods for setting up an efficient build system to convert our assets into an efficient format for loading. Chapter 6, "Processing Assets," covers the actual techniques used to process the assets into platform-dependant formats.

THE INTERMEDIATE PHILOSOPHY

During the course of development, the final in-memory formats for most of the game's data is bound to change at least once. When this happens, it can really stall the development process, as all of the assets must be reprocessed and re-exported to the new format. Because this is so problematic, such format changes are often postponed, sometimes indefinitely. This is especially true as the project nears completion and time becomes tight; the artists probably have much better things to do than try to track down every single asset they built for the game in order to re-export it in the new format.

The intermediate philosophy tackles this head-on. The philosophy is simple: make it so that the artists only ever have to export an asset once, no matter how many changes the format of the final data might go through. This is actually really simple to accomplish. When exporting an asset, find every last piece of data that you possibly can about it, whether or not you think you will need it (you nearly always will eventually), and write it all into a simply formatted, intermediate text file. After this file has been exported, the only time it should ever need updating is if the artists change something in the source asset.

These intermediate files are then processed by a simple build system into the final, platform-dependent format. This build system would always have access to all of the intermediate files and would be able to make partial builds, rebuilding only the elements that have changed. This technique leaves the programmers free to make as many changes as they want to the final format of the asset. It also literally guarantees that no artist will ever have to go and re-export every single asset that he or she has ever built for the project.

PLATFORM DIFFERENCES

A modern game project is more often than not developed simultaneously for multiple target platforms. These platforms often have wildly different data requirements, memory capacities, and even byte-ordering. Any asset management system that we build must be amenable to building the assets into a different format for each target machine. It must also be able to change the specifications of each asset to meet the various memory requirements and rendering capabilities of the target.

Although we will not attempt to address byte-ordering in this chapter, it is easily added once the final routines for processing the data have been developed. Simply wrapping all memory reads and writes to the final data areas in an overloaded function call enables us to write the data with the correct endian-ness as we create it. Although this might seem intrusive, it actually is the most feasible way of accommodating different byte-orders, since whether or not consecutive bytes must be swapped depends on the type of data within them. For example, four consecutive characters will retain their ordering, whereas the four consecutive bytes that make up a 32-bit value will not.

DATA GROUPS

Before we look at the types of data that usually occur in a game project, we should first examine more closely the different subtypes of data that occur within each data type. By categorizing the different groups of data that make up each asset, we can better understand the most efficient way to store it for fast retrieval.

Most assets consist of two or more groups of data. The first group, metadata, is common to almost all assets and is the easiest to deal with. Metadata, more commonly known as a *header*, is data about the data. A good example of this is the metadata for a texture; it contains a description of the actual texture image—its dimensions, pixel format, number of mip-map levels, and so on. Without this metadata, we'd just have a collection of pixels with no idea of what to do with it (since we'd only know its length); unless you work for SETI, this is not a situation that you want to find yourself in.

The second group of data is the raw data itself—the pixels in the aforementioned texture. The aim of this chapter is to emphasize the importance of having this data in a readily usable form. A complex asset might have multiple pieces of raw data. For example, a mesh will usually have a data set representing the individual vertices and another data set representing the indices used to construct the triangles for the mesh. Additionally, the mesh might include a list of materials or a skeleton definition and might sometimes be forced to split the vertex or index data sets into multiple parts (e.g., if a mesh contains more than the maximum number of addressable vertices).

Each of these examples represents a different instance of raw data. However, they are not all handled in the same way. How the raw data is used often dictates where it must be placed in memory. An example of this is the pixels of a texture; these must usually reside in an area of memory addressable by the video card. Depending on the destination platform and the API used, this might or might not be directly addressable by the CPU. Under the DirectX API, for example, a texture object of the correct format and size must be created before the pixels can be loaded into GPU-addressable memory. On a console such as the Xbox®, however, we can load the texture data directly into GPU-addressable memory with little work.

Things are even more complex than this, however. Some areas of memory are volatile and might not be completely entrusted with the sole copy of any data that is placed in it. This is especially a problem on the PC, where the game might not be the sole application running, and where it might lose focus, and hence access to the video hardware, at any time. To combat this, some types of indirectly loaded data might need to either be duplicated in nonvolatile memory, or be quickly and easily reloaded from disk. Whoever said writing games was fun?

Looking at all the assets that have to be drawn into a game, each of the subtypes of data usually falls into one of the following groups:

- Metadata
- Data that can be loaded into general memory
- Data that can be directly loaded into nonvolatile specialized memory
- Data that must be indirectly loaded into nonvolatile specialized memory
- Data that must be loaded indirectly into volatile specialized memory

The type of specialized memory that they reside in can further subcategorize each of the last three data groups. Some examples of specialized memory are video card memory, AGP memory, and dedicated sound card memory. By recognizing the type of each chunk of data that makes up an asset, we can group all of the similar data from different assets together and so reduce the amount of memory allocations required. This forms the basis of our data format.

A FILE FORMAT FOR GROUPING ASSETS

As we saw in the previous section, the key to creating a robust data format that can contain multiple assets is to recognize and group together similar chunks of data from each individual asset. Each of these groups then forms a large block of contiguous data within our data file. Each of these blocks requires an index so that we can locate the individual data chunks for each asset. We also require a way of finding the first, pivotal chunk of data for each asset, which is the parent of all other data chunks. This implies that we need a second index for this purpose.

To locate an arbitrary piece of data in the file, we need two things: the index of the block where it resides, and an identifier for finding the chunk in the block's table of contents. The identifier within each block could simply be an index, but doing this could cause problems later, when we attempt to merge multiple data files of this format together to form a single large file. To understand why this is a problem, we must look at how we represent pointers between different data chunks within the file.

To be able to successfully store pointers in the file, we need to turn them into a form that can be recovered easily and that consumes the same amount of memory or less, so that it can be stored over the original pointer. This seems easy enough; just combine the block index and data identifier into a single, 32-bit locator ID and replace the original pointer with this locator. A simple structure for this purpose that includes a placeholder for the underlying pointer is given here:

```
typedef union
{
```

```
    struct
    {
        u16    blockId;
        u16    chunkId;
    };
    u32    id;
    void   *pData;

} LOCID;
```

In fact, this works quite well until you try to combine two data files in this format into a single file. In this situation, if the data identifier is an index within each block, then when you attempt to concatenate similar blocks, the indices of the data within the second source block are changed. Unfortunately, the ex-pointers that must be changed to reflect the new locator ID are, for all intents and purposes, distributed randomly among the other data chunks. Unless we possess intimate knowledge of each chunk so that we can locate and correct these pointers (which we do, but we don't want to admit it just now, because it will make our job harder), then we need to ensure that this doesn't happen.

The solution to this is to give each chunk of data an identifier within each block that is not dependent on its position in the block. However, because of the need to combine the block index with this identifier to form a locator ID that will fit within 32 bits, we now only have 24 or so bits of data to store an ID in. Anyone who has read the section on hash collisions in Chapter 3, "Hashes and Hash Functions," will now be breaking into a cold sweat. This will only get worse when they consider that there will be many more chunks of data than there are assets, with a corresponding need for a larger hash space to avoid collisions.

The simple solution to this problem is to increase the hash space for the locator ID. However, we need it to fit in 32 bits so that it can exactly replace a pointer in the data. The only way to do this is to find another identifier that is easily found whenever a locator ID is found that can be appended to the locator ID to effectively expand the hash space available. Luckily, this data has already been calculated and is readily available: the hash of the asset's name (which is used to locate the asset in the first place). Since this hash is *guaranteed* to be unique (see Chapter 3) for each asset to avoid hash collisions when searching for assets, we effectively have a separate 32-bit hash space for each of the chunks of data that comprise an asset.

Using this 64-bit composite hash value to represent each chunk of data gives us the following structure for the index entry of each chunk in the block:

```
class BlockIndexEntry
{
public:
    HASH    nameHash;
    LOCID   locatorID;
    U32     blockOffset;
    U32     dataLength;
};
```

Each block's index is effectively an array of these items, sorted by the 64-bit hash contained within each. Finding an item within a block is then simply a matter of searching the index for the correct hash. Since this list is sorted, the search can be a binary search and so has an $O(\log n)$ time complexity. To finish the definition of a block's header, we need to store a few more pieces of data. The first of these is the *type* of the block, which defines the type of memory it must be loaded into. We also need the required alignment and overall length of the block, which define how much of that memory to allocate for it. Finally, we need the count of the chunks of data in the block so we can successfully negotiate the index. The final block index structure is shown here:

```
class BlockIndex
{
public:
    u32     blockType;
    u32     blockAlignment;
    u32     blockLength;
    u32     numItems;
```

```
// BlockIndexItem items[numItems];
};
```

Now that we can define the individual chunks that comprise a given asset, the only other thing that is needed is a way to locate the primary chunk for an asset, which usually consists of the metadata that describes the asset. These can be stored in a single master index for the entire file that is sorted by the hash of the asset's name. To be able to process the asset at load time, we also need to know the type (texture, mesh, sound, etc.) of each of the assets. This is also stored in the master index entry for each asset. Given these requirements, we end up with the following structure for an entry in the master index:

```
class MasterIndexEntry
{
public:
    HASH    nameHash;
    HASH    typeHash;
    LOCID   primaryChunk;
};
```

In a similar way to the block index, we must also define a structure to hold data about the master index. However, since the master index is the key to the entire file, we will also store some extra information about the file that will help us load it faster. By storing the length of the master index as the first item in it, we can quickly and easily determine how much memory to allocate for it during loading. Similarly, by storing the total size of all of the block indices, we can load them all in a single operation. Finally, if the data file has an optional dictionary attached to it (for storing the names of the assets), its length is also stored here:

```
class MasterIndex
{
public:
    u32     indexLength;
```

```
    u32      totalBlockIndexLength;
    u32      dictionaryLength;
    u32      numBlocks;
    u32      numItems;

// MasterIndexEntry items[numItems];
};
```

Figure 5.1 shows the final layout of our data file. Notice that all of the indices are concatenated together at the start, followed by each block's data segment in turn. Finally, the file is terminated with an optional dictionary containing the names of the assets.

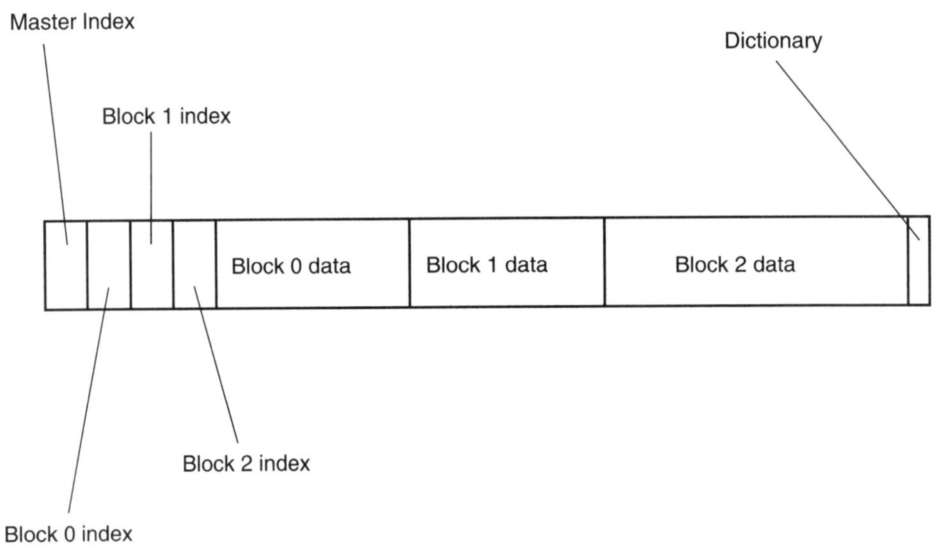

FIGURE 5.1 Composite data file format.

Loading a Composite Data File

Now that we have designed our file format, we need to figure out how to load it back from disk. Since all the assets in the file have already been processed, this should be pretty simple. The first step is to load the master index. This is simple, since the first 32 bits of the master index structure contain the length of the entire master index. After reading this length from the file, we simply allocate a block of memory of the correct size and load the data into it. The allocated memory should come from a heap designed for long-lived allocations of regular memory, because we'll be keeping this index around for the lifetime of the assets.

After loading the master index, we now need to load the indices for all of the blocks of data in the file. However, unlike the master index, these indices will not be needed after we have finished the loading process, so the memory required for these should be taken from a short-lifetime heap. As with the master index, the amount of memory required is readily available, stored in the `totalBlockIndexLength` member of the master index. After allocating the required amount of memory, we then fill it with the block index data from the file.

The next step is to iterate through each of the blocks, allocating the correct type of memory and loading the data into it. The length and memory type of each block of data is stored in the corresponding block index. As explained earlier, some memory types are not directly addressable by the main CPU, and so some blocks might need to be loaded into main memory and then somehow copied into the correct area of memory. In this case, the main memory allocated for the block should be deleted immediately after it is no longer needed.

The final phase of reading the file from disk is to read the names dictionary, if it is both present and required. Again, the total length of the dictionary is stored in the master index header, so loading it should be straightforward. After the dictionary is read, or not, then we are finished with the file and can close the file handle.

Now that our file resides totally in memory, we can begin to reconstruct the assets contained within it. This is simply a matter of recreating the links between the various chunks that make up each asset. We achieve this by iterating through the entries in the master index, calling a setup function for each asset, based on its type. These setup functions know the underlying structure of the asset and so know the location of the pointers that need to be restored. The base address of each data chunk can be found by using the locator ID that replaced the pointer to it to find first the correct block, and then the correct offset within the block.

The setup function also instantiates any runtime data that needs creating for the asset. Doing this might allow us to forget about the original data. For example, on a Direct3D-based platform, the setup function for a mesh could retrieve a pointer to the vertex data chunk and then use this to construct a vertex buffer containing the data. The pointer to the vertex buffer can then replace the locator ID of the chunk in the structure, and the original data block is no longer needed.

After the setup function has completely restored the asset, it returns a pointer to the asset. This pointer might or might not be the pointer that it was given as the primary data chunk, depending on the format of the asset. If the API used for an asset can maintain all of the data for an object for us, we might not need to store anything but a pointer to the API object. The pointer returned by the setup function then replaces the locator ID of the primary chunk in the master index.

Once all of the assets in the data file have been set up correctly, the block indices are no longer needed and can be freed. Similarly, any blocks of data that are no longer used can also be freed at this time. A good example of this is a block of memory containing only vertex data, which is loaded into Direct3D's vertex buffers; after loading, nothing needs to access the original vertex data again, and so the whole block can be freed.

ASYNCHRONOUS LOADING

Loading data can take a while, even when it is already fully processed and in a form that is easily restored. This is especially true on platforms where the data will be loaded from optical media, and seek and access times are horrendous. We can make our games look more professional by displaying moving text and images on the screen during the loading of the data. However, we can't rely on the speed of reading bits of data from the file, and so can't simply read from the file in small chunks, processing the loading animation between file accesses. Attempting to do so usually results in choppy animation and uneven frame rates; exactly what we don't want, since we are trying to look good by doing things during loading. This is where asynchronous loading comes in.

Although the exact method of achieving asynchronous loading varies from platform to platform, the concept is always the same. Instead of issuing a load command that completes before returning to the main process, with asynchronous loading our load command returns after simply placing the name of the file we requested in a list of files that are waiting to be loaded. We can then happily go away and smoothly run our loading animation, oblivious to the behind-the-scenes loading of the file.

The simplest way to implement asynchronous loading on most platforms is through the use of the built-in multitasking features of the operating system. It is a simple task to create a *thread*[1] that *blocks*[2] itself until given a filename, at which point it loads and processes the file. After it is done processing the file, it places the file in a list that the main game can access, and then *blocks* itself until it receives another file request.

When writing multitasking code, care must be taken to ensure that variables that are accessed by more than one thread are not accessed at the same time by multiple threads. An especially bad example of this occurs during list accesses. Imagine that thread A is iterating through a list when its time slice ends, and thread B then deletes the list entry that A is currently examining while thread A is asleep. Then, when thread A reawakens, it will find itself either accessing freed memory or iterating through the free list, neither of which are healthy activities. Although this seems that it would be fairly easy to test for, this problem can potentially occur whenever two threads access or alter the same memory location.

So, how do we overcome this problem? Any simple method that we can use to signal that a thread is about to access a shared variable potentially involves modifying a shared variable, which puts us right back where we started. Luckily, the operating system has to overcome this problem and so supplies a solution that we can use, called *critical sections.*

A critical section is an object that the operating system maintains that only one thread can have ownership of at any one time. When a thread attempts to gain control of the critical section, hereafter called *entering* the critical section, it must do so through an operating system function call.

This function call is guaranteed not to return until the calling thread has sole ownership of the critical section. If a thread requests access to a critical section that a second thread currently owns, then the first thread is *blocked* (taking no processor time) until such a time that the second thread relinquishes ownership of the critical section (*exiting* the critical section).

By careful placement of critical section objects around all of the vulnerable access to shared variables, we can successfully remove bugs due to contention over shared variables. However, critical sections are not foolproof; care must be taken that a thread that owns a critical section does not block it in such a way that it can only be awakened by another thread inside the same critical section. But hey, that's why programmers get paid the big bucks!

FILE COMPRESSION

By careful tailoring of our data files so that they are in the correct format to be loaded and used in place, we have reduced the *load-time* processing cost and memory footprint for the data. This effectively reduces the time it takes to load a given set of data. However, we have yet to look at the most costly part of loading the data—reading it from whatever media it is stored on. If the data is stored on a hard drive, then this cost is negligible, but if we are developing a game for a console, then chances are that the data will be stored on CD or DVD, with correspondingly appalling seek times and transfer rates.

We have already addressed the seek times for our data by putting all of it in just a few files, read sequentially in large blocks, thus reducing the number of seeks needed. However, this does nothing for the transfer rate of the data. A simple way to increase the transfer rate is to compress the files as they are authored and transparently decompress them as they are loaded. This reduces the amount of data that must be read and hence increases the *apparent* transfer rate.

Although some of our data might already be compressed (e.g., textures could be stored as any DXT compressed textures and sounds could be stored as ADPCM data), it is compressed in such a way that it can be decompressed quickly on-the-fly. In the case of compressed textures, the compression is designed for efficient random access of the image data and to give a constant number of bits per pixel. Although this effectively reduces the data size somewhat, the data still has a pattern and predictability to it, and this makes it conducive to further compression.

There are many compression libraries available for licensing, with varying prices, speeds, compression rates on different types of data, and compatibility. Our main requirements for compression are that it works on a data stream (i.e., that we can start decompressing before the file has fully loaded) and that the compression is loss-less. This narrows the field somewhat, but there are still a fair number of libraries available.

One compression library is freely available and usable without fee, even in a commercial application. This library is widely used in many commercial applications, and you have probably used it unknowingly on several occasions. The library is called Zlib, and was written by Jean-loup Gailly and Mark Adler.

ON THE CD

A full Zlib distribution, of the version currently available at time of press, is included on the companion CD-ROM, in the folder `common/compression/zlib`. *Please read the license included in the source code at the top of the main include file, zlib.h. More information about Zlib can be found at [ZLIB].*

Using Zlib

Like most compression libraries, Zlib treats the incoming data as a stream and outputs a corresponding stream with its result. This means that the data, whether it is to be compressed or decompressed, must be sent to Zlib sequentially; there is no random access inside a compressed file. If you think about it, though, this makes perfect sense: since the number of bits needed to compress a section of data varies by that data's contents, it is impossible to know in advance how much space the compressed version of it will take. It follows, then, that since we cannot know how much space the compressed form of the data preceding the data we are interested in takes, we cannot know where to begin decompressing from to get instant access to our data. We must instead decompress the whole file up to that point and continue from there.

The thing that makes Zlib so useful to us is that it has been written to work on partial streams. Zlib basically has three buffers: an incoming buffer, an outgoing buffer, and an internal buffer to hold unfinished results. To compress or decompress a stream of data, we must first tell Zlib the location and sizes of the incoming and outgoing buffers. Once we have done this, we can tell Zlib to either compress or decompress the incoming stream. Zlib will then proceed to perform the requested action, drawing data from the incoming stream as needed and writing data to the outgoing stream as it is completed. It carries on doing this until it runs out of space in one of the buffers, at which point it returns. However, it still has intermediate results stored in its internal buffer, and can use these to resume its compression once there is either more data to operate on, or more room to output results. As you can see, this makes it very useful to us, since we can use the streaming nature of Zlib to operate on large files in small chunks.

To compress a file, we simply allocate a small buffer for Zlib to write to, and then keep passing chunks of data to it until this buffer is full. At this point, we flush the output buffer to disk, and then continue adding more data. Once all the data is compressed, we need to instruct Zlib that it is finished so that it can dump any partially complete values stored in its internal buffer to the output buffer for one final disk write. Care must be taken with this final step, since flushing its intermediate buffer might cause the output buffer to become full and so might need more than one disk write.

To decompress a file, we again allocate a small buffer, but this time the small buffer is Zlib's incoming stream. Each time we request data from Zlib, it pulls bytes from this input buffer to try to deliver the data we requested. Whenever the input buffer becomes empty, we simply refill it with the next section of data read from the file and carry on as before. Decompressing a file is actually easier than compressing it, since we don't have to worry about flushing the intermediate data out of Zlib when the compressed stream ends.

ON THE CD

A class for reading and writing compressed data files is provided on the companion CD-ROM in the folder common/compression. The base class is called Xfile and has two subclasses: XFileWrite for compressing data and XFileRead for decompressing it. These classes supply a simple interface to Zlib for reading and writing compressed files in small sections. The classes are written so that they hide the Zlib header files from the rest of the program, which helps speed compile times and reduces the maze of header dependencies.

A RESOURCE PIPELINE MODEL

Now that we know the overall format of the file we will be storing our assets in, we need to create a method of processing the source assets for the game and combining them into a single, composite data file. We will refer to this as our *resource pipeline*, since it can be viewed as a pipe that delivers resources from the artists to the game. The pipe analogy is a good one, because ideally we want everything to just work, without worrying about the myriad of tools the data goes through along the way.

Although artists and designers are very good at producing masses of high-quality content, they are usually not too concerned with learning the process of putting their assets in the game. Any process that can't be summed up in two steps on the back of an envelope is going to come back and bite you again and again, especially with each new hire or loaned employee. Murphy's law has never been more true than with unseasoned colleagues trying to get their work into the game; if anything can go wrong, it will certainly go wrong, many, many times over.

In truth, artists and designers should not have to worry about running this tool or that tool, or about the order in which tools are run. They should worry about producing their content and having the fast turnaround times that it takes to fine-tune that content. By keeping the resource pipeline simple, you increase the speed, volume, and quality of their work and enable them to make your game truly shine; any time spent simplifying the pipeline will pay off a thousand-fold later in the project, especially as deadlines loom.

For this reason, we are going to design an automated build process that will allow the artists to put their data in the game with a single mouse click. In addition, to decrease turnaround time, we are going to concentrate on facilitating minimal rebuilds; only data that changes and data that depends on it will be rebuilt.

We want to define our automated build process in such a way that it can handle multiple projects with multiple data files, containing multiple data formats, for multiple platforms. As you can tell, this can quickly become very confusing, so before we start we should define some terminology:

Project: A project is a collection of data files. A project is responsible for setting up the entire resource pipeline and recording its state.

Project path: The base path of the project. All relative paths have this as their base.

Platform: A platform describes the target machine. Each project can be built for several different platforms.

Data format: A data format is a supported type of data. Each data format must be assigned a handler for each platform type that it can occur in.

Include path: An include path is a directory where files should be looked for. Include paths can be enabled or disabled by data format and platform type. For example, if textures were stored in one directory and sounds in another, then it would be wasteful to search for sound files in the texture directory.

Data file: A data file is the final output of the resource pipeline, ready to use in the game. A data file is fully described by an accompanying command file. The data file is dependent on all intermediate files generated while processing the command file. If any of the intermediate files are newer than the data file, then the data file must be recreated using the intermediate files.

Command file: A plain-text file containing commands to build data in various formats. A command file can reference other command files.

Source file: A binary file containing raw source data; for example, a texture or sound file.

Intermediate file: A binary file containing a single piece of data described in a command file. This file is dependent on the command file that created it, any source files that contributed to it, and the format of the data it contains. If any of these are newer than the intermediate file, then the intermediate file must be recreated.

Intermediate path: The base path where all intermediate files are stored. The intermediate files are actually stored in subdirectories by platform, data file, and data type.

Image path: The base path where the final data files are placed. This is definable by platform.

The project file contains all of the settings for the pipeline, including the include, intermediate, and image paths. The location of the project file is called the *project path* and should be the root of all of the paths used. If this is the case, then all of the paths given in the project file can be stored as relative paths, and the project can be freely moved. Any paths given that are not descendants of the project path must necessarily be stored as absolute paths, and so might prevent the project from being easily relocated or copied.

As explained previously, different platforms can have wildly different capabilities and data needs. Additionally, each platform can define key constants differently. Since we are trying to process the data into a format directly usable by the game, these constants might need to be embedded in the data. This leaves us with a conundrum: either we duplicate the code needed to process the command files in several executables that can each handle one or more data formats for a single platform, or we find a way to *safely* include the headers for each platform only where they are needed.

By making one or more DLLs for each platform, each containing code to build one or more data formats for that platform, we neatly sidestep this problem. Each DLL can freely include the header files for the single platform it was written for, and all the DLLs use a common interface provided by the build tool to perform common tasks. This guarantees safety for the platform-specific headers and allows us to share common code through the base tool, reducing code replication.

Each DLL has a single exported function, `Register()`, that is used to tell the build tool which data formats are implemented and for what platform. Since the DLLs dynamically add functionality at runtime, this method also lets us easily add new data types, both at the project level and at the platform level. Additionally, by including the timestamp of the appropriate DLL in the dependency check for each intermediate file, we can automatically rebuild only the resources that we need to when a data handler changes.

Building a Data File

When the build tool is told to build a data file from a given command file, it creates two lists—a list of command files to process and a list of intermediate files generated—and adds the given command file to the first list. It then processes each command file in the process list, adding command files to the end of the process list as instructed. Each command file contains a series of instructions to either add or exclude another command file to the list or create intermediate files of a given data format, as described previously.

As the data handlers declare each of the intermediate files, they are added to the list of intermediate files, which is also the list of dependencies for the final data file. When every command file in the process list has been fully processed, the timestamp of the final data file is compared against the timestamp of each intermediate file generated. If any intermediate files are newer than the final data file, then it is recreated by combining all of the intermediate files.

Command Files

The data files that make up a project are each represented by a command file, which is a plain-text file. We can use the parser developed in Chapter 4, "Scripting," to tokenize the command file prior to processing it.

To be able to transparently change the contents of any command file based on the platform, we must preprocess each command file after tokenizing it. In this preprocess path, we will descend the syntax tree searching for a `PLATFORM` command. When a `PLATFORM` command is found, the contents of its parameter list is compared against the current target platform to see whether to include the commands contained in the platform block. The `PLATFORM` command's parameter list is *either* a list of platforms for which this block is to be included or a list of platforms for which this block is to be excluded. If a parameter to the `PLATFORM` command begins with either a `~` or a `!` character, then the specified platform is to be *excluded*; otherwise, it is to be *included*.

When the current platform is included in the parameter list, then the PLATFORM command is removed from the tree, and its command block is pasted in its place; otherwise, the platform command is removed along with its block. In the following example, we define a texture that has a different size on the PC platform than on any other platform:

```
Texture("face")
{
    PLATFORM("PC")    SIZE(512,512);
    PLATFORM("~PC")   SIZE(128,128);
}
```

After preprocessing for the PC platform, the texture's size parameter will be defined as 512x512, but for any other platform it will be defined as 128x128. Any underlying data handler will not then have to worry about processing the PLATFORM command, since they will all have been removed prior to the data handler's invocation.

The only other commands that the build tool understands natively are the AddFile and ExcludeFile commands. The first of these commands tells the build tool to add the specified command file to its list of files to process; the other instructs it to ignore the given command file if it is subsequently added. These commands allow us to string together a list of command files to make a single data file. Any command that is not natively recognized by the build tool is looked up in the list of data handlers for the target platform derived from the DLL files. This data handler is then invoked to process the command.

Data Handlers

Each data handler is invoked with both a pointer to the command that caused it to be called and a pointer to an interface object supplying common functions. The data handler is responsible for processing the command it is passed and any commands in its block.

The first thing that the data handler must do is parse its input commands, using the supplied interface object, to determine what it is being asked to do. This should yield information such as the name of the intermediate file that this handler should create and any source files that must be used to create it. At this point, the data handler needs to create the full pathnames of any source files referenced. It does this by using the interface object to query for files in the relevant include paths (by resource type and platform name). If any of the source files cannot be found, then an error is reported and the data handler exits.

The full pathname of the intermediate file is also generated using the interface object, but this is deterministic (i.e., it exactly specifies a single file that might or might not exist). The timestamp of the intermediate file is then compared against the timestamp of the current command file, the timestamp of the DLL that the data handler resides in, and the timestamps of any source files specified. If the intermediate file is older than any of these, then it is recreated from the given data.

Finally, the intermediate file is added to the build tool's list of intermediate files.

THE DATACON BUILD ASSISTANT

ON THE CD

A sample implementation of a build system is supplied on the companion CD-ROM, in the Chapter5/DataCon folder. This simple dialog-based MFC application, when coupled with the required DLLs, is all that is required to make a robust data build system that satisfies our goal of a single-click, minimal rebuild resource pipeline.

The first time you use DataCon, you must select a project. On subsequent uses, however, DataCon remembers the last project that was selected (and the last options for it) and automatically reselects this project. To select a project, click the Change button in the upper-right portion of the DataCon dialog, and then choose the project path from the file selector that appears. If a project already exists in the path chosen, it is loaded; otherwise, a new project is created and the Project properties dialog appears. Figure 5.2 shows some of the different tabs of the Project properties dialog.

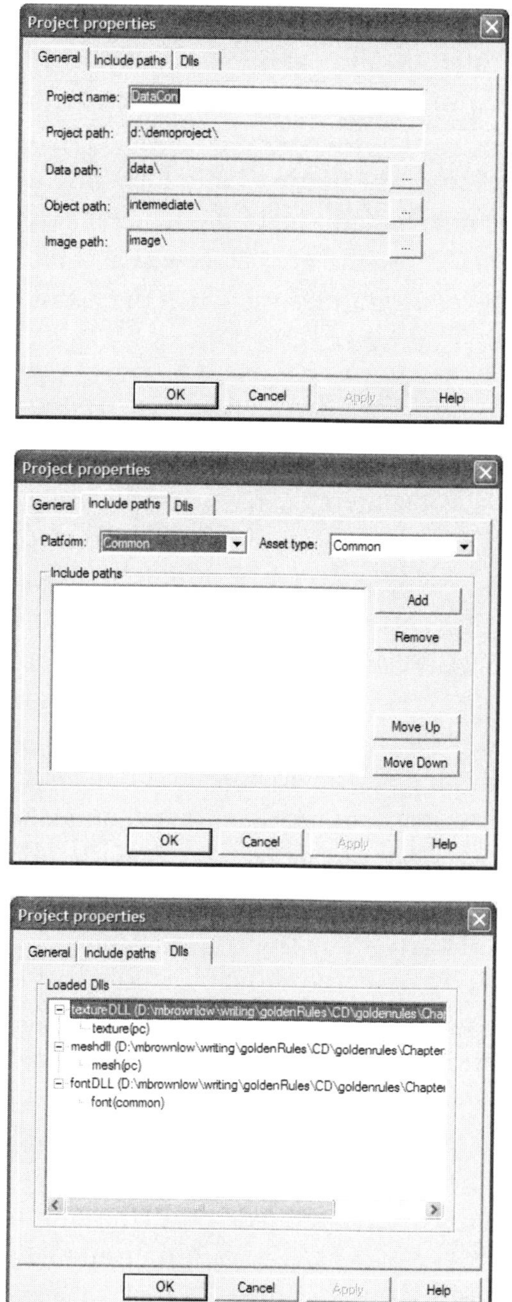

FIGURE 5.2 DataCon Project properties.

In the General tab of the Project properties dialog, you can set the data, object (intermediate), and image paths to control where the output from the build process goes. Be careful to make sure that these folders are below the project path; otherwise, the project might not be transferable between machines since the destination folders might be in a different place on the new machine. In addition to the General tab, there is a tab for changing the include paths for the project as well as a tab for listing the DLLs that are currently loaded (and from which the list of available platforms and asset formats are derived).

The Include paths tab allows you to add and remove include paths to the project, as well as rearrange the order in which they are checked. Include paths are gathered into groups by a pairing of a platform and asset type. When DataCon attempts to locate a file of a given type, it looks through the specified include paths until it finds the correct file. The paths are checked in order by grouping, and four groups are checked in all. The first group of paths to be checked is that for the destination platform and asset type. Next, DataCon checks the group for the destination platform and the common asset type. If the file is still not found, it checks the group for the common platform and the specific asset type. Finally, it checks the group for the common platform and the common asset type. If after all this checking the file is still not found, then it is presumed to not exist.

The DLL tab of the Project properties dialog lists all of the DLLs that have been loaded by DataCon to achieve its functionality. If you expand an entry in the DLL list, DataCon will show all of the registered functions for that DLL, by asset type and destination platform. This is useful for tracking down instances where DataCon doesn't know what to do with an asset.

Figure 5.3 shows the main DataCon dialog (please note that the majority of the controls in the dialog do not become active until a valid project has been chosen). The first thing that must be done to build a data file is to choose the destination platform. This is done using the Target Platform combo box, which is located toward the upper-right of the main dialog. Simply select the desired target platform from the drop-down list to begin building data files for that platform. Initially, the common platform is selected.

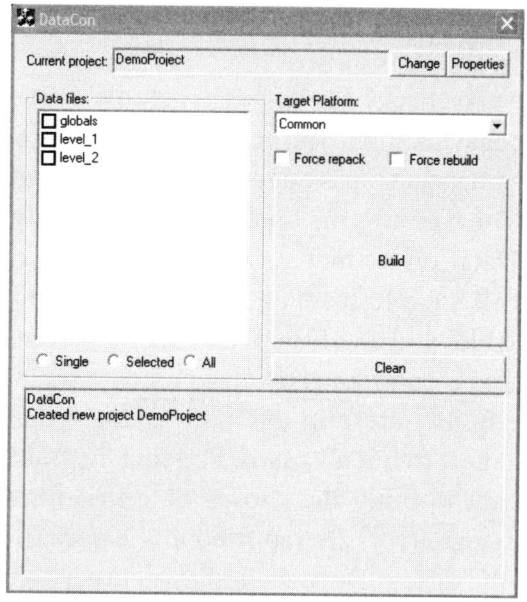

FIGURE 5.3 Main DataCon dialog.

The window labeled "Data files:" lists all of the command files that were found in the data path for the project. Each file in this list builds into a single output file, located under the project's image path, in a subfolder with the same name as the target platform. This enables us to build the same data files for different platforms without getting them mixed up. Immediately below this window are three radio buttons, marked "Single," "Selected," and "All." Selecting one of these determines the action of the Build button. With the Single radio button selected, only the data file that is selected in the list (marked by a black box around it) is built when the Build button is pressed. The Selected radio button tells DataCon that we want to build every data file in the list that has a check mark next to it. Finally, the All radio button makes DataCon build every single data file in the list.

Note that although DataCon can be asked to build multiple files, whether those files are actually built depends on whether they are up to date.

Files that are up to date do not need to be rebuilt, since the end product would be the same as the file already present.

The two check boxes immediately above the Build button modify DataCon's behavior slightly. The "Force repack" check box makes it always see that the final data file is out of date, and so makes it always recombine the intermediate files into the final data file. Similarly, the "Force rebuild" button makes DataCon see that all intermediate files are out of date and so makes it rebuild all the intermediate files. The Clean button deletes all of the intermediate files and all of the final data files, even the ones not selected in the list, and so is good for starting a new data build with a clean slate.

The Build button in the main dialog is the largest button present, and also the most frequently used. Pressing the Build button will cause DataCon to attempt to build the chosen data files for the chosen target platform. Progress and errors are reported in the grayed-out window at the very bottom of the dialog. During a build, all other controls in the DataCon dialog are grayed out.

Extending DataCon

ON THE CD

Three simple DLLs for the data formats explained in the next chapter accompany the version of DataCon supplied on the companion CD-ROM. These DLLs only add functionality for processing the data for the PC platform type. However, extending DataCon is as easy as writing a new DLL, following the template of the DLLs supplied with it.

The first thing that a DLL needs to do is define the `Register` function, which is the only function exported by the DLL. Inside this function, we must call back into DataCon with the supplied `IRegister` interface once for every platform, asset type, and function call triplet. Doing this declares to DataCon that this DLL processes the given asset types for the given platform with the given function. Then, every time DataCon comes across a command in a command file that it does not recognize natively, it searches through its list to find a function that handles the specific asset type (the name of the command) for the current destination platform, invoking it when found. In this manner, we gain control of the build pipeline to process the asset type that we have declared that we know how to process.

Each function that we declare takes four arguments. The first argument is a pointer to an `IProject` interface. Using this interface, we can jump back into DataCon to do common tasks, and other tasks such as finding files in the include paths for the project, checking file times, and writing to the output file. The second argument is a pointer to the section of the parsed command file that we are expected to process. The final two arguments are the destination platform and the asset type that caused us to be invoked.

Once invoked, our function must process the section of the command file passed to it. DataCon uses the generic scripting format that we developed in Chapter 4, and so the same methods can be used to process this as described in that chapter. The only difference here is that the functions we will use to parse the commands have been wrapped into the `IProject` interface to reduce the amount of linkage points between DataCon and its DLLs.

Once all of the commands have been parsed, we are in a position to let DataCon find all the files that we need to process them. This is done through the `IProject` member function, `GetSourceFile`. This function takes four parameters: the name of the file we are searching for, the current platform, the current asset type, and a pointer to an array of characters to be filled with the absolute filename of the first matching file found. It uses the platform and asset type provided to create a list of directories to search, and then searches through them all for the given filename. If the file is found, its absolute path is written into the provided character array, and the function returns true. Otherwise, the character array is cleared and the function returns false.

Next, we must tell DataCon about our intermediate file. This is done through the `SetOutputFile` member function. This function takes the same four parameters as the `GetSourceFile` function, but instead of searching for the file (since it might not exist yet), it simply constructs the expected absolute filename for the given parameters. Calling this function also adds the given file to the list of intermediate files needed to create the final data file. Failure to call the `SetOutputFile` function will cause the given file to be omitted from the final collation step, and hence stop the asset from appearing in the final file.

Once we have the absolute filenames for our output and input files, we can check to see if the output file is up to date. To do this, we use the `FileIsNewer` member function of the supplied interface. This function returns true if the file represented by the first parameter is newer than the second parameter. If the output file is newer than all the input files, then we do not need to do any more work, and can return control to DataCon. We also must check the output file against the DLL file that we are in and the command file that our commands come from; a change in either could change what should appear in the output file. Luckily, this is simple to accomplish using the `FileIsValid` function, which checks for just this contingency, and also for whether the given file exists.

If we find that our output file is either out of date or nonexistent, then we must rebuild it using the commands that we parsed earlier. To rebuild the file, we must first get an interface to an object that will ease its creation. This is done using the `CreateOutputFile` function, which takes the absolute pathname of the output file as its only parameter, and returns an `IOutputFile` interface. Using the `IOutputFile` interface, we can finally construct our output file from the various input files that we were given. This interface has just three methods:

`AddChunk`: Used to add a data chunk to a block of data.

`AddItem`: Used to add our main resource item to the master index.

`Close`: Closes the file and deletes the interface object.

As detailed earlier in the chapter, each asset can be broken into several chunks of different kinds of data. These data chunks are grouped by type into blocks of data that all use the same kind of memory. The `AddChunk` function takes five parameters. The first two parameters are the name of the item (used to create the name hash portion of the data chunk's locator ID) and the type of block that it must be placed in (so that it can be grouped with similar data). The last three parameters are a pointer to the data, the size of the data, and its required memory alignment, respectively. This function returns a 32-bit locator ID that can be used later to retrieve the data. This locator ID is made from a combination of the block ID (which is basically the block type) and a chunk number, which increments with every chunk added to the file. As each chunk is added, its data is copied into a memory buffer that is internal to the `IOutputFile` implementation, and so can be safely freed.

Once all of the data chunks have been added, we can finally add the item to the master index using the `AddItem` function. This function takes three parameters: the name of the asset, the type of the asset, and the locator ID for the primary chunk of data, as returned from one of the `AddChunk` calls. A final call to the `Close` member function writes the file to disk, closes it, and deletes the `IOutputFile` interface.

Congratulations! You've just extended the functionality of DataCon!

Now that we have a simple, yet powerful and extensible build system that can handle multiple data formats for multiple platforms, we need to look at methods of processing the most common types of asset. These are covered in the next chapter.

FURTHER READING

[ZLIB] Zlib home site. Available online at *www.gzip.org/zlib/*.

ENDNOTES

[1]A thread is an instance of the CPU executing a program.

[2]When a thread blocks, it stops execution unless it is awakened by external stimuli. While blocked, a thread takes no processor time.

6 Processing Assets

In This Chapter

- Rule #6: "Don't Use a Square Peg for a Round Hole"
- Processing Textures
- Processing TrueType Fonts
- Processing Meshes
- Automatically Generating Triangle Stips
- Putting It All Together
- Further Reading

In the previous chapter, we looked at how combining data segments of similar types into blocks helped speed the loading process. We also looked at ways of automating the build process and enabling minimal rebuilds. Following on from this, in this chapter we will look at how to efficiently process the data for each asset, prior to adding it into our composite data format.

RULE #6: "DON'T USE A SQUARE PEG FOR A ROUND HOLE"

As we stated in the previous chapter, the assets created for our games seldom come in an appropriate format for efficient loading and use. We created the DataCon build assistant to establish a specific build process. Now all we need to do is figure out exactly what we need to do to the incoming data to create the final assets that our game can load and use with as little extra processing as possible.

Data comes in many forms; far too many, in fact, to cover them all in the space granted by a single chapter (or even a single book). Additionally, your game might involve custom-generated data that would not be applicable to another game, so even if we tried, we could never create an all-encompassing reference guide. For these reasons, we will limit ourselves to discussion of three forms of data that pretty much every 3D game will need to process at some point: textures, fonts, and meshes. So, without further ado, let's begin.

PROCESSING TEXTURES

Images come in many different formats—jpg, gif, png, bmp, tga, tiff, etc.—and at first glance, it would seem that they are simple to use, especially for the potentially uncompressed file formats such as tgas. However, looks can be deceiving. Most of the hardware platforms that games target have severe restrictions on image dimensions and pixel formats for textures. Even when a piece of hardware is relatively forgiving, there can be terrible performance penalties for choosing the wrong image type. The situation is especially bad for a game targeting PCs; different PCs will almost definitely have different video hardware, with different supported texture sizes and formats, and a different "sweet spot" where maximum performance can be achieved.

Nevertheless, effective preprocessing can be done on image data. All that needs to be done is to recognize the limits of the output format in the image preprocessor tool. The basic things we need to know are:

- What restrictions are there on texture size; do all textures have to be a power of 2 in width and/or height?
- Do all textures have to be square, or is there some other limit on the aspect ratio?
- Which texture formats are supported? How broad is the support for each format?
- In what situations does the image quality/render speed/image size trade-off make each texture format worthwhile to use?
- What is the "magic" texture size for each texture format?

It is important to disseminate this information to the artists working on the game so that they can take this into account as they author the art. Artists don't take kindly to a programmer arbitrarily scaling their magnificent 2031 by 3763-pixel, 16-million color image (depicting the main character's face) down to a measly 32x32-pixel, 256-color texture.

Defining a Texture

Although each image file is easy to locate and load, there is not enough information in it to enable us to create the best texture possible. Each image usually only contains data about its width and height, and maybe its pixel format (when it's not presumed to be 32-bit). We need a little more than this to be able to use it effectively.

Each texture must be declared in a command file using the `Texture("<name>")` command. This command declares that we are going to define a texture called "name" in the block of commands immediately following it. We must begin the texture block by defining the size and pixel format of the final texture, as well as the number of mip-map levels that we want and various other properties. This is done using the following commands:

Size(<x>,<y>);: Defines the required size of the texture. If this command is omitted, then the size of the texture is taken from the first image loaded. If no images are loaded for this texture, then this command cannot be omitted. This command must appear before any images are loaded.

Format("<format>");: Defines the required pixel format of the texture. The valid values of format depend on the target platform. The easiest thing to do is to present the artists with a list of texture formats, taken from all of the destination platforms, and then prepare a lookup table that converts each format name to the closest format on the target platform. If omitted, the texture is created as a 32-bit texture.

Levels(<num>);: Declares the required number of mip-map levels for the texture. The default value if this command is omitted is 0, which actually means, make as many mip-map levels as possible. To disable mip-map generation for a given texture, specify 1 for the number of levels.

Filter("<filterType>");: This command allows the artist to override the filter type for this texture. Valid values are generally point, bilinear, and trilinear. If omitted, this usually defaults to bilinear or trilinear.

Wrap("<wrapType>");: Changes the wrap mode for the texture (what happens when the graphics hardware tries to read off the edge of the texture). Valid values include wrap, clamp, and mirror. If omitted, this defaults to wrap.

Color(<r>,<g>,<b>,<a>);: Defines a color for the pixel elements that are not drawn from an image. If this is omitted, then the default color is opaque white (255 for each component).

Once we have defined what type of texture we want, we must declare where to get the image data for the texture. This is done using one or more instances of the Image command. The first parameter to the Image command is the filename of the image to be read. There are four more optional parameters to the `Image` command that define what data is put into each pixel element. These are, in order, the red, green, blue, and alpha components. If any components are omitted, then the default action is to just copy the corresponding channel from the incoming image. The valid values for these components are:

`“red"` / `“green"` / `“blue"` / `“alpha"`: These declare that the value that goes into the current component comes from the given component in the image. Using these values allows us to effectively swap color channels around inside an image. These values can also be specified by just their first letters.

`“none"` or `“n"`: Declares that the current component should not be altered by this command.

`“max????"` / `“min????"` / `“avg????"`: The maximum, minimum, or average value of the given source channels is used to fill the current color component, respectively. The ?s in the command definition can be filled with either r, g, b, or a in any order. There must be at least two of them, and at most four, with no repeats.

`“nx"` / `“ny"` / `“nz"`: Declares that the value of the given component should be taken from the corresponding component of the normal map generated by treating the incoming image as a grayscale height map.

`“gray"`: Causes the grayscale value of the pixel from the source image to be written into the current component. This is calculated by Equation 6.1:

$$gray = (0.30 * red) + (0.59 * green) + (0.11 * blue) \tag{6.1}$$

The examples that follow illustrate this functionality.

Example 1: 256x256, 32-bit texture with constant alpha of 192.

```
Texture(“Example1")
{
    Size(256,256);
```

```
        Format("A8R8G8B8");
        Color(255,255,255,192);
        Image("example1.jpg","r","g","b","n");
    }
```

Example 2: 128x128, 16-bit texture, whose alpha comes from the grayscale value of the input image. Texture uses point sampling.

```
    Texture("Example2")
    {
        Size(128,28);
        Format("A4R4G4B4");
        Filter("point");
        Image("example2.jpg","r","g","b","gray");
    }
```

Example 3: Compressed texture with color channels coming from one image and alpha coming from the grayscale value of a second image. Size of the texture is taken from the color image.

```
    Texture("Example3")
    {
        Format("DXT2");
        Image("example3color.jpg");
        Image("example3alpha.jpg","n","n","n","gray");
    }
```

Example 4: 32-bit texture whose alpha component comes from the maximum value of the input color components. Size of the texture is taken from the image and no mip-maps are generated. Texture wrapping is disabled.

```
    Texture("Example4")
    {
        Wrap("clamp");
```

```
        Levels(1);
        Image("example4.jpg","r","g","b","maxrgb");
    }
```

Example 5: 128x128, 32-bit auto-generated normal map texture whose alpha component comes from the grayscale value of each of the input pixels.

```
    Texture(“Example5")
    {
        Size(128,128);
        Image("example5.jpg","nx","ny","nz","gray");
    }
```

Processing the Texture

The six main steps to converting an image are:

1. Load the source images.
2. Convert each to 32 bits per pixel (or higher).
3. Composite the source images together.
4. Resize the image (including mip-mapping).
5. Convert to the required pixel format.
6. Save the processed image data.

Step one sounds deceptively simple, but there are so many different image formats, and so many different subformats per image type, that writing a generic image loader can quickly become a daunting task. Imagine if you will, with a deadline rapidly approaching, an artist complaining that no matter what he does, the conversion tools for the game will not load a certain image . . . <shudder> . . . for this reason, we recommend using a third-party image library to load any images. Such libraries often come with built-in image conversion and resizing functions, and their use is also strongly recommended.

Step two involves taking the loaded image data and converting it to a large enough bit-depth so that any of the following steps do not degrade the image quality due to rounding errors. This usually means promoting the image to 32 bits per pixel (8 bits each for red, green, blue, and alpha), but higher pixel depths should also be considered, especially if you need to write your own image manipulation routines. With modern SIMD (single instruction, multiple data) instructions and 128-bits per pixel images (a 32-bit floating-point value for each color component), image manipulation becomes very simple and fast. Using floating-point data like this with each color component in the range 0 to 1 means that there is never a need to renormalize each color component after a multiplication. Moreover, color precision is kept intact through multiple operations with little to no effort.

The third step is to composite all of the textures that we have loaded together in the manner specified. This is done at the highest bit-depth and resolution possible in order to avoid artifacts. Any special effects required are also applied here.

The fourth step is to resize the image to the final size that is required by the game. This is done at a high bit precision and with a high-quality filter to prevent inaccuracies from manifesting. Mip-maps are also generated at this time (see the section Mip-Map Generation later in the chapter).

Step five takes the high bit depth image and converts the pixels to the correct format required by the hardware. This usually involves at least a color bit-depth conversion, but might also require a color palette to be generated. Moreover, depending on the destination platform, format, and API combination, the output pixels might need to be swizzled or compressed.

Finally, once we have the image data in the correct format and at the correct resolution with all required mip-maps generated, we must save the data to disk in a format that the game can quickly and easily load.

Using D3DX

As previously mentioned, due to the large number of image formats and subformats, it is desirable to use a preexisting image library to perform texture conversions, and preferably one that is both free and easy to use. Although your game (or indeed your target platform) might not support Direct3D, the free DirectX SDK from Microsoft ships with a built-in suite of image manipulation functions that can load images in a variety of formats, resize them with various sampling methods, and perform color conversions. Since this library is widely available, easy to use, and free, we will focus on its use to perform our image manipulation functions. The library is called the D3DX library and ships with all versions of Direct3D from v8 onward, although the exact function names and parameter definitions might change with subsequent versions of DirectX.

ON THE CD

`IImage`, *a sample class that uses D3DX to load, resize, and reformat images can be found on the companion CD-ROM, in the common/image folder. This class handles all of the communication with the D3DX library, and the pixels to the texture are always immediately available in a simple 32-bit format.*

To load an image using `IImage`, we use the static member function `LoadImage`. This takes a single parameter, which is the absolute filename of the image that is to be loaded. The supported image types are those supported by D3DX, which at the time of writing are bmp, dds, dib, jpg, png, and tga. This function returns a pointer to an `IImage` object, or 0 if the file failed to load. The `IImage` class contains a static member variable, which contains a pointer to a software Direct3D device. Each time an `IImage` is instantiated, if this pointer is empty, the constructor creates a new Direct3D device; otherwise, the existing device's reference count is incremented. The destructor decrements the device's reference count and empties the pointer when the device is no longer referenced.

To create an empty image using `IImage`, the static member function `CreateImage` is used. This function takes six parameters; the width and height of the image, and four values in the range 0 to 255 that get placed into each color channel (red, green, blue, and alpha), respectively.

Resizing an image is simple using the member function `Resize`. This function takes three parameters: the x and y dimensions of the resized texture and the filter that we need to use, from a list of filters defined in "iimage.hpp." This function does not alter the instance it is invoked upon, but rather creates a new `IImage` class containing the result and returns a pointer to it.

Other image manipulation functions work in the same way; they all return a pointer to a new image rather than alter the existing one. Other member functions include:

`Duplicate();`: Returns a new `IImage` instance that is an exact duplicate of the instance it was invoked on.

`Monochrome( f32 r, f32 g, f32 b, f32 a );`: Creates a new `IImage` instance in which each pixel contains a monochrome value derived from the components of the same pixel in the source object. The monochrome value is calculated by Equation 6.2:

$$mono = \left(r * red\right) + \left(g * green\right) + \left(b * blue\right) + \left(a * alpha\right) \tag{6.2}$$

`Grayscale();`: Performs the function Monochrome(0.30,0.59,0.11,0.0); and returns the result.

`NormalMap( f32 height );`: Generates a normal map from the input image. The normal map is generated by first converting the image to grayscale, and then using it as a height map. Each pixel in the resultant normal map represents the normal vector of the height map at this point. The alpha channel contains 0.

The final function in the `IImage` class that we will cover here is the `Reformat` function. This function takes two parameters: a D3DFORMAT value representing the desired format, and a pointer to a variable (u32) that will hold the length of the data. It returns either a 0 if the function was unsuccessful or a pointer to the raw converted data. If it returns a valid pointer, then the length of this data will be written into the supplied variable. The memory allocated by this function and returned to the caller can be freed using the standard `free()` function.

Mip-Map Generation

Mip-maps are lower-resolution and filtered versions of the larger source texture that are used in its place at a distance. More correctly, the mip-maps are used as each pixel on the screen covers more than one pixel in the texture (texel). Mip-maps are necessary to prevent the high resolution texture from sparkling as it recedes into the distance, or becomes more oblique to the viewer. Sparkling occurs when each pixel on the screen covers more than one texel. Small movements in the eye position can then cause the rendered pixel to map to a different texel, causing the rendered pixel to change color, sometimes dramatically.

Mip-maps offset this by making the GPU use a smaller texture when a rendered pixel covers more than one texel on the larger texture. This increases the texel-to-pixel ratio and so stops the rendered pixels from sparkling. The mip-map level used by the GPU depends on many things, but in layperson's terms, the GPU simply chooses the mip-map level that results in a single on-screen pixel covering approximately one texel.

Each mip-map level is half the size of the previous level in both width and height. This means that each mip-map level takes exactly one quarter of the memory of the previous one. Over a complete mip-map chain (which goes down to a 1x1 texture), this adds up to approximately one third of the memory for the original texture—a small price to pay to stop our game from having a chronic case of the sparklies.

To generate a mip-map chain, simply resample the previous level (the original texture is presumed to be the first mip-map level) to half of its original width and height. Repeat this for the desired number of mip-map levels, or until both of the dimensions become one pixel in size (for the purposes of mip-map generation, we consider that half of one pixel is one pixel). Although this is the easiest way to generate mip-maps, it is by no means the only way. In fact, we can take advantage of the behavior of the hardware to generate some cool effects. A simple example would be to apply a color transition to each successive mip-map level. Using this technique we could make distant objects appear in pastel tones, or make them brighter, or fade to gray . . . the list is almost endless.

Sometimes, though, the only way to achieve a specific effect is to have an artist generate each mip-map level by hand. If this is the case then we need a simple way to organize the artist-generated data so that it can be easily pulled into our data pipeline. The simplest way is to have the artist extend the size of the original image enough to put all of the mip-maps onto it in a predefined pattern. Figure 6.1 shows one possible layout for this.

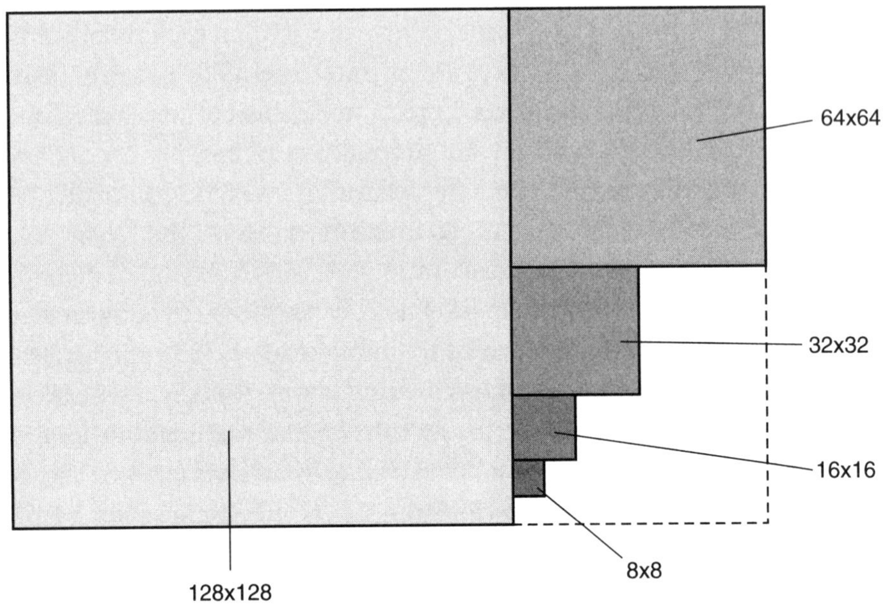

FIGURE 6.1 Possible image layout for a pregenerated mip-map chain.

ON THE CD

A DLL for the DataCon build assistant to process textures declared in the form described in this section is located on the companion CD-ROM, in the Chapter5/datacon/textureDLL folder. This DLL uses the `IImage` *class, and hence D3DX, to do most of its image processing.*

PROCESSING TRUETYPE FONTS

In a perfect world, it would be really fast and simple to render text on the screen using default operating system functions. Unfortunately, the reality is that, depending on the target system, the operating system calls are either missing or slow and cumbersome to use. However, TrueType fonts have many great features that it would be a shame to lose; they are proportionally spaced, they scale smoothly, and can be easily anti-aliased.

The simplest way to take advantage of these features is to render the TrueType font at a given point size into a texture, with each character occupying a rectangle that overlaps with no other characters. An artist can easily do this with Photoshop or some other art program, and with careful placement of guiding lines, the artist can even help you capture the proportional spacing information. However, any changes to the font (to change point size or add new characters) require that the artist do a lot of work to produce a new image. Additionally, fonts whose characters overlap when rendered, such as italicized or cursive fonts, are very difficult to prepare using this method.

Our artists' lives would be so much easier if we could find a way to automatically render the required font onto a texture at the required point size. They would be more likely to try different fonts in order to find the best-looking font for use in each situation in the game. By having access to the spacing information, we can even make use of the aforementioned italicized and cursive fonts.

Using TrueType Fonts in Windows

Before we can hope to convert a TrueType font into a usable format, we must first discover how to render a character or string of characters using the font. Luckily for us, Windows has some handy built-in font routines. A full description of all the font functions, and indeed the entire Windows API, can be found online on the MSDN home page [MSDN].

Before any characters can be printed, it is necessary to create a font with the required parameters. This is achieved using the `Win32` function, `CreateFont()`. Although this function has 14 (count 'em) parameters, its use is actually pretty straightforward, since for our purposes we won't need to use most of them.

The first parameter is the height that the font is to be rendered at; it is important to note that this is measured in "logical units," not pixels. The second parameter is the average width that you want the characters to be. Luckily, we can pass 0 for this parameter, and Windows will choose a value correctly in proportion to the requested height. The next two parameters allow you to rotate the font away from the axis; simply use 0 for these.

The fifth parameter is the weight that you want to render the font at. This is basically the thickness of the font, and is measured between 0 and 1000. There are several values defined in the Windows header files, the most useful of which are `FW_NORMAL` (400) and `FW_BOLD` (700). The next three parameters specify whether the font is to be *italic*, underlined, or ~~struck out~~, respectively.

For parameters 9 through 11, we can just use the default values: `DEFAULT_CHARSET`, `OUT_DEFAULT_PRECIS`, and `CLIP_DEFAULT_PRECIS`, respectively. The twelfth parameter controls anti-aliasing for the font; choose either `ANTIALIASED_QUALITY` or `DEFAULT_QUALITY`.

The penultimate parameter controls the pitch and family of the font, and should be set to `DEFAULT_PITCH|FF_DONTCARE`. The final parameter is the name of the font that you want to render; a list of installed fonts can be retrieved using the `EnumFontFamilies()` function.

The following code segment creates an italicized, antialiased font object using the Arial font with a height of 48:

```
HFONT newFont;
newFont = CreateFont( 48, 0, 0, 0, FW_NORMAL,
                      1 /*italics*/,
                      0 /*no underline*/,
                      0 /*no strikethrough*/,
                      DEFAULT_CHARSET,
                      OUT_DEFAULT_PRECIS,
                      CLIP_DEFAULT_PRECIS,
                      ANTIALIASED_QUALITY,
                      DEFAULT_PITCH|FF_DONTCARE,
                      "Arial");
```

Once you have successfully created a font of the correct size, you must select the font into the device context for the surface you want to render the font to. You can do this using the `SelectObject()` function. This function returns the handle of the old font, which you should restore after you are done rendering with your font. Now we can finally render some text with our new font, using the `TextOut()` function with the device context we just selected the font into. The following code segment renders a character string to a device context at (0,0):

```
const char *lpString = "This is a test";
HDC         dc;
HGDIOBJ    oldFont;
oldFont = SelectObject(dc,newFont);
TextOut(dc,0,0,lpString,strlen(lpString));
SelectObject(dc,oldFont);
```

Some of the more useful font commands are `GetTextExtentPoint32()`, which allows you to calculate the size of a string if printed in the current font, and `GetTextMetrics()`, which can be used to get a plethora of size information about the currently selected font.

As you can see, this can be a bit of a handful at the best of times.

Understanding ABC Widths

Windows achieves proportional spacing by using something that it calls ABC widths. These are three numbers that are attached to each character, defining how far to move the cursor before the character is drawn (A), how wide the character is (B), and how far to move the cursor after the character is drawn (C). Both the A width and the C width can be negative, meaning that the cursor is moved to the left instead of to the right. This allows the characters in a font to overlap each other slightly, to achieve effects such as italicization. Figure 6.2 shows an example of the ABC values for the letter I, in both regular and italic versions.

We can see from Figure 6.2 that when drawing the character I in the normal font style at the given point size, we must first move the cursor right by two units (A). Next, we draw the character, which is 17 units wide (B) and so moves the cursor by the same amount. Finally, we move the cursor right another two units (C) to put it in the correct position to start rendering the next character. The italicized I character, however, is drawn

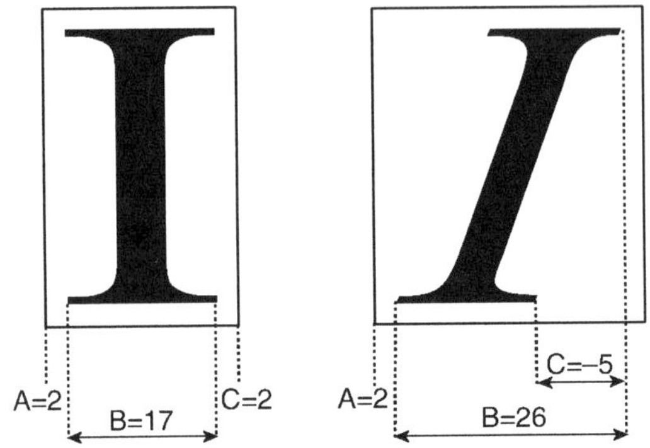

FIGURE 6.2 ABC values for the letter I in two font styles.

in a slightly different manner. We first move the cursor right by two units, and then draw the 26-unit-wide character. Finally, we move the cursor back to the left by five units. This has the effect of making the next character overlap the current one slightly.

As you can see, the ABC width convention easily allows different sized characters to overlap each other in well-defined ways, enabling a variety of effects such as italics and cursive.

The ABC widths for characters in a font are queried using the `GetCharABCWidths()` API. This function returns the ABC widths of a sequence of characters from the font currently selected into the given device context.

Automatically Creating a Font Texture

Given the information gleaned from the Windows functions listed previously, we should be able to automatically create a texture containing any characters that we want from the font. Using the ABC widths and the font height (from the `GetTextMetrics()` function) we can auto-arrange all the characters we need as efficiently as possible in the confines of the texture. We can even do this multiple times to find the maximum font size that will fit in the given texture space.

Before we go any further, we would be remiss if we did not point out that various companies hold the copyright on most of the fonts residing on your computer; they are not free for you to distribute. Luckily, it is a simple matter on a Windows machine to see the copyright information for a TrueType font; simply double-click on the font to display information about it. The copyright message, if one exists, should be right below the version number.

ON THE CD

There is a sample MFC application on the companion CD-ROM that will take any of the fonts on a machine and automatically arrange it semi-optimally onto a texture of a given size. The source code to this application can be found in the Chapter6/makefont folder. If you run this application (a precompiled version exists in the bin directory on the CD-ROM), you will see the dialog from Figure 6.3.

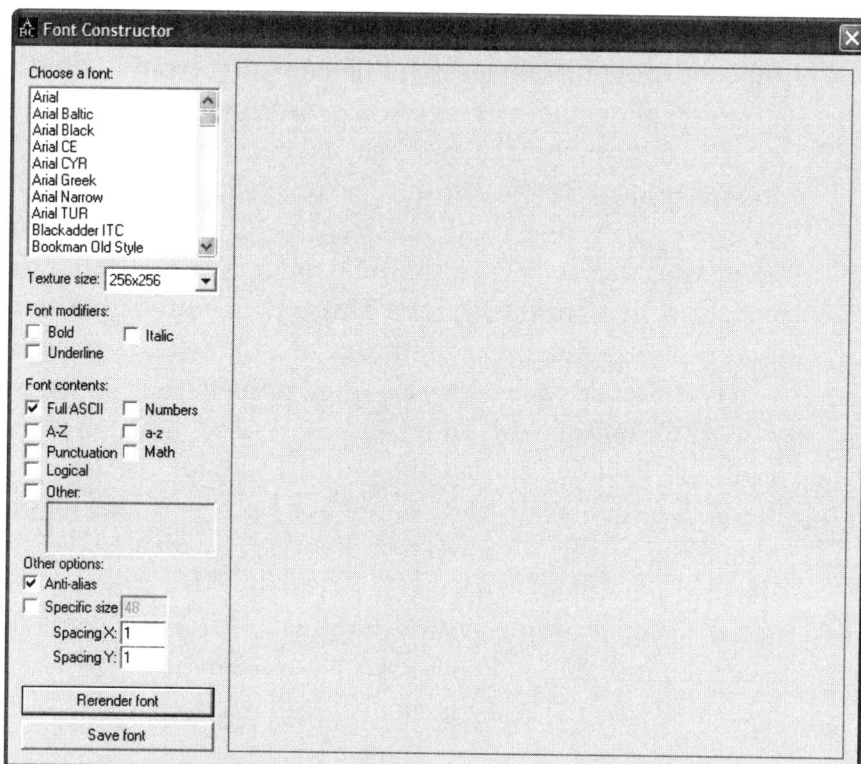

FIGURE 6.3 Makefont application.

The controls located on the left-hand side of the dialog allow you to select which font you want to render (from a list of every font on your machine), the style of the font (**bold**, *italic*, underline), and which characters from the font will appear in the texture. You can also choose whether to anti-alias the characters, and add a border between the characters (to make it easier to display the font cleanly using bilinear filtering). Notice that as you make changes to the parameters, the font displayed in the right-hand section of the dialog changes size and layout to automatically fill as much of the texture as it can. When you have found the correct settings for the font you want to use, simply click the Save button to save out an 8-bit, grayscale TGA image of the font. Along with the TGA, the makefont application also writes out a text file describing the font in a format readable by our resource generation system.

So, how does it work? The bulk of the work is done in the `MapFont()` function of the dialog class. This function first creates a font from the given TrueType file at the given size, using the Windows API functions. Then, for each character to be displayed, we first query its ABC widths, and use these to reserve space in the texture. The total width reserved for a character is calculated using its B width plus its A and C widths, if they are greater than zero (a negative A or C width would move the character into the neighboring character's reserved space). This is done until either all the characters have been allocated space on the texture, or the texture space is exhausted. Since we don't actually draw anything at this stage, this is pretty fast. However, as the font size gets larger, the `CreateFont()` function takes longer to execute, so in order to find the optimal size for the font on the texture, we need to pull a few tricks out of our hat. The makefont program uses a simple binary search variant to find the largest size that the font can be rendered at and still fit on the texture. This algorithm allows the makefont program to efficiently calculate the best size for the font; on a 1.8-GHz machine, it takes well under a second to compute the best layout for even a 512x512 texture. The algorithm is as follows:

1. Set the last successful font size to 0 and the current font size to 16.
2. Call the `MapFont()` function with the current font size.

3. If the function returned `true`, set the last successful font size to the current font size, double the current font size, and go back to step 2.
4. Set the best result equal to the last successful font size.
5. Start a binary search between the last successful font size and the current font size.
6. At each step in the binary search, call the `MapFont()` function with the test value. If it returns `true`, record this value as the best result so far and choose the top half of the tree; otherwise, choose the bottom half of the tree.
7. When the search is finished, we should have a best result that is the maximum font size that can fit on the given texture.

Once the font has been mapped, it is a simple matter to render each character into a bitmap of the same size as the texture. It should be noted that when drawing a character, if its A width is negative, then we must step right by the absolute value of the A width before drawing the character to keep it in its assigned region of the texture. After all characters have been rendered, the finished bitmap is displayed in the right-hand window for the examination of the user.

Processing the Makefont Output

The output from the makefont program still needs some more processing, however. In continuing with the philosophy that we write all the data we can in a simple format to the disc and process it later, the makefont program writes the font description as a simple text file that can be used as a command file for the DataCon build tool. This text file first describes how to process the texture, as described previously in this chapter. Following this is the font description. The first thing the font description contains is a reference to the correct texture and some basic size information about the font. Next, the total number of characters is declared, and each character is defined, in order of ASCII value, in the block attached to this declaration. For each character, we define which character it is, where it is on the texture, how large it is on the texture, and finally, two values that are called preadvance and postadvance. The preadvance value is the amount to move the cursor before drawing the character, while the postadvance is the amount to move the cursor afterward. These are derived from the ABC widths for each character, but take into account the spacing of the character inside the specified rectangular section of the texture.

ON THE CD

The DLL for DataCon to process the output from the makefont tool is included on the companion CD-ROM in the Chapter5/datacon/fontDLL folder. Additionally, to fully process the font file, DataCon will need the texture processing DLL, described in the previous section.

PROCESSING MESHES

Meshes are usually generated in third-party modeling software. These packages are usually written with the movie industry in mind, and so support many more features to a much greater degree than most game engines can currently support. The data files output by these packages are correspondingly complex and convoluted . . . any chance of successfully parsing a raw data file from a modeling package disappeared with the advent of 3D Studio Max. Even if the packages support a plain-text or similar output, many of the advanced features might not be exported in a file of this format, rendering them next to useless.

All is not lost, however, since these packages also support the development of user-created plug-in modules to do pretty much anything, including exporting data into an arbitrary format. Using the plug-in SDKs, it is possible to access, and indeed modify, pretty much any aspect of a model existing in the software. Most of these systems also allow arbitrary data to be attached to a model, either through the SDK or sometimes even through the default user interface. This can be used to attach both game-specific data (e.g., how many hit-points a character using the current model has) and instance-specific data (e.g., what format a texture should be spat out of the model conversion process).

There are generally two types of proprietary plug-ins that game engines use when it comes to modeling packages. The first type allows the artist or designer to attach data to the meshes that the game engine will then use to modify an object's behavior. Obviously, any data attached to a mesh in this way will need to be propagated into any file that we output from the package. The second type of plug-in is the exporter, which takes the mesh (or complete scene) from the modeling package and outputs it to disc in a format friendly to our game or resource path. Following our intermediate philosophy, any exporter plug-in that we write should not attempt to process the data in any way; it should merely dump as much data about the scene as it can into a plain-text file that can be processed at our leisure later.

Unfortunately, a detailed overview of plug-in writing techniques and modeling package APIs is beyond the scope of this text. For more details on creating plug-ins for 3D Studio Max, see [MAX]. For more details about plug-ins for Maya, see [MAYA].

Common Scene Elements

No matter which package is used to author the meshes and scenes that your game will use, the elements that make up the final data are generally the same. A scene has a list of meshes and instances (duplicated meshes that differ only in placement). A mesh has lists of materials (including texture definitions), bones (skeletal information), vertices, and triangles. Each of these elements is made up of predictable forms of data. This knowledge allows us to design an output format that will work for almost any modeling package, and is easily extensible to accommodate extra data as needed.

We already developed a generic scripting format and parser in Chapter 4, "Scripting," and using this will allow us to read our intermediate file directly into the DataCon build tool described earlier. Since our base hierarchical syntax is already defined, we merely need to determine what data there is to be stored, and where in the syntax tree it should occur. Although modeling packages generally allow entire scenes to be constructed featuring multiple meshes, instances, and animations, in this section we will concentrate on exporting a single mesh and leave the exporting of everything else as an exercise.

So, what kind of data does a mesh contain? As stated earlier, the data in a mesh usually consists of several materials, bones, vertices, and triangles. Each of these elements can contain several different types of data, which must be represented somehow in our definition. Since there's no better place to begin, let's start at the top: the definition of the mesh itself. To begin the definition of a mesh, we will use the command `Mesh("<name>")`. This simple command begins a block of commands that define the components that make up a mesh. Every mesh has exactly one name, and so this is the data item that we have chosen to put into the command. In this way, even if an empty block followed the command, we would have defined a legitimate mesh, albeit one with no data attached.

Storing Skeletal Information

The first thing that we need to describe in our file format is the skeletal information for the mesh, if it has one. Most meshes that can be animated will have skeletal information. A skeleton consists of a list of named bones and their default positions and orientations. Each bone also has a parent bone, from which it inherits its position. Move the parent and you move the children. Change the orientation of the parent and you change the position and orientation of the children. We start the definition of the mesh's skeleton with the `Skeleton(<numBones>)` command. As you can see, this command takes the number of bones that are described within its block as its only parameter. Immediately following this command is a block that contains `numBones` bone definitions.

A bone is defined using the `Bone("<boneName>")` command. As described previously, each bone contains data regarding its position and orientation, as well as the name of its parent bone in the hierarchy (if it has one). Although we could include more data here, such as each bone's position relative to its parent bone, this is easily calculated at process time and so should be omitted. To define the different elements of the bone, we will use some simple commands:

`Parent("<boneName>");`: This command defines the parent of the given bone. The named bone must appear somewhere in the skeletal definition, ideally before the bone that is its child, since this makes later processing easier.

`Position(<x>,<y>,<z>);`: Defines the initial position of the bone when it was added to the skeleton.

`Rotation(<x>,<y>,<z>,<w>);`: Defines the initial rotation of the bone when it was added to the skeleton, stored as a quaternion.

Although more data could be stored for each bone, such as its length and a list of its children, this data can be easily reconstructed from the data that we did store. By removing easily recalculated data, we reduce the size of the intermediate file.

Storing Materials

Next, we declare the list of materials that occur within the mesh. Each material describes how to draw any faces that use it: which textures to apply, its opacity, how it responds to lighting, whether it is double sided, and so on. Each material is usually generalized into a list of properties of a common form factor. Each of these properties usually supplies a value for how strongly it affects the final result, and either a color, a texture map (including information on which texture coordinate channel to use), or a procedural texture.

To declare the list of materials, we use the `Materials(<numMatls>)` command. This block immediately following this command individually defines each of the materials contained in the mesh. Each material in the block is defined by the `Material("<matlName>")` command, which is followed by a block of commands that further define that material's properties. The first things that we should list are the generic properties for the material. These include:

`FillMode("<fillMode>");`: Defines how the faces drawn with this material should be filled. The default value is solid. Another typical value for this is none, which declares that the triangles should not be filled. Used in conjunction with the Edges command, this enables us to define a material that is only drawn in wireframe.

`Edges("<edgeMode>");`: Declares how the edges of the faces drawn with this material should be displayed. The default value is none, which means that no edges are drawn. Another typical value for this is solid, which causes the edges to be drawn.

`Winding("<windingOrder>");`: This command declares the winding order for faces drawn with this material. The winding order determines whether the front or back face of a polygon is facing the viewer. The default value for this is counterclockwise.

`Culling("<cullMode>");`: Declares how faces drawn with this material are culled. The default value, back, declares that faces should not be drawn when they are facing away from the viewer. The possible values for this command are back, front, none, and all. None causes the faces to be double sided, and all causes them to never be drawn.

Once the generic properties for a material have been declared, we can go on to list the properties of the material that take a common form. To declare an instance of one of these properties, we use the `Property("<propertyName>")` command. A block that declares the parameters attached to this property immediately follows this command. Common property names include diffuse, ambient, and specular (which define the lighting response of the material), bump, and reflection (which define advanced rendering techniques). Each property block uses the following commands to declare its properties (depending on the modeling package, there might be more properties needed):

`Amount(<value>);`: Specifies the amount that the given property affects the final pixel. Usually in the range 0–100.

`Texture(<channel>,"<name>");`: Declares that the property should use the given texture name to get its color contribution to the final pixel. Also defines which channel of texture coordinates should be used to perform the texture lookup.

`Color(<r>,<g>,<b>,<a>);`: Directly defines the color that the property contributes to the final pixel. This is usually only present when no texture is defined.

Storing Vertex Data

Now that we have declared the skeletal information and the materials, we can start to declare the meat of the mesh: the vertex information. Each vertex in the mesh can contain several different types of data. Some of this data is always present (a vertex must always have positional information), some of it is usually present (normal information and texture coordinates), and some of it is seldom present (tangent and binormal data for bump mapping and other advanced effects).

To start the declaration of our list of vertices, we use the command Vertices(<numVerts>). The block of commands immediately following this command defines each vertex individually. The vertices in the block should be defined sequentially and there should be exactly numVerts of them. The declaration of a single vertex is performed using the Vertex(<index>,<x>,<y>,<z>) command, where index specifies the index of the vertex in the array and (x,y,z) defines the position of the vertex. Although the vertex index is given in the declaration, it must occur in sequence with the other vertex definitions. By defining the position of the vertex in its declaration command, we ensure that even if the command has no following block, we still define a valid vertex.

An optional block that defines additional vertex properties follows each Vertex command. To define these properties, we will use the following simple commands:

Normal(<nx>,<ny>,<nz>);: Defines the normal vector for the vertex. The normal vector points directly away from the mesh's surface at the vertex's position, and is usually scaled to have a magnitude of 1.

TexCoord(<channel>,<u>,<v>);: This command defines a texture coordinate that is attached to the current vertex. Since a material can contain multiple textures, there needs to be multiple sets of texture coordinates for each vertex.

Color("<type>",<r>,<g>,<b>,<a>);: Defines a color that is attached to the vertex. Depending on the modeling package, there could be multiple types of color attached to each vertex. The most common types are diffuse, specular, and ambient.

Bone("<boneName>",<weight>);: Declares that this vertex is affected by skeletal animation. Specifically, the given bone affects this vertex with the given weight. Modeling packages usually allow an arbitrary number of bones to affect each vertex, and so there will probably be multiple bone definitions in each vertex block.

Tangent(<nx>,<ny>,<nz>);: Defines the tangent to the mesh's surface at the given vertex. This, along with the normal and binormal, is used in bump mapping, and so if this command is present, the vertex must also have a normal and binormal defined.

BiNormal(<nx>,<ny>,<nz>);: Similar to the tangent, this command defines another value to be used in bump mapping. Again, if this value is declared, then the vertex must also declare a normal and a tangent.

Storing Triangle Data

Triangle, or connectivity, data describes how the individual vertices are connected to each other to form units that can be drawn, usually triangles. Each face, triangular or otherwise, has at a minimum a list of vertices (by index) that make up the face and the material with which to draw it. A face can also include a normal vector for lighting purposes. To keep things simple, we will limit ourselves to a list of triangular faces, declared using the Triangles(<numTriangles>) command.

As you will no doubt have guessed by now, the block of commands immediately following this command contains a definition for each triangle. Individual triangles are declared in this block using the Triangle("<matlName>",<v0>,<v1>,<v2>) command, where matlName is the name of the material with which to draw the triangle, and v0, v1, and v2 define the indices of the vertices composing the triangle. The order of the indices in this command is important, as defined by the Winding() property of the given material.

Immediately following the Triangle command is an optional block of commands that specify optional properties of each face. The only command currently valid inside the triangle block is the Normal(<nx>,<ny>,<nz>); command, which defines the normal vector for the given face.

Processing the Mesh

Now that we have defined the intermediate file format for our meshes, we need to construct a section of code to process this intermediate file into our final, platform-dependent format. The very first thing that our processing routine must do is to parse the given intermediate file into a data structure that we can then manipulate. To keep this step as simple as possible, it should not attempt to process the data in any way, but instead merely create a more easily addressed representation of the intermediate file.

Once we have created this data structure, we can begin to process it into a format more easily digested by the target platform. We'll start by looking at the materials for the mesh.

Processing Materials

As stated earlier, most modeling packages were developed to produce movie-quality renderings, and so support many more material features than we probably support in our game engine. The task of translating an arbitrary material into a series of commands that approximate the expected appearance of the material is a daunting one, and is the subject of much current research. For most engines, the task is too great; it is better to choose a small subset of material options and closely approximate these. Just make sure that you notify your artists which options are supported, and how they would go about getting the expected results in the engine. Hopefully by now you will have decided to construct a fast pipeline that will allow the artists to get their work into the game quickly and easily.

One decision that should be made while processing the materials is whether to split the mesh into multiple submeshes by material or groups of materials. This can be done for several reasons, but the most compelling one is that different material configurations can require different elements to be present in the vertex definitions for the mesh.

A good example of this is a material that implements bump mapping. Bump mapping requires that each vertex have two extra vectors in addition to the usual normal vector. These vectors represent the tangent and binormal of the surface at each vertex, and can bloat vertices by as much as 24 extra bytes (two sets of three floating-point numbers). However, this data is only usually required to be present in the vertices while bump mapping is enabled; on materials that don't have it enabled, this data is wasted.

If a mesh has 10,000 vertices, and only 100 of the vertices are attached to faces that are drawn with a bump-mapped material, then we have wasted 237,600 bytes with those two extra vectors. Obviously, this is not at all acceptable, and so serious consideration should be given to splitting the mesh into two or more submeshes, with bump-mapped vertices in one submesh and non-bump-mapped vertices in the other.

Processing Vertices

The first thing we must do is decide what portion of the supplied vertex data is needed to be able to properly display the mesh. This depends on several things: the data supplied in each vertex, the materials used, the limits of the target platform, and any dynamic rendering options (such as turning objects transparent as they block the camera) that we might have. The simplest example of this is to omit the vertex normals from the vertex data if none of the materials in the mesh responds to lighting in any way. Since a normal vector is made up of three floating-point numbers, we have suddenly saved 12 bytes per vertex, a not-inconsiderable amount of memory on many systems.

Once we have determined which portions of the vertex data we are going to keep, we must then do some work to make sure that these pieces of data take up as little memory as possible. Modern graphics cards can automatically perform some simple data conversions for us as they load vertex data. For example, the video hardware might support the expansion of an unsigned byte into an equivalent floating-point value between 0 and 1. Some common conversions are listed in Table 6.1, although the exact set of conversions supported depends on the destination platform.

TABLE 6.1 Common Vertex Compression Data Types

Data Type	*Input Range*	*Output Range*
s8	−128 to 127	−1.0 to 1.0
u8	0 to 255	0.0 to 1.0
s16	−32768 to 32767	−1.0 to 1.0
u16	0 to 65535	0.0 to 1.0
u32:10:10:10	3 of 0 to 1023	3 of −1.0 to 1.0

As you can see, with careful use of the built-in conversions listed in Table 6.1, we can make a serious dent in the amount of memory taken up by our vertex structures. An example vertex structure and its compressed equivalent, including position, normal, diffuse color, two texture channels, and bump-mapping information, are given in Table 6.2.

TABLE 6.2 Uncompressed vs. Compressed Vertices

Uncompressed Vertex	*Size*	*Compressed Vertex*	*Size*
typedef struct		typedef struct	
{		{	
`float pos[3];`	12	`u32 pos;`	4
`float normal[3];`	12	`U32 normal;`	4
`u32 diffuse;`	4	`U32 diffuse;`	4
`float tex0[2];`	8	`U8 tex0[2];`	2
`float tex1[2];`	8	`U8 tex1[2];`	2
`float tangent[3];`	12	`U32 tangent;`	4
`float binormal[3];`	12	`U32 binormal;`	4
`} Vertex;`		`} Xvertex;`	
Total size:	68	Total size:	24

As you can see, the compressed form of the vertex takes up only 24 bytes as opposed to the uncompressed form's 68 bytes. We reduced our vertex size by a whopping 65 percent. Admittedly, we included a lot of data in our original vertex that won't be present in most of the vertices that we usually render, but the principal remains the same.

To take advantage of these compressed formats, we must first arrange for all of our compressible vertex elements to be in the correct range. Actually, this is a pretty simple operation. By finding the axis-aligned bounding box for each of the values, we can work out a scale (multiplication) and bias (addition) vector for each of the compressible elements that maps it proportionally into the desired range. If we have already worked out the bounding box for a given axis of a given element (the axes for each element can be treated independently), then the scale and bias for that axis are given in Equations 6.3 and 6.4, respectively:

$$scale = \frac{(bboxMax - bboxMin) + value}{(rangeMax - rangeMin)} \tag{6.3}$$

$$bias = bboxMin - (rangeMin \times scale) \tag{6.4}$$

Notice that the numerator for the scale of the axis contains the addition of an extra, undefined value. This is to prevent the scale ever becoming 0, since it is used as the denominator when compressing an element. This value should be 0 unless the bounding values for the axis are close to each other, in which case it should be increased to prevent a division by 0. After these values have been worked out, we can use them to transform a vertex element into the compressed range and back again, using Equations 6.5 and 6.6:

$$xElement = \frac{(Element - bias)}{scale} \tag{6.5}$$

$$Element = (xElement \times scale) + bias \tag{6.6}$$

The value of the element in the correct range can then be used to calculate the final, compressed value that is to be written into the vertex data. Although the graphics hardware will uncompress our vertices for us, the result will be in the compressed range, not the range we started with. Unless we compensate for this elsewhere, our meshes will not draw correctly. There are two main ways to compensate for this. The first is to build the scale and bias into the matrices used to transform the data. However, not every element compressed in this way might have a built-in transform that can be used for this purpose. Another problem with this method is that if we add a scale and bias into our world transform matrices, these matrices might also be used to generate lighting information, and so will generate incorrect lighting. This means that the lighting matrices will need to be stored separately from the transform matrices. Depending on whether you store these separately or not, this might not be a problem for your game.

The second method relies on the availability of vertex shaders or some other method of manipulating the vertex data before it is passed to the rasterizer. Using this method, we store the scale and bias for each element somewhere where the graphics card can access them, and then apply them to the correct elements before their first uses. The cost of doing this is usually more than compensated for by the bandwidth savings of having compressed vertices.

Obviously, the compression method that we must use for each vertex element depends on the range of values that it is expected to take, and its granularity. For values that encompass a large range and must have a higher precision, we should use one of the compression modes that keeps as much precision as possible, or even store the element uncompressed. The problem with this is that in different meshes, the same elements might have different storage requirements than others. Sometimes, even in the same mesh, two elements of similar types (e.g., two different texture channels) might have different compression requirements. The solution to this is to base the final compressed form not on the expected range of values, but on the actual range of values. Doing this enables us to keep precision where it is required, but to compress elements with a really small range as much as possible.

This implies that two meshes with otherwise identical vertex formats can vary in the size of their vertices. Moreover, if we are defining vertices as structures, the number of possible combinations of elements in a vertex rises dramatically, as each element can take one of a number of data types. For this very reason, when a platform supports vertex data compression in this way, it must also support a data-driven way of defining where to find each vertex element, and its expected size. We can use either the same method or a similar one to define the format of our vertices on a per-mesh basis, and then use this data to define how we read from and write to the vertex data area.

In addition to being able to compress vertices, some platforms also allow us to split the vertex data into multiple streams. Each stream contains a subset of the vertex data and is loaded from different sections of memory. Since the amount of data for a vertex that is stored in the stream is not constant, each stream also needs to know the stride between vertices. This is the number of bytes between the first element of any vertex in the stream and the first element of the next vertex. Splitting the data for each vertex into streams allows us to omit reading from some streams when the data within them is never accessed. A good example of this is a stream containing the extra vertex information required to draw a model with bump mapping enabled; whenever the model is drawn without bump mapping, we can make the graphics hardware refrain from reading data from this stream and so save memory bandwidth.

Processing the Faces

Although possibly the simplest way to store a mesh is as a series of triangles, each with a material index and three vertex indices, it is woefully inefficient to draw it from this representation. To draw a mesh efficiently, we must reduce two things:

- The number of rendering commands issued
- The amount of data sent to the graphics card

Each rendering command requires a certain amount of time spent initializing the graphics hardware for its new configuration. Even just submitting a new batch of triangles for rendering with the same graphics pipeline configuration will require a certain amount of hardware reinitialization. More complex rendering commands, such as material changes, can become very complex and might require a large amount of data to be sent to the graphics hardware, or pulled into its cache. For example, a change in the texture being applied to a batch of triangles will at the very least require that parts of the texture be pulled into the texture cache. In the worst case, the whole texture might have to be uploaded to the card in addition to the population of the texture cache.

At first glance, reducing the number of rendering commands would appear relatively simple, and indeed, with the preceding representation of our meshes, it is. Simply sorting the triangles in the mesh by material reduces the number of material changes needed, and allows us to batch all of the triangles that use the same material into a single rendering command.

Table 6.3 gives an example of sorting the triangles in a mesh by material. As you can see, even in this simple example, we have reduced the number of rendering calls by a third.

TABLE 6.3 Advantages of Sorting a Mesh by Material

	Before Sorting:	***After Sorting:***
1.	Change to material "head"	Change to material "head"
2.	Draw 13 triangles	Draw 25 triangles
3.	Change to material "body"	Change to material "body"
4.	Draw 15 triangles	Draw 15 triangles
5.	Change to material "head"	
6.	Draw 12 triangles	

To reduce the amount of data sent to the graphics processor, we must first understand what information we are currently sending, and which parts of it are redundant. Figure 6.4 shows an example of a simple mesh of 11 triangles. If we consider this mesh to be a single material, then it could be rendered in a single rendering command: "Draw 11 triangles." However, what is really sent to the graphics card for this simple command?

To draw this simple mesh as a series of distinct triangles (a triangle list), the graphics processor needs to receive 11 sets of three indices. If indices are 2 bytes each, that is 66 bytes of traffic to draw 11 triangles, not including the command bytes to set up the graphics processor to draw a triangle list. If the triangles were submitted in a roughly clockwise order, then the command stream might look something like this:

Draw 11 triangles

Triangle 1: (0,1,11)

Triangle 2: (1,2,11)

Triangle 3: (11,2,10)

. . . And so on . . .

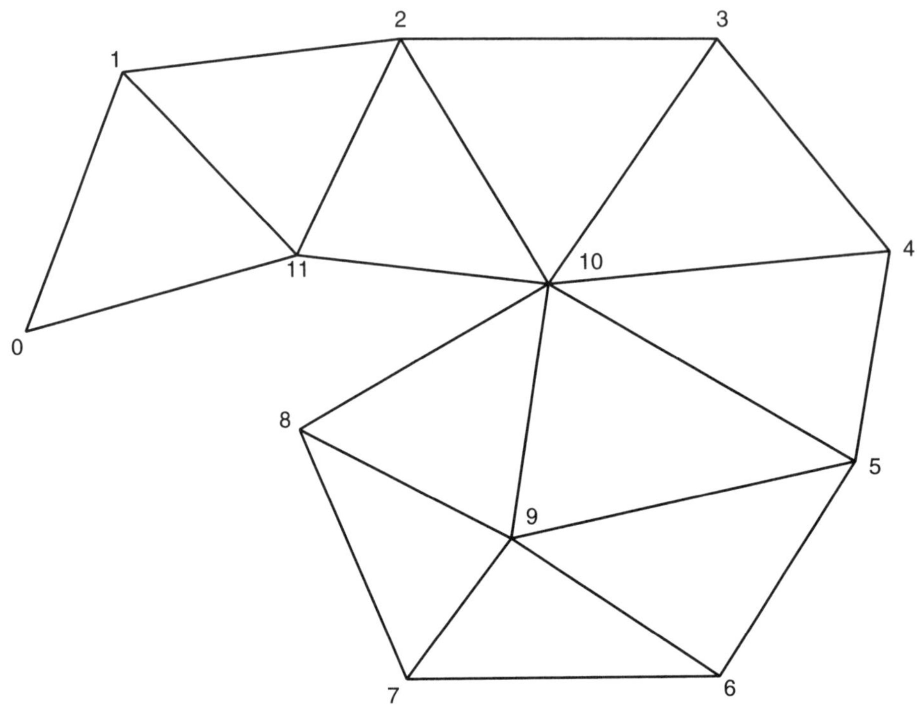

FIGURE 6.4 A simple mesh.

As you can see, much of this data is repeated several times in the command stream. In this simple example of only three triangles, the index 11 is resubmitted three times. There is a better, more compact way to represent this geometry, and that is by using triangle strips.

A triangle strip is a primitive that defines a series of triangles as a single sequence, taking advantage of shared edges between triangles to reduce the number of indices submitted. In a triangle strip, any three consecutive indices represent a single triangle. That is, each additional triangle after the first (which still takes three indices to describe) adds only a single extra index to the command stream. Compare this to a triangle list, where each consecutive group of three indices represents a triangle, and every additional triangle adds three indices to the command stream. In mathematical terms, for a mesh with n triangles, an optimal triangle strip representation of the mesh requires only n+2 indices, whereas a triangle list representation requires n*3 indices. So, our example mesh, if we could create an optimal strip for it, would take only 26 bytes to represent it (11 triangles means 13 indices at 2 bytes each).

One important property of triangle strips is that every other triangle has its winding direction reversed. That is, if you are defining triangles as forward facing when the vertices are given in a clockwise direction relative to the viewer, then every other triangle in a triangle strip is actually defined in a counterclockwise direction. This is very important to remember when reading triangles from a stripped index stream. For example, the first three triangles from our simple example, written in strip form would be (0, 1, 11, 2, 10). To read the first triangle, simply read the first three indices: (0,1,11). However, the second triangle must be read with two of the elements swapped to take into account its reverse ordering. Therefore, instead of (1, 11, 2), the second triangle should actually be read as (1, 2, 11). For the third triangle, we are back to the default clockwise orientation, and so it should be read as (11, 2, 10).

As we progress trying to create a triangle strip from our example, we hit a problem after the fifth triangle has been added. So far, the index stream looks like this: (0, 1, 11, 2, 10, 3, 4). If you look at the last two indices in this stream, you can see that the next triangle in the strip should take the form (3, 4, x). However, there is no such triangle present in the mesh. There is a triangle (4, 5, 10), though, and we can use this with a little extra work. By repeating the last index—in this case, the index 4—we are able to swap which edge we exit the previous triangle on. Our index stream becomes: (0, 1, 11, 2, 10, 3, 4, 4, 10, 5). Reading out the triangles in this list, starting at the fifth, we get the following triangles (with the given winding orders):

(10, 3, 4)—clockwise

(3, 4, 4)—counterclockwise

(4, 4, 10)—clockwise

(4, 10, 5)—counterclockwise

This operation is called, funnily enough, a swap, since we are swapping the edge that we exit the triangle on. Notice that in the preceding list, two of these triangles (numbers 2 and 3) do not represent valid triangles, since two of the points in them have the same index and so are coincident. This type of triangle is called a degenerate triangle, and on most current hardware they take almost zero time to process, for reasons that will be explained later. Cunning use of swap operations allows us to represent the entire example mesh as a single strip with 15 triangles (four degenerate triangles) represented by 17 indices. This can be represented in 34 bytes at 2 bytes per index, an almost 50-percent space saving over the original 66 bytes for the triangle list.

The Post-Transform Vertex Cache

The reason why degenerate triangles are, for all intents and purposes, free on modern graphics hardware is a little piece of technology called the post-transform vertex cache. This is an area of cache memory on the graphics card that stores the results of the last few vertices that were transformed. The exact behavior of this cache changes from video card to video card—some caches behave in a First-In-First-Out (FIFO) manner, and some operate in a Least-Recently-Used (LRU) manner. The size of the cache will also change from card to card and sometimes from render-mode to render-mode on the same card. The general result, however, is always the same: if a vertex resides in the cache, then that vertex will not need to be transformed again until it is pushed out of the cache. This means that when creating a strip, the optimal strip layout will take into account the recently transformed vertices and direct the strip to reuse those vertices over introducing new vertices that will have to be fully transformed.

A FIFO cache can be thought of as a circular buffer; once a vertex has been added, its position never changes, no matter how often it is reused while in the cache. A vertex that is added to the cache will be overwritten after n new vertices have been added, where n is the size of the cache. For example, with a four-element FIFO cache, rendering the strip (a, b, c, d, e) will cause vertex e to overwrite vertex a in the cache. However, when rendering the strip (a, b, c, d, a, e), despite the vertex a being reused, it is still the first vertex to be overwritten when the vertex e is placed in the cache.

An LRU cache, however, operates in a different manner. Each time a vertex that already exists in the cache is accessed, its cache entry gets refreshed. When a new vertex is added to the cache, it overwrites the entry that was least recently used. Using the same two examples given previously, rendering the strip (a, b, c, d, e) still causes the vertex a to be overwritten in the cache by the vertex e. However, in the strip (a, b, c, d, a, e), the second use of the vertex a refreshes its cache entry, and so it is vertex b, now the LRU cache entry, that is overwritten by the vertex e.

Even a software renderer has, in effect, a post-transform vertex cache. The way a software renderer usually works is to find the range of vertices that will be accessed by this draw command and transform them all according to the current state of the renderer. These are then looked up and passed to the rasterizer (whether hardware or software) as needed to draw the triangles. As each vertex's transformed data is read from the buffer, it is placed into the CPU's data cache. Future reads of this vertex will then be very fast, since the data for it will already be in the data cache. In effect, then, a software renderer uses a kind of LRU cache by virtue of a modern CPU's architecture.

On some hardware that uses a FIFO cache, there are actually some bad cache entries. Accessing these cache entries can cost more than if the vertices weren't in the cache at all. An example of this is the GPU used in the Microsoft Xbox console. In these cases, the bad cache entries are usually located at the tail end of the cache. This means, for example, that a FIFO cache might have 20 entries, but the last 5 could have a penalty associated with using them. Any vertex selection algorithm must take this into account.

The upshot of all this is that vertex selection is very important when creating a strip, whatever the method used to render the strip. Unfortunately, unless we are creating strips for a fully known and stable hardware configuration (i.e., a console), there is no way to know in advance what kind of caching system, if any, will be used in the destination system. Therefore, we must make some assumptions and do trial-and-error performance measurements to find the overall best-performing vertex cache configuration when the final destination hardware is not known.

AUTOMATICALLY GENERATING TRIANGLE STRIPS

You might have noticed by now that in all our talk of triangle strips, not once have any vertex properties been discussed except index. This is because, if we assume that all duplicate vertices have been coalesced into a single vertex, we do not need to know any of their properties except their indices. This makes an effective point of abstraction when creating an automatic triangle strip generator. Beyond this point, all we need to know are how many triangles we have to process and the indices that make up each triangle.

Our basic approach to creating triangle strips for the input geometry is very simple, and can be summed up in the following steps:

1. Create a new strip and choose a starting triangle for it that has not yet been used in a strip.
2. Add the current triangle to the strip.
3. Pick one of the neighboring triangles not yet assigned to a strip (if there are any).
4. If we picked a triangle in step 3, move to it and go back to step 2.
5. End the current strip.
6. If there are more unassigned triangles, then go back to step 1.

The first thing that we will need to be able to implement this algorithm is a list of triangles that have yet to be assigned to strips. As we assign triangles to strips, we can keep this list updated, and hence reduce the amount of work that steps 1 and 6 must do. This list is very simple to construct from the input data. We should at this point also create room for additional data that can be attached to each triangle. We will define exactly what this data will be later.

Additionally, we will need a way to quickly find all triangles that neighbor any given triangle, for use in step 3. A triangle is defined as neighboring another triangle when the two triangles share an edge. If a triangle has three component indices (i0, i1, i2), then it also has three edges, made by connecting each vertex to its subsequent vertex when traversing the triangle clockwise. We will call these edges e0, e1, and e2, respectively. Figure 6.5 shows two triangles, (i0, i1, i2) and (I0, I1, I2), where i0=I2 and i1=I1. These triangles share two points and a single edge. Notice that the shared edge is defined in the opposite direction in each of the two triangles. We must take this into account when finding the shared edges in our input data. Failure to consider this can result in strips where the winding order of the triangles changes unpredictably, and which will not display properly.

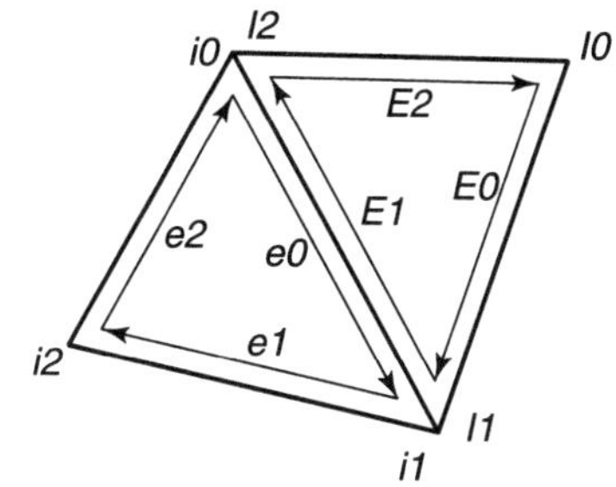

FIGURE 6.5 Two triangles sharing a single edge.

We can use a hash tree, as presented in Chapter 3, "Hashes and Hash Functions," to efficiently find the shared edges in our geometry. By using a hash tree during the creation of this list, we change an $O(n^2)$ operation (since each edge on each triangle needs comparing to every other edge on every other triangle) into an $O(n\log n)$ operation. If we limit our indices to 16 bits each, then we can create a unique 32-bit hash for each edge by concatenating the indices of the two end points together. This hash can be created in two ways, depending on the direction that we traverse the edge in and hence the order of the indices. We can use the following algorithm to find all the shared edges in the input data:

1. Start at the first triangle's first index, *i0*.
2. Get the current index and the next index (the next index for *i2* is *i0*).
3. Create a hash from these two indices and look this up in the hash tree.
4. If an edge already exists with this hash, then assign it to this triangle and remove it from the tree (since it now is assigned to two triangles). Now go to step 7.
5. Reverse the order of the indices and create a new hash.
6. Create a new edge, assign it to this triangle, and add it to the tree with the hash calculated in step 5.
7. If not on index *i2*, move to the next index and go back to step 2.
8. If not on the last triangle, move to the next triangle and go back to step 2.

So, how do we best choose a starting triangle for our strip? To generate the maximum number of long strips, we need to avoid isolating triangles by using all of their neighbors in strips. To accomplish this, we should start our strip on one of the triangles with the least amount of neighbors. By choosing our starting triangle in this way, we ensure that we process the triangles that are most likely to become isolated first, and hence avoid isolating them later.

This gives us our first piece of data that must be attached to each triangle definition—the number of neighbors it has that are yet to be assigned to a strip. We can count the number of neighbors for each triangle as we create the list of edges; as each edge has its second triangle attached, increment the neighbor count for both triangles. Then, when a triangle is assigned to a strip, decrement all of its neighbors' neighbor counts to show that they have one less available neighbor.

With the first triangle of the strip selected, we must now look at its available neighbors and select which one to add to the strip next. Several factors affect which neighbor we should pick, but in general we want to select triangles that best enable the strip to continue, while avoiding isolating any unassigned triangles. Additionally, any vertices added by the triangle we select should have as low a cost as possible, where cost is defined as the processing time for the vertex. Two things that affect vertex cost are whether the vertex is in the post-transform cache, and whether the vertex introduces any degenerate triangles.

When selecting the second triangle in the strip, the decision we make has a much greater effect on the triangle strip at much less cost than selecting any subsequent triangle to add. This is because we can choose any of the first triangle's neighbors as the second triangle, with no possibility of creating any degenerate triangles; whichever triangle we choose sets the initial direction of the strip. When selecting subsequent triangles for the strip, we must pay close attention to the edge that the strip is expected to leave the current triangle on, since choosing the other edge will introduce degenerate triangles.

By assigning different weights to each of the factors listed, we can derive a total cost for each candidate triangle. Then, the candidate triangle with the least cost is the one that should be added to the strip next. We can radically change the output of the strip generator by changing these weights, so by exposing them through the API, we get a way of tailoring the strip generation to a given target platform or application.

Stitching Strips Together

Once we have assigned all of the triangles present in the mesh to one strip or another, there is still more optimization that can be done. Even though each strip is an almost-optimal representation of the triangles within it, a series of strips is not optimal, since we have to go through the overhead of sending another command to the graphics processor every time we start to draw a new strip. Luckily, we can easily overcome this by "stitching" strips of the same material faces together.

Stitching strips together is similar to the swap operation, in that we introduce degenerate triangles into the strip. However, two strips stitched together do not have to share any vertices in common. Additionally, in order to maintain strip winding, the number of degenerate triangles introduced depends on the current winding of the strip (derived from the number of vertices currently in the strip). Figure 6.6 shows a simple example of three distinct strips of miniscule length that we are going to stitch together. The first of the three strips is two triangles long and can be written as (0,1,2,3). The second strip is three triangles long and is written as

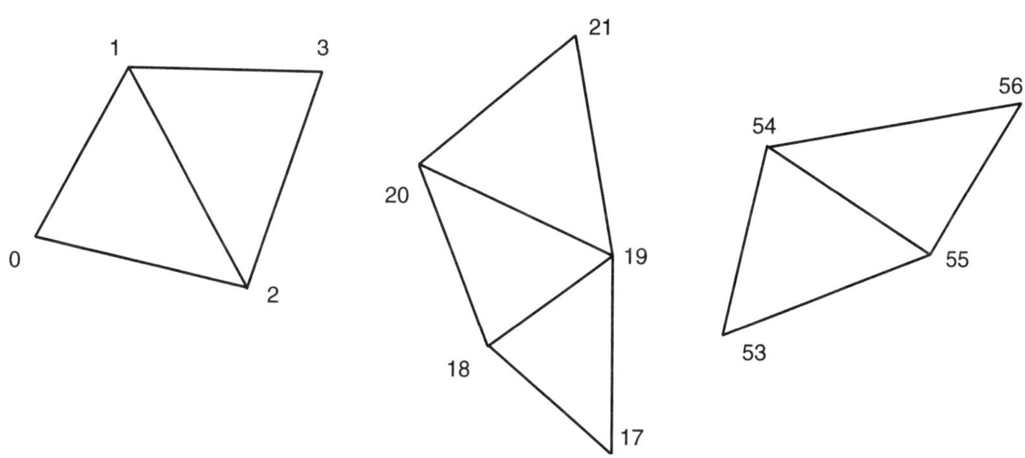

FIGURE 6.6 Three distinct triangle strips.

(17,18,19,20,21). Finally, the third strip is again just two triangles long, and can be written as (53,54,55,56).

To stitch the first two strips together, we must introduce enough degenerate triangles to allow us to move between the last triangle of the first strip and the first triangle of the second. We also need to know the expected winding for the next triangle in the first strip (clockwise) and the actual winding of the first triangle in the second strip (again, clockwise). Because both of these triangles share the same winding, and the winding of a given triangle is decided by the position in the strip of its first vertex, we must use an even number of points to stitch the strips together.

The first point that we introduce must be a repeat of one of the last two vertices in the strip in order to make a degenerate triangle. Additionally, we need the next index that we add to also produce a degenerate triangle. We can see that unless we reuse the last index in the first strip, any new index that we add after that will not produce a degenerate triangle. For example, repeating the index 2 and then adding index 17 gives us (0,1,2,3,2,17). As you can see, the very last triangle here is not degenerate, but neither is it one we want to draw. However, repeating the index 3 and then adding 17 does not repeat this problem; in (0,1,2,3,3,17), the last two triangles do produce the degenerates that we need.

Similarly, we must repeat the first vertex of the second strip twice to avoid introducing any unwanted, nondegenerate triangles. Since we have then added exactly two indices to the first strip, our winding order is preserved, and we can continue adding the rest of the vertices for the second strip. This gives a resultant strip of (0,1,2,3,3,17,17,18,19,20,21), which contains four degenerate triangles: (2,3,3), (3,3,17), (3,17,17), and (17,17,18).

However, the same trick does not work when adding the third strip onto the end of this one, since we now expect a counterclockwise triangle definition, and the third strip starts with a clockwise definition. Unfortunately, as our winding orders of the two strips are different, we need an odd number of points to be added, but as we saw earlier, we need two repeated points to successfully stitch together two strips. In this example, there is no choice but to repeat the last point of the first strip not once, but twice. The first repeat turns it into a strip that ends with the correct winding order, and from there we use the method for stitching two similar winding-ordered strips.

Our result, then, is a strip with 18 indices, 7 valid triangles, and 9 degenerate triangles: (0,1,2,3,3,17,17,18,19,20,21,21,21,53,53,54,55,56). Notice that this is still more efficient than a triangle list for those seven triangles, which takes 21 indices to describe.

If we presume that every strip starts with a clockwise triangle, then every even-numbered triangle (added by index n+2) is also clockwise. Given this, our algorithm for stitching strips together becomes simply:

1. If the first strip has an odd number of points (and hence expects the next triangle to be counterclockwise), repeat the last point.
2. Repeat the last point of the first strip.
3. Add the first point of the second strip twice.
4. Add the rest of the second strip.

Now that we know how to stitch two arbitrary triangle strips together, we need to find a way to determine the order in which we stitch the strips together. We still must be wary of the post-transform vertex cache, since it can give us performance penalties for choosing the wrong strips to stitch together. A simple, yet effective way to determine which strips to stitch together is to fill the vertex cache with the vertices from the first strip, in the order they are to be drawn. Then, simply count the cost of adding each vertex in the second strip to the cache, until we either completely flush the cache or run out of vertices. Divide the total cost of this by the number of vertices added to get an average cost per vertex for stitching the two strips together. Whichever two strips have the lowest per-vertex cost for being stitched together should then be the ones stitched first.

Post Stripping Optimizations

So, now that we have the triangles for our mesh in a single strip per material form, we're done, right? Far from it; in fact, some of the best optimizations are yet to come. Although we have represented the triangles for the mesh in the best form we can, we are still going to be wasting bandwidth by reading unwanted and uncached data from the vertices for the mesh. To understand why, let's look at a simple example.

For the sake of this example, let us presume that our vertices are 18 bytes each, and that the graphics card reads from AGP memory in 32-byte chunks. Can you see where this is going? Unless we read from the vertices sequentially, each time the graphics card reads from AGP memory, its wastes a minimum of 14 bytes by reading part of a vertex that it is not going to use immediately. Obviously, this is not our desired behavior.

To get around this, we are going to rearrange the order of the vertices in the original mesh so that they are read sequentially. Obviously, we must also change the indices in our strip to reflect the new position of each vertex. For example, if we have five vertices and a strip of five indices in the following order (3,4,2,1,5), then we should rearrange our vertices so that what was the third vertex is now the first, the fourth vertex becomes the second, and so on. After changing the indices in the strip to reflect the new order, our strip looks like this: (1,2,3,4,5). Much better! The graphics card now reads these vertices sequentially, and every single byte of each 32-byte read from AGP memory now contains vertex information that is used immediately. Congratulations, you've just doubled your vertex throughput!

Although this looks like an all-around win when just considering a single strip, what happens when we try to do it with a second? Any vertices in the second strip that were also in the first would need to be repeated, thus adding more vertices through repetition. However, is this bad? We already saw that our throughput would be increased dramatically, so what does it matter that we introduced a few extra vertices?

In fact, unless memory is really tight, this is a very good practice to use. Direct3D's draw API functions actually need a mesh in this format to work optimally for a software transform and lighting (TnL) pipeline, and even some hardware TnL cards work better this way. Unless the API knows the complete range of vertex indices that the draw call accesses, it must either transform the whole buffer or wait until right before each vertex is sent to the rasterizer before transforming it. In the first case, multiple draw calls from a single buffer will cause the whole buffer to be transformed multiple times. In the latter case, each vertex can be transformed multiple times within a single draw call. Neither of these is a very attractive option (although the latter option is what is implemented in most hardware TnL cards, albeit very heavily cached).

By collating and rearranging all of the vertices for a single strip into one contiguous block, we know the exact range of vertices that need to be transformed to properly draw the strip. We also know that every single vertex that is transformed will definitely be used, at least once. If we then pass this information along to the API along with the draw command, the transform engine (be it hardware or software) can transform only these vertices, resulting in faster vertex processing.

Implementing a Triangle Stripper

To effectively implement a reusable triangle stripper, we must reduce the data that we have to send it to its most simple form. Doing so allows it to be reused without having to worry about modifying any triangle structures so that their sizes and member names and offsets are compatible with the ones the stripper expects. So, this begs the question: exactly what data does the triangle stripper need, and what should we be expecting to get back from it?

In fact, the triangle strip generator doesn't need to know about the values for each vertex. Moreover, if we only pass the triangle stripper faces that share the same material, it doesn't need to know about materials, either. The only two pieces of data that the triangle stripper needs is the number of triangles that it is being passed and the indices for these triangles. To keep things simple, the stripper should expect to receive a linear array of indices, with each three consecutive indices describing a single triangle.

The final output of the stripper should be a list of strips. Although the triangle stripper, if unrestricted, would produce a single strip, some platforms, notably the PlayStation 2, place severe restrictions on the amount of geometry that it can process in a single chunk, hence reducing the maximum data length for a single strip. This list is represented as a single list of numbers. The first number in the list is the total number of strips in the list, followed by the data for each strip in turn. The first number in each strip is the number of indices it contains, followed by the indices themselves. Therefore, the following output stream would contain two strips of four vertices each:

(2, 4, 0, 1, 2, 3, 4, 4, 5, 6, 7)

Additionally, our triangle stripper needs a way to instruct it about the restrictions of our target platform, such as what kind of post-transform vertex cache it has, the size of this cache, and weighting values for each of the vertex selection heuristics.

ON THE CD

You can find an example of an efficient triangle strip generator on the companion CD-ROM in the folder common/mesh. This code implements all of the optimizations discussed here, and its behavior is modifiable via a configuration structure. Using this structure, we can modify the weights attached to each vertex selection heuristic, and modify the maximum strip length, both in indices and vertices. This allows us to use the strip generator for platforms such as the PlayStation 2, where geometry must be cut into small sections due to memory constraints.

PUTTING IT ALL TOGETHER

As you can probably tell from the length of this chapter, properly massaging the assets for a game is a huge topic, and we have barely scratched its surface. Many dissertations can be found scattered around the Web on various related topics, and some areas are actively being researched even now. Some of the topics that we have not addressed here, but that you probably need to consider at some point for your game, include:

- Level of detail (continuous and discrete)
- Intelligently sectioning large meshes for better culling
- Portals
- World database representation
- Sounds
- Music
- Animation

However, the topics covered here should be enough to point you in the right direction, and the framework presented early in the chapter allows any of the preceding data to be easily processed.

ON THE CD

As a final word, we will end this chapter with a demo project that demonstrates examples of all the data types presented so far. This project can be found on the companion CD-ROM, in the folder Chapter6/DemoProject. The project uses the DataCon build assistant and the DLLs we developed for it to process its data to run under DirectX9 on the PC.

FURTHER READING

The following books and Web pages, referenced in the two previous chapters, provide further information on the topics presented.

[MSDN] Microsoft Corporation, "Welcome to the MSDN library." Available online at *http://msdn.microsoft.com/library*

[TTT] "TrueType Typography: Info about TTF fonts & technology." Available online at *www.truetype.demon.co.uk/*

[Kommann99] Kommann, David, 1999, "Fast and Simple Triangle Strip Generation." Available online at *www.dlc.fi/~dkpa/strip/strip.html*

[MAX] Bicalho, Alexander and Feltman, Simon, "Maxscript and the SDK for 3d Studio Max," *Sybex*, 2000.

[MAYA] "Maya API / SDK." Available online at *www.aliaswavefront.com/en/products/maya/complete/apisdk.shtml*

7 Finite State Machines

In This Chapter

- Rule #7: "Exploit Your Data"
- What Is a Finite State Machine?
- Explicit vs. Implicit FSMs
- A Scripting Language for FSM Development
- Everybody Was Kung Fu Fighting
- Removing Redundancy and Avoiding Replication
- FSM Scripting Language Reference
- Compilation
- Implementation
- Let's Get Ready to Rumble!
- Other Uses

Character control logic is often written as a large switch statement or series of `if-else` statements. The code inside each case generally handles the special cases required for the logic state defined by the conditions required to get into the case. This quickly becomes ungainly as more and more conditions are added, and more and more special cases are generated. The main problem, though, are the general case functions; things that must be done except when these few things are true, or only when this other set of conditions is true. As more and more cases are added, care must be taken to update all of these general cases so that everything is still executed (or not) in the right cases. This would be bad enough, but functions outside of the main logic loop also have conditionals attached to them:

- Damage should not be done to a creature if it is dead.
- A character cannot fall if it is flying.
- A character should not go into a damaged animation if it is in an attack animation.

. . . and so on, *ad nauseum*. Errors breed like maggots in code like this.

RULE #7: "EXPLOIT YOUR DATA"

However, there is a better way. Each character has a limited number of states that it can be in. Each of these states has a different behavior; for example, whether the character can move in the current state. They also react to differing sets of inputs in different ways, causing the current state of the character to change. There is a well-known data construct that exhibits these characteristics: a *finite state machine* (hereafter FSM).

By transforming as much of the code as we can into data, we can reduce the code complexity while at the same time enabling other members of the team (specifically designers) to easily chop and change the behaviors of the game objects. In a sense, we are exploiting the data to keep our code simple and robust.

WHAT IS A FINITE STATE MACHINE?

Simply put, an FSM is an enclosed system that can be in a limited (hence, finite) number of states. Each state is linked to a limited number of other states through discrete events. An ATM is a good example of an FSM. When in the idle state, the only thing an ATM responds to is a card being inserted. This event (the card being inserted) causes the ATM to change state into the "waiting for PIN number" state. This state has three events that can happen. The first is if the user presses the Cancel button—this causes the ATM to briefly enter a state that ejects the card and then returns to the idle screen. The second is if the user enters a bad PIN number; this causes the ATM to change to the "bad PIN number" state, which tells the user that he entered an invalid PIN. The final event happens when the user enters a valid PIN number; this causes the ATM to change state to the "main menu" state.

EXPLICIT VS. IMPLICIT FSMS

So, what makes an FSM explicit or implicit? In simple terms, an explicit FSM is a "black box" object that has only events as its inputs. The explicit FSM need know nothing of the object that it is maintaining the state for. It cannot be cajoled or fudged into changing state except through the predefined events and transitions. Maintaining this formalism helps focus the code and reduces runtime bugs that occur due to unforeseen state interactions. Anything that does not conform to this model is an implicit FSM.

It is important to identify potential FSMs as they are created. Accidentally creating an implicit FSM can be costly in terms of time, code size, and bug count. Anything in the game that has a set of core behaviors that changes based on the current state of the object is probably better represented as one or more FSMs.

Since an explicit FSM does not need to know anything about the object that it is maintaining the state for, the code for the FSM itself can be reused for many different types of object. Additionally, the description of the states, events, and transitions become abstracted from the object, allowing these items to be expressed purely as data. This has several important consequences:

- The source code becomes smaller and easier to maintain.
- The behavior of game objects can be altered quickly and easily without recompiling code.
- The designers are now free to experiment with object behaviors without bothering the programmers.

Now that we have identified that the states for an explicit FSM can be represented purely as data, we need to decide on a way to quickly and easily declare that data. This can be done either graphically in a specially designed application, or through a text file and parser tool combination. For now, we will concentrate on defining a scripting language to enable the design of our FSMs.

A SCRIPTING LANGUAGE FOR FSM DEVELOPMENT

We have already identified that an explicit FSM has certain data requirements. An FSM contains a number of states, with each state containing a number of event handlers, which are generally transitions to other states. Each FSM also requires its initial state to be defined. Adopting a simple C-like syntax, a possible implementation of the states of the ATM looks something like this:

```
FSM("ATM")
{
    InitialState("Idle");

    State("Idle")
    {
        On("event_card_inserted")
            Transition("EnterPin");
```

```
        }

        State("EnterPin")
        {
            On("event_cancel")
                Transition("ReturnCard");
            On("event_correctPin")
                Transition("MainMenu");
            On("event_invalidPin")
                Transition("InvalidPin");
        }

        State("InvalidPin")
        {
            On("event_timeout")
                Transition("EnterPin");
        }

        State("ReturnCard")
        {
            On("event_timeout")
                Transition("Idle");
        }

        State("MainMenu")
        {
            On("event_cancel")
                Transition("ReturnCard");

            // more events here
        }
    }
```

The first thing that should be noted is that arbitrary strings define all of the states and events. This allows easy comprehension of the FSM definition and enables nonprogrammers to be able to quickly pick up the language. By using one of the hash classes introduced in Chapter 3, "Hashes and Hash Functions," this becomes trivial to implement. As we expand the scripting language to incorporate more features, having arbitrary strings becomes invaluable.

The `FSM` command delimits the definition of the FSM and defines a name by which the FSM can be identified. The `InitialState` command defines the initial state that the FSM should be in when reset. The `State` command defines a block of code that represents a single state and also declares the name of the state. Within the state block, the `On` command defines an event handler. Currently, only one command is valid in an event handler; the `Transition` command tells the FSM to change to a new state.

Given this definition, it is the responsibility of the ATM machine to issue events for all inputs; when the Cancel key is pressed, it gives an `"event_cancel"` event, regardless of which state it is in. If the state does not handle the `"event_cancel"` event, then the event is ignored. It is also the responsibility of the ATM machine to examine the state it is in and:

- Display the correct UI screen
- Handle any state-unique inputs (e.g., inputting the PIN #)
- Handle any state-unique operations (e.g., ejecting the user's card)

Executing Arbitrary Code from a State

As you can see, the language as defined so far is no real improvement over implementing an implicit FSM, since the ATM machine needs to examine its current state to see what it is expected to do. Clearly, then, we need to implement some way to tell the ATM which pieces of code to execute for each state. Examining the requirements of the ATM, we can see three distinct times that code needs to be executed:

When a new state is entered. This is used to reset the PIN each time the `"enterPin"` state is entered, or to return the user's card when the `"returnCard"` state is entered.

When a state is exited. This is used to reset the number of times that a bad PIN has been entered when the `"idle"` state is exited.

Iteratively, while a state is active. This is used to run the code to handle the entering of the PIN.

This implies that we need three new events that we can detect in the FSM data. We will call these events "state_enter", "state_exit", and "state_run", respectively. We also need a way to attach something other than a state transition to an event in the scripting language. We can accomplish this by simply adding new commands to be used in place of the Transition command. This has the effect of making the data for an event handler a stream of commands that must be interpreted, instead of just the state to transition to.

The first of these new commands is used to invoke a function in the code. We will call this command Execute. Using this command allows us to move the brunt of the control logic for the ATM into the FSM data. For example, the "EnterPin" state now looks like this:

```
State("EnterPin")
{
    On("state_enter")
        Execute("ClearPin");
    On("state_run")
        Execute("RunPinEntry");

    On("event_cancel")
        Transition("ReturnCard");
    On("event_correctPin")
        Transition("MainMenu");
    On("event_invalidPin")
        Transition("InvalidPin");
}
```

This says that when the state is first entered, a function called "ClearPin" should be invoked, and that for each iteration of the main loop that occurs while in this state, the function "RunPinEntry" should be executed. We can then move all the pin entry logic in the ATM code into these two functions.

We should also move the responsibility for generating the "event_correctPin" and "event_incorrectPin" events into the "RunPinEntry" function.

To execute arbitrary code, we need to make a runtime dictionary of functions that can be called from the FSM. This dictionary contains a name and a function pointer for each function that can be invoked from a state. At code startup, the game will fill the dictionary with available functions and their associated strings. Although it is best to keep the string for a function to be the same as the function name, it is by no means necessary. Similarly, it is possible to link a single function to more than one function name. If we had a static member function in the FSMINSTANCE class called DeclareFunction, then the following code would add the functions that we need to the FSM object:

```
FSMINSTANCE::DeclareFunction( ReturnCard, "ReturnCard" );
FSMINSTANCE::DeclareFunction( SetTimeout, "SetTimeout" );
FSMINSTANCE::DeclareFunction( ClearPin, "ClearPin" );
FSMINSTANCE::DeclareFunction( RunPinEntry, "RunPinEntry" );
```

At this point, it might prove useful to leverage the power of macros to make sure that the function name and the string used to invoke it are identical. The # operator in a macro takes the argument immediately following it and makes it into a quoted string (see Chapter 1, "Embracing C++"). This enables us to create a macro like this:

```
#define DECLAREFSMFUNCTION(A) FSMINSTANCE::DeclareFunction(A,#A)
```

Thereafter, we use the following to add functions to the FSM (provided we want their dictionary names to be the same as the function name):

```
DECLAREFSMFUNCTION( ReturnCard );
DECLAREFSMFUNCTION( SetTimeout );
DECLAREFSMFUNCTION( ClearPin );
DECLAREFSMFUNCTION( RunPinEntry );
```

One downside of this runtime binding of functions to the FSM is that missing functions or mistyped function names cause errors that cannot be detected until execution time. However, by storing within each FSM a list of all the functions that it can invoke, this can be compared against the runtime function dictionary at instantiation time. Any omissions can then be reported as soon as an FSM is instantiated, rather than waiting until the `Execute` command fails to find the function it is trying to invoke.

EVERYBODY WAS KUNG-FU FIGHTING

Now that we have a basic method for defining an FSM, let's look at a real gaming example. Simultaneously, we will continue expanding our FSM scripting language to handle any required behaviors that it can't currently handle. The example that we will work through is a simple animation logic FSM to be used in a character-based multi-opponent fighting game. In this example, the player controls a character that must negotiate through an environment while simultaneously combating one or more opponents. In this first FSM design iteration, the enemy characters will have exactly the same capabilities as the player. In future iterations, we will look at expanding the FSM to endow the player with extra animation logic.

The first thing we must define is the division of responsibilities between the code-driven game and the data-driven FSM. If we list the things that the character system must be able to do, we can see three distinct classes of operations:

- Those that are performed every frame in most states.
- Those that are performed every frame in just a few states.
- Those that are only called once for each state in which they occur.

In our language as defined so far, we can accomplish all three of these. However, it will quickly become cumbersome to have to include all those execute commands for every single state. We need to concoct a solution that allows us to declare that one or more operations need to be performed every frame while in a given state. A natural way to do this would be to define these operations as *behaviors*, and to require each state to declare the behaviors it expects to be active.

Behaviors

We define behaviors as tasks that are running in parallel to the FSM, and that are not readily dependent on a single state or any events. Some good examples of behaviors for this example game are animation, world physics, and character control; none of these depends on being in a single state, and each has work to do every frame.

In our example, the animation behavior is processed every frame. Its responsibilities are to process the animation data for the character to provide position and orientation for every bone in the character, to provide movement data that is applied in the physics behavior, and to process any action frames embedded in the animation data. An action frame in this context is a frame in the animation that is marked as needing an operation; for example, a strike frame in an attack animation is the frame at which the character's attack is considered to strike its opponent. Using the FSM for all state transitions allows us to simplify the animation system with respect to action frames; instead of having to determine which function to call based on the type of action, the animation system now just has to send an event to the FSM. This simplifies the animation system and makes it much more reusable—it now does not need to know anything about the object the animation will be applied to, since the action frame function mappings are handled by the FSM.

We can implement behaviors in many ways, but the simplest is probably a series of bit-flags. We can expose this to the FSM scripting language as a command that takes a variable number of string arguments, representing behaviors that are active for this state. We will implement this using the `Behavior` command, which can only be used inside a state definition. As an example, the command `Behavior("animate", "controls" );` inside a state definition defines a state in which both the `"animate"` and the `"controls"` behaviors are active. Omitting the `"controls"` behavior would disable the controls while the character is in this state. The problem with this is that the `"animate"` behavior must be specified for almost every state, and repetition breeds errors. There are two ways we could get around this:

- Specify a behavior where the character does not animate (`"noanimate"`).
- Specify default behaviors inherited by all states, and make the `Behavior` command turn additional behaviors on and off.

To preserve clarity, we will choose the second option; we should always keep the behaviors as intuitive as possible since we want the designers to be defining the FSMs. To implement this, we need to add a `DefaultBehavior` command to be used outside of a state definition, and we need to change the `Behavior` command so that it turns behaviors on and off. To accomplish this, we say that if the behavior string starts with a ~ or a !, then the behavior should be turned off. For example, the command `Behavior( "~animate", "controls" );` says that in this state, the `"animate"` behavior should be turned off, and the `"controls"` behavior should be turned on.

To keep our FSM compiler tool able to compile different types of FSM, each with a different set of behaviors, we will add a second parameter to the `FSM` instruction that represents the type of FSM that we are defining. This type can then be used to change the mappings of the behavior strings to the actual bit-flags and hence the available behaviors.

So, applying all the features that we have just defined, and adding a command, `SetAnimation`, to start playing an animation on a character, our initial fighting game FSM looks like something this:

```
FSM("DefaultCharacter", "Character")
{
    InitialState("Stance");
    DefaultBehavior("animate", "physics");

    State("Stance")
    {
        Behavior("controls");
        On("state_enter")
            SetAnimation("Stance");
        On("input_attack")
            Transition("Attack");
        On("event_damage")
```

```
        Transition("Damaged");
    On("event_death")
        Transition("Die");
}

State("Attack")
{
    On("state_enter")
    {
        Execute("ChooseTarget");
        SetAnimation("Attack");
    }
    On("state_run")
        Execute("FaceTarget");
    On("anim_done")
        Transition("Stance");
    On("keyframe_strike")
        Execute("DoDamage");
    On("event_damage")
        Transition("Damaged");
    On("event_death")
        Transition("Die");
}

State("Damaged")
{
    On("state_enter")
        SetAnimation("Damaged");
    On("event_death")
        Transition("Die");
    On("anim_done")
        Transition("Stance");
}

State("Die")
```

```
        {
            Behavior("dead");
            On("state_enter")
                SetAnimation("Die");
            On("anim_done")
                Transition("Dead");
        }

        State("Dead")
        {
            Behavior("~animate","~physics","dead");
        }
    }
```

Examining this, the first thing we see is the changed `FSM` command, saying that this is defining an FSM called "DefaultCharacter," of type "Character." This allows the FSM compiler to choose appropriate behavior flag definitions and which event commands are valid in the event handlers. The `DefaultBehavior` command tells the FSM that unless explicitly turned off in a state, the `"animate"` and `"physics"` behaviors will always be in effect. This allows us to effectively forget about these behaviors unless we have to turn them off. In fact, examining the `"Dead"` state, we can see that these behaviors are turned off on entry to this state.

Notice that only in the `"Stance"` state is the `"controls"` behavior enabled; this implies that the characters will not obey movement commands in any other state.

The `"Attack"` state bears scrutiny, since it makes use of several new features. The first thing to notice is that the event handler for state entry contains more than one instruction, surrounded by curly braces. This is analogous to the standard C syntax, where an `if` statement can be followed by either one instruction or a series of instructions, delimited by curly braces. The event handler block first calls the `ChooseTarget` function to choose which of the surrounding characters, if any, the attack is directed at, and then uses the `SetAnimation` command to apply the attack animation to the character.

Four new event handlers have been added to this state, two of which are thrown by the basic character logic (`"event_damage"` and `"event_death"`), and the other two are thrown by the animation behavior (`"anim_done"` and `"keyframe_strike"`). The damage event is thrown when a character has been damaged—ignoring this event does not stop the damage to the character; however, it does stop the character reacting to it—and the death event is thrown when a character has been damaged so much that he has been killed. Because most of the character logic runs via the FSM, ignoring the death event will not have unintended consequences other than a character running around with no health, since whether a character is actually marked as dead is the responsibility of the FSM.

The animation behavior triggers the `"anim_done"` event when a character reaches the last frame of its current animation, and it throws the `"keyframe_strike"` event when the character's animation passes through a frame marked as a strike. Within the `"keyframe_strike"` event handler, we see that the FSM invokes the `DoDamage` function. Notice that as described previously, although the animation system is responsible for detecting the designated action frames, it knows nothing about what the actions mean or what to do with them. This makes the animation code more portable and less prone to bugs, since no matter what action frames it encounters, all it has to do is throw an event to the FSM handler.

Using the FSM to Detect Errors

One unexpected use of the FSM is to detect error states. That is, we can mark some areas of the FSM as unreachable given proper execution of the game, and if the FSM ever reaches these states, then we know an error has occurred. For example, we know that for every attack animation, there should be at least one strike frame. If we ever reach the end of an attack animation without passing a strike frame, then either the animator has forgotten to place the action frame, or the wrong animation has been used as an attack animation. This can be detected by transitioning out of the `"Attack"` state and into a similar state when a `"keyframe_strike"` event is detected. Then, if the `"anim_done"` event is received while still in the original state, we know that no strike frame was present, and can either call an error function or transition to a state marked as an error state.

Although this is a useful feature, in this form it is very awkward to use, since each state that behaves in this way must have a similar sister state to transition into to avoid the error. What we really want to be able to do is flag the strike event as having happened, and then check this flag to see if it did happen at a later time in the same state. By keeping these flags local to a state and putting all commands to manipulate them in the scripting language, we can avoid having to define them in the compiler, since nothing outside of the state block needs to access them. This lets our designers go to town with descriptive flag names without having to bother the programmer to put them in the language.

Flags are defined at the state level by the `Flags` command. This command takes a variable number of arguments, representing the names of each flag that we want to define. All flags defined in this way default to being in the off state. The order in which the flags are defined in determines which bit they are assigned to represent them. This has important ramifications later, when we look at inheritance. There can be any number of `Flags` commands in a given state, and each `Flags` command can be positioned anywhere in the state code, as long as the following two conditions are met:

- Each flag is defined before it is used in an event handler.
- There are no more than 32 flags defined in a single state.

The new commands we will add to the event handler syntax are `SetFlags`, `IfFlags`, and `Error`. The first two work in a similar way to the `Behavior` command, in that they take as parameters a variable number of string arguments, representing which flags to turn on and off. Additionally, the `IfFlags` command makes the command (or block of commands) immediately following it conditional upon all of the given flags being set (or clear, if the ~ or ! characters precede the flag name). Finally, the `Error` command takes a single string as a parameter that is used as the error message to output. Using these new commands, we can detect errors in an attack state like this:

```
State("Attack")
{
    // define the flags that we will use
    Flags("strikeHappened");
    On("state_enter")
    {
        Execute("ChooseTarget");
        SetAnimation("Attack");
    }
    On("state_run")
        Execute("FaceTarget");
    On("event_damage")
        Transition("Damaged");
    On("event_death")
        Transition("Die");
    On("keyframe_strike")
    {
        Execute("DoDamage");
        SetFlag("strikeHappened");
    }
    On("anim_done")
    {
        IfFlags("~strikeHappened")
        {
            Error("Attack missing strike key-frame");
        }
        Transition("Stance");
    }
}
```

Examining this, we can see that the event handler for `"keyframe_strike"` sets a flag called `"strikeHappened"`. This flag is checked in the event handler for `"anim_done"`. If the flag has not been set at that point, then the animation has finished without hitting a strike frame, and the FSM throws an error, since no damage was done during the attack animation.

Creating Combos

A common feature of fighting games is that the player can link multiple attacks together to form deadly strings of attacks; these are often called *combination attacks*, or simply *combos*. Although at first glance they would seem trivial to implement—if you're in *this* attack animation and the user presses *this* button, change to *that* animation—in practice, it's not so simple. The problem is that at the time the input event happens, the character is probably not at a place in the animation conducive to changing state. In practice, there is only a narrow window of timing where the animation can be seamlessly changed to the next one in the sequence. What we need to do is record that an input event has occurred, and then act on it at the correct time to produce a seamless animation change. Luckily, we just introduced the very commands that allow us to do this completely inside the FSM with no external code assistance required.

In our example fighting game, the designer wants to create a two-hit combo that starts from the `"Attack"` state. This combo is initiated by pressing the Attack input key, and then pressing it again while in the first attack animation. The animator has set up the animations such that the second attack in the sequence must start at a point in the first animation that he has marked with a `"link"` frame. If the Attack button has been pressed again when this frame is hit, then the second attack in the sequence should start; otherwise, the first animation should play through as normal.

We would achieve this in the FSM by setting a flag when the `"input_attack"` event occurs in the `"Attack"` state. Then, when the `"keyframe_link"` event occurs, we check this flag, and if it is set, we transition to the state containing the second animation in the sequence. This adds the following event handlers to our `"Attack"` state:

```
State("Attack")
{
    Flags("strikeHappened","userHitAttack");

    // unchanged event handlers omitted

    On("input_attack")
```

```
        {
            SetFlag("userHitAttack");
        }

        On("keyframe_link")
        {
            IfFlags("userHitAttack")
                Transition("Attack2");
        }
    }
```

If we were being pedantic, we should also check the `"strikeHappened"` bit in the event handler for the link frame; it isn't much of a combo if the first animation never connects due to a missing strike frame. In practice, however, the combo isn't always initiated, leaving some times when the first animation will finish and causing the flag to be checked.

Working with Animation Blending

An aspect to be wary of when using animations specifically designed by the animator to link together from certain frames is animation blending. This is where the animation system detects a change in animation and saves the current orientation (and maybe also angular velocity for an advanced blending system) for each bone before changing to the new animation. This then allows it to blend in the new animation from the last position generated from the old animation over a short period of time. In general, this works great; it allows you to not have to worry about changing animations. For example, you could change to the damaged animation from any frame in the attack animation and things will look smooth and natural on-screen. The alternative would be to have an extremely visible snap as the animation changes and many limbs move a great deal in a single frame.

However, there are some situations where we don't want animation blending to occur. Probably the most important of these is, as mentioned previously, when the animator has specifically designed two animations to run into each other, or to link to each other from a certain frame. Therefore, a way is needed to turn animation blending off for certain animation changes. Luckily, this is trivial to do from the scripting language; we can just add extra optional parameters to the `SetAnimation` command that specify behaviors that we want to enable.

Notice the use of the word *behaviors* again; this is because we want to reinforce this method of doing things, to leave one less thing for the designers to learn. Therefore, the extra parameters to the `SetAnimation` command will take the form of strings defining the behavior of the command, and behind the scenes in the compiler these will be translated into behavior flags specific to this command. Although the functionality we want to add is enabling the animation system to not blend into the new animation, this is probably best described as turning off the default behavior of blending to the new animation. This means that the behavior to specify to stop animation blending should be `"~blending"`.

Another behavior that is needed in the `SetAnimation` command is that of not starting the new animation at the first frame. However, since animations can change (and since we are going to look at adding a layer of indirection to the animation lookup later), neither do we want to start an animation from a specific frame. This is needed mainly when changing from a walk animation to a run animation and back again, to avoid an untimely wait in the animation change (to line the legs up) or a major amount of blending (blending from the left foot forward in the walk animation to the right foot forward in the run animation). The way we get around this is to add a behavior called `"keepframe"` that chooses a frame number in the new animation that is proportional to the current frame number in the old animation. For example, if the character is 25 frames into a 100-frame animation and then changes to a 50-frame animation with the `"keepframe"` behavior, then the new animation will start at frame 12 (since frame 25 out of 100 is 25 percent of the way through the old animation, we want to start the new animation from 25 percent of the way through). This allows the animator to make all of the movement animations start and end on the same feet, meaning that the legs should be about in the same location and moving in about the same direction at proportionally the same frames. By doing this, we limit the amount of blending that needs to be done when changing from a walk to a run (or a run to a walk) while keeping the ability to change immediately between these animations at any time.

Finally, for completeness, we will add two extra behaviors; the first we will call `"reverse"` and simply makes the animation run backwards. The second allows us to turn off animation repeats; with this flag enabled, the animation will just hold at the last frame. We will call this behavior `"~repeat"`. This implies that there is a default `"repeat"` behavior that is always on.

Linking FSM Objects

It sometimes becomes necessary for two FSMs to be able to communicate with each other. A good example of this is when a character in our fighting game attempts to throw another character. For a throw to be initiated, the character being thrown must be in a state susceptible to being thrown. If he is, then the throw is begun, a link between the two FSMs is formed, and the FSMs can pass events to each other through the link to affect each other's state. During the throw itself, if something happens to one of the characters that can break the throw, that character breaks the link and the throw fails. If the throw finishes successfully, the throwing character breaks the link, since it is no longer needed.

In addition to the two-way link, it is also possible to create one-way links, in which the FSM that forms the link can send events to the target FSM, but the target cannot send events back. Additionally, we can create broadcast links, in which the creating FSM can send messages to multiple targets. A broadcast link can also be one- or two-way, but in a two-way broadcast link, each of the target FSMs only sees the link back to the FSM that created the broadcast link.

Another important property of links is whether a link is consensual. In a consensual link, the target FSM needs to actively accept the link in order for it to be formed. When a consensual link is attempted, the linker sends an event to the target (`"link_`*`linkname`*`"` where *linkname* is the name of the link specified in the `CreateLink` command), during which the target must invoke the `AcceptLink` command. If the target does not accept the link during this event, the link is not formed. This is the type of link that is needed in our throwing example, since the state of the target character determines whether the link is successfully formed. In a nonconsensual link, the link is always formed, no matter the state of the target FSM. All types of link (one- and two-way, broadcast or not) can be either consensual or not.

Ideally, all this would be achievable with no external code calls, since this is purely an FSM to FSM communiqué. In practice, however, we need at least one external function call in order to provide the pointers to the FSMs that we want to link to.

To create a link between two FSMs, we need to introduce the `CreateLink` command. This command takes two or more parameters, the first of which is the name of the link—each FSM can have a potentially unlimited number of active links and so a way is needed to direct events down a specific link. The second parameter is an external function name, which is invoked as the link is attempted, and is responsible for providing the FSMs that are to be the targets of the link. The number of FSMs reported by this function (there might be zero or more) determines whether this link is a broadcast link. Any extra parameters are modifiers that change the behavior of the link. The `"oneway"` modifier (off by default) makes the link a one-way link; the default for all links is to be two-way. The `"always"` modifier (off by default) makes the link nonconsensual.

After a link has been created, it is usually necessary to test whether the link was successful, especially in the case of consensual links. This is done via the `IfLink` command, which tests the named links for their presence (or not). This command takes a variable number of parameters, each corresponding to the name of the link to be tested. If the name of the link is preceded by a `~` or a `!` character, then the result is true if the link is *not* present; otherwise, the result is true if the link *is* present. The commands inside the block following the `IfLink` command are only executed if *all* of the tests specified in the command are true.

Now that we have created a link between one or more FSMs, we need to be able to use them to send communications between the FSMs. This is done using the `SendEvent` command. This command takes two parameters; the first is the name of the link down which the event is to be sent, and the second is the name of the event. The effect of this command is that all FSMs connected to this one by links whose names match the first parameter will immediately receive the event specified by the second parameter. Care should be taken to avoid an infinite loop, where the receiving of one of these events triggers another sending, which in turn triggers another sending, and so on. Although this could be easily prevented in the FSM implementation (by not receiving events from links while sending an event), doing so could prevent legitimate uses of chaining messages.

Finally, after a link is no longer of use, we need to break the link. The `BreakLink` command is used for this purpose. It takes a variable number of parameters, each parameter corresponding to the name of a link to be broken. One-way links are just broken, but two-way links must notify the target of the link that it is being broken, which it does via the `"unlink_linkname"` event. This event handler is not required, and handling the event or not in no way affects the outcome of the `BreakLink` command.

REMOVING REDUNDANCY AND AVOIDING REPLICATION

The scripting language that we have developed so far is already a powerful tool for defining the behavior of a character and simplifying the underlying code. However, even in our simple examples, we are approaching a point where there is a lot of replication in the script for each FSM state. This goes directly against our stated goal of simplifying the definition of each character; it does us no good to simplify our code and pass on the complexity to the designers. As programmers we are much better prepared to handle massive logic knots and code repetition, and still we manage to make a mess of it. How do we expect a designer to do better?

In this section we will look at some simple features that will enable the designers to reuse a single FSM as much as possible, and to avoid repetition within a single FSM. Using these language features will allow the designers to more easily navigate through the FSM code, and to more easily introduce variations in character behavior.

State Groups

The first issue that we need to address is that of the repetition of event handler code between similar states. Obviously, this could become a breeding ground for errors unless it is addressed. It is easy to see that the states that share the most event handler code are usually closely related in function, and we can use that to our advantage by arranging similar states into explicit groups that share certain event handlers and behaviors. To do this, we need to add two extra commands to our FSM description language.

The `Group` command defines a group block, within which all the child states inherit the group properties. Although the group command takes a string as a parameter, this parameter is ignored, since groups have no meaning in the final FSM. Groups can be nested to any depth.

Within the group block, the `GroupState` command defines the common, inherited event handlers and behaviors for the group. This command works in exactly the same way as a `State` command, except that no state is generated. Instead, every state within the group automatically inherits anything defined by the `GroupState` command. There can only be one `GroupState` command per group block, and if present it must be the first thing defined in the block, although this is purely for ease-of-compilation reasons.

Indirect Animation Lookups

To make a given FSM as reusable as possible, it is necessary to refrain from explicitly naming any resources. If we were to simply use the resource names of our animations, then every character in the game would need an explicit FSM referencing its unique set of animations. If many of these characters shared the same basic states, this would be a huge amount of replicated FSM code. As we have asserted many times during this chapter, repetition breeds errors.

Fortunately, the solution to this problem is relatively simple. If we alias each of the possible animations to a generic name, and supply a different lookup table for each character, we can de-reference the alias to produce the specific animation required for a given character. Doing this allows us to use a single FSM for each class of character, regardless of how different their animations look.

Inheritance

The final, and probably most important, feature of the FSM scripting language is that of inheritance. We already saw how using indirect animation lookups enabled us to reuse a single FSM for multiple characters, as long as they shared the same basic functionality of animations. However, the Achilles' heel of this is that characters that differ in their animation functionality only slightly must implement an entirely different FSM. For example, suppose that your game already includes a character type called "soldier." This character can stand, run, jump, attack, and die. If the designer wanted to create an "advanced soldier" character that could do a combination attack, there are two approaches that he could take:

- Include all the states required for the combination attack in the "soldier" FSM, and ask the programmer to ensure that these states never get entered unless the character is indeed an "advanced soldier."
- Implement a new FSM for the "advanced soldier" by first copying the "soldier" FSM, and then editing it.

Neither of these options is very appetizing. The first option is an example of the very thing that we are trying to escape from (implementing large `if-else` statements at the code level to determine behavior) and should be treated as such. The second option moves the programmer's burden onto the designer, and should also be treated with disdain. Remember: repetition breeds errors.

Fortunately, the very solution we need is a tried and tested technique included in many modern languages, including the one that your game is probably being written in. That solution is, of course, inheritance: the ability of one class of objects to inherit its default behaviors from another class of objects, and to extend and modify those behaviors as needed.

The only command needed to enable inheritance is the `Parent` command. This command takes a single parameter—the name of the FSM that supplies the base functionality for the current one. There are two restrictions on this command, neither of which can be detected until runtime (this is because we will be compiling the FSMs singly and in isolation from each other):

- The parent FSM must be of the same type as the child FSM (the type of an FSM is declared in the initial `FSM` command.

- The parent class cannot be a child of any FSM that inherits from the current FSM (this avoids an infinite loop).

Declaring a parent for the current FSM automatically adds to it every state that is defined in the parent. This means that initially an FSM that inherits from another exhibits exactly the same behavior as its parent. This behavior is changed when we begin overriding the parent's states with new implementations specific to the child. Doing this is as simple as declaring the state again in the child. Whenever a state is declared in the child, the behavior of any event handler defined in the child's state supercedes that of the handler in the parent. Any event handlers that are not overridden in the child remain unchanged from that of the parent.

How does this work? Each FSM has a data entry that contains a pointer to its parent. Any state lookup in the child FSM will first check for the state in the child's state list. If it is found, then this state is used; otherwise, the search moves to the FSM's parent. This continues until we either run out of parents (which is an error, since the state is not defined anywhere) or we finally find the state declaration. Each state in the FSM also contains a pointer, but this time a pointer to the corresponding state in its parent (or its parent's parent and so on). Whenever an event occurs, the corresponding event handler is looked up in the current state; again, if the handler is not found, the search moves to the parent state and is retried.

Sometimes it might be desirable to completely override a state in the parent FSM. There are two ways to do this. The first is to declare every event handler that occurs in the parent state in the child state. This works great until a new event handler is added to the parent—unless the child is updated to override this event handler, then it will inherit this functionality, potentially breaking the child FSM. A better way to completely override a parent state's functionality is to use the `Orphan()` command. This command declares that the current state should be orphaned; it should inherit nothing from its parent.

There are some things that cannot be inherited (since we compile each FSM in isolation—see the section on compilation later in this chapter). The most significant of these are the behaviors for the parent state. These are stored as an absolute bit-flag and so must be redeclared in every overridden state, whether or not the behavior is different from its parent. The groups of the parent state cannot be inherited either, since these do not survive compilation in any recoverable form. However, this is not so important since the event handlers in each group are rolled into every state contained within the group.

State-specific flags (used by the IfFlags and SetFlags commands) cannot be inherited either, as these are dynamically mapped to bits at the compile stage. However, this can be worked around easily by redeclaring the flags in the same order in the inherited state. Failure to declare the flags in the correct order, or missing a flag out of the declaration, can result in strange behavior as inherited states have the flags that their functionality depends on changed outside of their controls.

Even with these restrictions, inheritance is a powerful tool that allows varying behavior with the minimum of work. It reduces repetition and hence keeps the FSM code simple and less prone to errors.

FSM SCRIPTING LANGUAGE REFERENCE

Unless otherwise stated, each parameter to a function takes the form of an arbitrary character string, enclosed in double quotes; for example, "state_enter" is a valid parameter, but state_enter and 'state_enter' are not. The use of <block> in the command definitions represents either a single command that is valid in the described block type, or a sequence of valid commands, delimited by curly braces. This is similar to the C convention of describing a block of related commands.

Whenever the parameter is defined as <modifier>, this can be replaced by any of the modifiers listed in the command description. If any of the given modifiers is preceded with either the ~ or ! characters, then that modifier is turned off. The default value for each modifier is listed in the command description. Finally, if a command ends with the <...> parameter, this means that the previous parameter can be repeated an arbitrary number of times. This is usually used in conjunction with modifiers to fully describe the behavior of a command.

The Global Level

The global level is the default level for the FSM compiler (and any other tool it is embedded in). Only one FSM-related command is valid at this level:

```
FSM(<name>, <type>) <block>
```

The preceding code defines an FSM called <name> of type <type>. The type of FSM determines the mapping of the behavior flags and can also be used to add or remove valid commands from the event handler. The block of code immediately following this command comprises the complete definition of the FSM. This block is called the FSM block and is described next.

The FSM Block

The FSM block is the block of code immediately following an `FSM` command. It must contain at least one defined or inherited state and a valid defined initial state. The following commands are valid inside the FSM block:

`DefaultBehavior(<modifier>, ...);`: This command defines the default behaviors that every state inherits, unless the state explicitly disables them. This command takes a variable length list of modifiers, the names of which are dependent on the declared type of the FSM. The set of valid behaviors depends on the <type> parameter of the FSM command. All behaviors default to being disabled. Multiple `DefaultBehavior` commands are valid at the FSM level, but the behaviors specified are unified into one set of behaviors in the order specified. This means that if a behavior is turned off and then on, the result is that the behavior is on, but if it is turned on and then off, the behavior will be disabled. This command is optional.

`Group([<name>]) <block>`: This command, which is valid in both the FSM block and the group block, defines a group of states that share one or more event handlers or behaviors. It is immediately followed by a block of code that comprises the entire definition of the group. This block is called the group block and is described in the next section. The name of the group is optional, and is disregarded. This command is optional.

`InitialState(<name>);`: Defines the initial state assumed by this FSM upon startup or upon being reset. A state called <name> must exist within this FSM or within one of its parents. This command is not optional, even when inheriting from another FSM.

`State(<name>) <block>`: This command is used to declare a single state, called <name> in the FSM. Similar to the `Group` command, it is valid in both the FSM block and the group block. At the FSM level, it inherits the default behaviors defined at this level, whereas at the group level it inherits the group state (see the section "The State Block"). <name> must be unique to the current FSM declaration, but can be the same as a state in any parent FSMs. In this case, the state declared here will completely override the state from the parent FSM. The block of code immediately following the state command is called the state block, and must fully describe the given state. There can be any number of states in a given FSM block, but there must be at least one state declared somewhere in the FSM or inherited from a parent FSM.

`Parent(<name>);`: This command declares that this FSM inherits all of the states and behaviors of the FSM called <name>. The parent FSM must exist and must be of the same type, although this cannot be detected at compile time. This command is optional.

The Group Block

The group block is the block of code that immediately follows the `Group` command. This block defines a set of states that share some event handlers and behaviors, and is also useful in the design and visualization of an FSM. The valid commands in the group block are:

`Group([<name>]) <block>`: For a description of the `group` command, see the FSM block command list. Groups can be nested to an arbitrary depth.

Each successive group inherits the group state from the group it is declared in. This command is optional.

`GroupState() <block>`: This command declares a dummy state that is local to the group it is declared inside. This dummy state defines the behaviors and event handlers that are inherited by all of the states defined in the group block. The block immediately following this command is a state block (see `State` command). This command is optional, but can only be used once in a given group block and must be the first thing defined in that block.

`State(<name>) <block>`: For a description of the `State` command, see the FSM block command list. There can be any number of states in a group block. This command is optional.

The State Block

The state block immediately follows a `State` or a `GroupState` command, and in combination with the values inherited from the group block and FSM block, completely describes the given state. The following commands are valid inside a state block:

`Behavior(<modifier>, ...);`: Similar to the `DefaultBehavior` in the FSM block, this command enables or disables behaviors inside this state. The set of valid behaviors depends on the <type> parameter of the FSM command. This command is optional.

`Flags(<name>, ...);`: Declares a series of state-specific flags that will be used in the event handlers for this state. The bits that the flags get mapped to are assigned in the order in which the flags are declared. Any flags declared in the `group` state are assigned mappings first. All flags must be defined via this command before they are used in an event handler.

`Orphan();`: This command, valid only in a state block, tells the compiler that this state should inherit no functionality from the parent FSM. This allows a child FSM to completely override a given state, without having to worry about new event handlers being added to the parent state.

`On(<event>) <block>`: This command declares a handler for an event called <event>. It is followed immediately by the event handler block of code, which fully defines the actions to be taken when this event is received in the given state. This command is optional; however, a state with no event handlers is pretty useless.

The Event Handler Block

The final block of code to be defined is the event handler block. This block immediately follows the `On` command from the state block. The following default commands are valid inside an event handler block, although the type of FSM could add or remove commands from this list, depending on the needs of the application and the type of the FSM.

`AcceptLink();`: This command should only occur in the event handler for a `"link_linkname"` event. Use of this command accepts the consensual link for which the event handler was invoked. Failure to invoke this command in the `"link_linkname"` event handler causes the link to fail.

`BreakLink(<name>, ...);`: The `BreakLink` command breaks every instance of the <name> link for this object. This causes any object that shares a link called <name> with this one to receive an `"unlink_<name>"` event. Regardless of whether this event is handled, the link is broken for both objects. If there are multiple links specified in the parameter list for this command, then each link is broken in sequence.

`ChangeBehavior(<modifier>, ...);`: Using this command, it is possible to turn specific behaviors on and off for the remainder of the duration of the current state. These changes are lost when a state transition occurs.

`CreateLink(<name>, <function> [, <modifier>, ...]);`: This command causes a link called <name> to be attempted between two FSM objects. The valid modifiers for this command are:

`oneway`	Makes the link a one-way link (default=off)
`always`	Makes the link nonconsensual (default=off)

`End();`: The `End` command causes the execution of the current event handler to immediately finish.

`Error(<message>);`: Causes an error message to be displayed for a short period of time.

`Event(<event name>);`: This command throws the named event in the current state. This is useful to avoid repeating code for multiple, similar events. This command stops the execution of the current event handler.

`Execute(<function>);`: Causes a function called <function> to be executed. This function must have been declared to the FSM handler at execution time, and so errors cannot be detected at compile time. If the given function causes (directly or indirectly) a state transition before control returns to the event handler, the event handler will finish execution immediately upon return from the function.

`IfFlags(<flagName>, ...) <block>`: The `IfFlags` command checks the status of the named flags. If all of the given flags are in the states defined, then the block of code following the statement is executed. If any of the given flags are in a different state from the one specified, then the block of code is not executed.

`IfLink(<name>, ...) <block>`: This command checks the status of the links named in the variable length parameter list. If all of the links exist, then the block of code following the instruction is executed; otherwise, the block is skipped. If any parameter is preceded by a `~` or a `!` character, then the link is checked for its absence.

`IfRandom(<probability>) <block>`: This command takes as a parameter a single floating-point value between 0 and 1. This parameter should not be enclosed in quotes. If a random number between 0 and 1 is lower than the specified value, then the block of code following the instruction is executed; otherwise, the block is skipped.

`SendEvent(<name>, <event>);`: This command sends an arbitrary event, called <event>, to every object that is linked to this one via a link called <name>.

`SetAnimation(<name> [, <modifier>, ...] );`: This command causes the animation called <name> to be found and then assigned to the object that this FSM is maintaining the state for. By default, this animation starts at frame 0 and runs forward until the end, at which point it repeats. Any keyframes marked with events will cause the corresponding event to be thrown to the state handler. The valid modifiers for this command are:

`Blending`	Turns animation blending on or off (default = on).
`Repeat`	Turns animation repetition on or off (default = on).
`Reverse`	Causes the animation to play backwards (default = off)
`Keepframe`	Keeps the same proportional frame from the previous animation (default = off)

`SetFlag(<flagName>, ...);`: This command sets or clears the named state-local flags. These flags are automatically cleared upon state entry, and so they all default to off. The flag names are declared at the state level by the `Flags` command.

`Transition(<name> [, <modifier>, ...] );`: This command initiates a state transition to a state called <name>. This command finishes the execution of the event handler; any commands after this one in the event handler will not get executed. The only valid modifier at present is `"state_exit"`, which enables or disables execution of the `"state_exit"` event handler for this state transition. If omitted, this modifier defaults to on.

COMPILATION

So far, we have managed to define a scripting language for creating a hierarchy of FSMs that can be used to declare the behavior of characters in your game. We must now look at compiling this language into a usable form, and finally using it.

The first thing we must do is compile each of the FSMs into a binary representation. Luckily, we already laid the groundwork for this in Chapters 4 and 5, and we will use the techniques developed there to help us now. Using the parser developed in Chapter 4, loading and parsing the FSM code becomes trivial. Before we continue, however, we must define the final data format for the FSM.

The `FSMDEF` class contains the definition of an FSM. Notice that in order to aid debugging, the name of the FSM is stored as both a hash and a pointer to a character string. The hash is used for quick lookup, but this alone makes it very hard to tell which FSM you are looking at when debugging, so we include the character string to help with this. Moreover, the parent FSM is stored as both a hash and a pointer to the FSM; this is because the parent FSM needs to be examined whenever a state or event handler is not found in the current FSM. Although hash lookups are very fast, we still do not want to be doing them several times a frame. The pointer to the parent FSM is filled in at load time. Finally, the class contains two `StaticHashList` structures that contain all of the states for the FSM, and all of the strings referenced by the FSM (including each event and state's name and any error strings used).

```
class FSMDEF
{
public:
    HASH            name;
    HASH            type;
    HASH            parentName;
    HASH            initialState;
    const char      *nameString;
    const FSMDEF    *parent;
    StaticHashList  states;
    StaticHashList  dictionary;
};
```

The FSMSTATE class defines a single state in the FSM. Again, for ease of debugging, the state contains both the hash of its name and a pointer to a character string containing its name. We also define here the behaviors that are active for this state (the mappings of the flags onto behaviors is dependant on the type of the FSM). Each state contains a pointer to the state it inherits any functionality from in the parent FSM. This is defined at load time by looking up the corresponding state in the parent FSM. If the FSM has no parent, or the given state is orphaned, then the parent pointer will be NULL. Finally, the event handlers for the state are stored in a StaticHashList.

```
class FSMSTATE
{
public:
    HASH            name;
    u32             behaviors;
    const char      *nameString;
    const FSMSTATE  *parent;
    StaticHashList  events;
};
```

Each event handler is stored as a stream of DWORDs representing the commands defined in the source code. This allows better performance and platform compatibility, since we will only ever read from memory 4 bytes at a time, and reads will always be aligned on a 4-byte boundary. Each command DWORD is encoded in the same way. The least significant 8 bits represent the command to be processed. The next 8 bits represent the length of the current command, in DWORDs, not including the command DWORD. This allows commands to be up to 1024 bytes in length. The meaning of the remaining 2 bytes varies by command, but is generally used to represent the number of consecutive DWORDs used to record things that are on, and the number of DWORDs used to record things that are off, respectively. However, in cases where there are only a small number of valid modifiers for the command, these can be stored here. Tables 7.1 and 7.2 show the encoding of two sample commands.

TABLE 7.1 An Example Encoding of the `SetFlag` Command

`SetFlag("strikeHappened", "~userHitAttack");`

Offset	*# Bytes*	*Value*	*Comment*
0	1	FSMCMD_SetFlag	`SetFlag` command
1	1	2	Length of this command
2	1	1	Length of flags to set
3	1	1	Length of flags to clear
4	4	StrikeHappened	The flags to set
8	4	UserHitAttack	The flags to clear

TABLE 7.2 An Example Encoding of the `SetAnimation` Command

`SetAnimation("walk", "~blending", "keepframe");`

tch:Offset	*# Bytes*	*Value*	*Comment*
0	1	FSMCMD_SetAnimation	`SetAnimation` command
1	1	1	Length of this command
2	1	AnimFlag_KeepFrame	Command modifiers
3	1	0	*Not used*
4	4	hash("walk")	The name of the animation to set

All commands are defined in this way, with the exception of the conditional commands. These differ in that the length of the command includes all of the instructions that are dependent on it, allowing easy skipping of the conditional block. This has the side effect of limiting the size of the block following a conditional command to under 1024 bytes, but this should be sufficient for all but the most complex event handlers. Table 7.3 shows an example of encoding a conditional command with a conditional block containing a single command.

TABLE 7.3 An Example Encoding of a Conditional Command

```
IfLink("throw", "~grapple")
    SendEvent("throw","event_thrown");
```

Offset	*# Bytes*	*Value*	*Comment*
0	1	`FSMCMD_IfLink`	`IfLink` command
1	1	5	Length of this command & its block
2	1	1	Length of active links
3	1	1	Length of inactive links
4	4	hash("throw")	First active link to check
8	4	hash("grapple")	First inactive link to check
12	1	`FSMCMD_SendEvent`	`SendEvent` command
13	1	2	Length of this command
14	1	0	*Not used*
15	1	0	*Not used*
16	4	hash("throw")	Link to use
20	4	hash("event_thrown")	Event to send

The event handler data stream is always terminated by an `End()` command; the compiler adds one if it is not present.

ON THE CD

A sample implementation of an FSM compiler is provided on the companion CD-ROM, located in the Chapter7/FSMcompiler directory. This implementation takes the form of a DLL that works in combination with the DataCon program developed in Chapter 5.

IMPLEMENTATION

Once we have a compiled version of our FSM, we can begin to use it to control the state of our game objects. This is done through the `FSMINSTANCE` class, which represents an instance of an FSM and its current state. Each object that requires its state to be controlled by an FSM should contain one or more FSMINSTANCE objects, representing each FSM that comprises the object's behavior. As you can see from the simplified definition of the FSMINSTANCE class that follows, the interface is very simple and enforces the separation of the object and its state definition.

```
class FSMINSTANCE
{
public:
    // initialization
    void        Init( void *pObject, const FSMDEF *pFsm );

    // query functions
    const char  *GetFsmName();
    const char  *GetCurrentStateName();
    u32         GetBehavior();
    void        *GetObject();

    // action functions
    void        Reset();
    FSMRESULT   Run();
    FSMRESULT   Event( const char *eventName );
    bool        CreateLink( FSMINSTANCE *pLinkTo,
                            const char *linkName = 0,
                            u32 linkFlags = 0 );
};
```

The first thing that should be done when initializing an FSMINSTANCE is to call the Init function. This function takes two parameters; the first is a pointer to the object whose state it is responsible for and the second parameter is a pointer to the definition of the FSM. This function first initializes itself and then calls the Reset() function to enter the default state for the FSM. Depending on the definition of the FSM, this can cause an event to be thrown, and so care should be taken to ensure that the underlying object is in a position to receive any callbacks that might occur.

The `Event` function is used to send an event to the FSM. This function is the main interface between the game object and the FSM. Calling this function can result in multiple changes of state and multiple callbacks, depending on the event handler defined in the FSM. The first thing that this function does it to locate the correct event handler. This is achieved by taking the hash of the event name and looking it up in the current state's event list. If an event handler is not found and the current state is not an orphan, then the event is looked for in the parent state. This continues until either the event handler is found or there are no more places to look. If an event handler is found, then the command stream for that event handler is used to resolve the event and take any actions necessary. The return value for the `Event` command is taken from the `FSMRESULT` enumerated type and represents the result of the event. The valid return values are shown in Table 7.4.

TABLE 7.4 The Possible Values of `FSMRESULT`

FSMRESULT	*Meaning*
FSMRESULT_NotFound	An appropriate event handler was not found
FSMRESULT_Succeeded	The event was successfully handled
FSMRESULT_ChangedState	The event was handled and caused a change of state

The `GetBehavior()` function simply returns the behavior flags for the current state. This allows the object to perform the behaviors specified by the FSM state. As described earlier, this allows the FSM to dictate which behaviors an object is responsible for providing in a given state. The meaning of the behavior flags changes based on the type of the FSM, and so it is important to validate that the FSM is of the type expected by the object before initialization.

The `CreateLink` function allows the creation of links between `FSMINSTANCE` objects. This function is usually called one or more times from within the callback function specified in the `CreateLink` event handler command (see previous definition of this command). The flags for this command affect how the link is created: whether the link is consensual and whether the link is two-way. The *linkName* parameter can only be 0 when this function is called from within a callback generated by the `CreateLink` event handler command. Whenever *linkName* is 0, *linkFlags* must also be 0, and the true values of these parameters are taken from the event handler command.

The remaining two interesting functions are `Reset()` and `Run()`. The first of these resets the object's state back into the initial state defined for the FSM. This is the only way that an object's state can be changed outside of an event handler. The second function, `Run`, is simply an easy way to send an "`event_run`" event, required by many states to be thrown each frame.

This gives us a simple process loop for an object with a single FSM:

1. Call `FSMINSTANCE::GetBehavior()` and apply the specified behaviors.
2. Call `FSMINSTANCE::Run()` to send the required frame event.

Callbacks

The one thing left to implement is the callback functionality exposed through the `Execute()` event handler command. This is simply a dynamic hash list of function pointers, stored by the hash of their identifier strings (which is usually the function name). Each function takes the following form:

```
void FunctionName( FSMINSTANCE *pInstance );
```

This rather sparse definition of a callback function allows us to use a single list of all the callback functions exported by the game. Any extra information that is needed by the callback function (such as a pointer to the object containing the FSM) can be obtained easily through the `FSMINSTANCE` pointer.

As indicated earlier in this chapter, the functionality for declaring callback functions is enabled through a static member function of the `FSMINSTANCE` class. Similarly, the functionality for locating a callback function is also provided through a static member function. These functions and their supporting data structures are defined as follows:

```
class FSMINSTANCE
{
public:
```

```
    // see unchanged member functions declared earlier

    static void     ClearFunctionList();
    static void     DeclareFunction( const char *name, FSMFN fn );
    static FSMFN    FindFunction( HASH nameHash );
    static FSMFN    FindFunction( const char *name );

protected:

    static HashList functionList;
};
```

Since the function list is defined statically, in order to avoid leaking memory we need a way to clear it out when our game is exiting, and so release any memory used. This is provided through the static `ClearFunctionList()` member function.

LET'S GET READY TO RUMBLE!

ON THE CD

You can find the simple fighting game example described in this chapter on the companion CD-ROM, in the Chapter7\game folder. This game uses two FSMs, defined in the files fsmCharacter.txt and fsmPlayer.txt. The first is a simple FSM defining just one attack move, and the second is a more complex FSM for the player that extends it by adding a simple three-move combo. The data files for the game are built using the DataCon tool developed in Chapter 5.

OTHER USES

Although the main FSM described in this chapter is used to define the animation and control logic for a fighting game, there are many more places that an FSM could be used to simplify your game's code. Some of them are listed here:

Strategic AI: An RTS game could implement a strategic AI as an FSM. This AI could create links to the FSMs of all the units under its command and broadcast its commands as events through this link.

Spell system: A magic-based game could use an FSM to represent each of its spells. Each spell would use the FSM to alter its behavior as it proceeds through its lifetime. By deriving all of the spells from a single parent FSM, multiple characteristics can be shared between similar, yet different, spells. In this way, a large library of spells can be created by combining a small set of predefined behaviors at different stages of each spell's life.

Menu system: A simple menu system could be defined as an FSM. Each menu would be a state, and the menu options would be the events used to navigate through the menus.

Game state: A sports game has a very limited set of game states, and each of these states has a definite behavior, with a distinct set of events linking them. For example, a football game could have an `InPlay` state that has several event handlers for events that include fumble, foul, tackle, and touchdown. Each of these events will transition to different states, and each of these states will direct the camera and players to do certain things. In this way, the designers can direct the flow of the game and which camera angles are used when.

Hopefully, these few examples will have given you some ideas of your own. Remember:

- Repetition breeds errors.
- Exploit your data!

8 Saving Game State

In This Chapter

- Rule #8: "Save Early, Save Often"
- Types of Saved Game
- Why Is It So Difficult?
- What Do We Need to Save?
- Savable Data Types
- Declaring an Object's Save Template
- The `SAVEOBJECT` Class
- Saving and Loading a Game
- The `SAVEFILE` Class
- Processing a Save Template
- Auto-Detecting Object Changes
- Implementation
- Further Reading

One of the most time-intensive and arduous tasks involved in creating a game would also appear at first glance to be the simplest: saving the state of the game to the disk. Unfortunately, this task is a long and arduous one. Worse, since the things that define the state of the game change during development, it is a task that is often postponed for as long as possible.

RULE #8: "SAVE EARLY, SAVE OFTEN"

All is not lost, however; by drawing on a few of the earlier chapters, adding a little ingenuity and a lot of automation we can create a robust and stable saved game system. From this base, we can then add features that make it easy to maintain, allowing us to create the system much earlier in the development process and be reasonably certain that the system we create will survive to the end of the project.

TYPES OF SAVED GAME

Before we start constructing a saved game system, we must first decide what type of saved game system we are going to create; what are we expecting it to do, and what must be saved to accomplish this. Two main flavors of saved games exist, each of which has distinct advantages and disadvantages. The choice of which type to use most often depends on the target platform; it is no use trying to save the entire game state if the storage medium does not have enough capacity to store it.

The easiest type of saved game to implement is what we will call the *progress* save. This saved game saves the minimum amount of data required to store where the player is in the game. This usually includes the player's position in the game, and a list of the things that he or she has accomplished so far. The player's position in this case is usually limited to a small number of distinct points throughout the game. Limiting the position in this way allows us to omit saving the entire state of the game; the player is led to expect to replay the current section by virtue of the fact that he is reset to the start of it on loading the game. This type of save is most common on consoles, where the size available for storage is severely limited.

The second type of saved game is what we will call the *full* save. This type of saved game, most common among PC games, attempts to save the entire state of the game into a single file. When the player reloads this game, he will find himself at the exact same point in the game that he saved at. Obviously, a full save is much harder to implement than a progress save, since we need to store the complete state of every system and object in the game. A full save is also more fragile than a progress save; a simple change to any number of things can render the information stored in the save file invalid.

With the arrival of the hard drive in modern console systems, and the explosion of capacity on their memory cards, there is now no technical reason to ever implement a progress save. However, this does not mean that a game should never choose to implement a progress save over a full save; to make this decision, the design team must look at ease of use and player expectations given prior games of a similar genre.

Even when the player expects only a progress save, it is still possible, and in some cases preferable, to use a full save. By allowing the player limited access to the save system based on his position in the game, we can make a full save better approximate the player's expectations. This method retains many of the advantages of a full save system—enemies remain dead, buildings remain destroyed, objects remain where the player left them—while keeping the look and feel of the progress save.

In this chapter, we will look at implementing a robust method for implementing a saved game system that does a full save.

WHY IS IT SO DIFFICULT?

As stated previously, a full game save is an inherently fragile thing that can be broken by any number of things changing. Normally, this is not a problem in a shipping game—very little, if anything, changes once a game has shipped—yet in development, this can become a major problem.

The first stumbling block comes as you realize that you are trying to hit a moving target; the game code is changing and evolving as the save code is written. Inevitably, this leads us to postpone the creation of the saved game system until the game code base is fairly stable. Usually, this means post-beta, when the only code changes happening should be bug fixes (although how you can reach beta without implementing the saved game system is another question entirely).

The next stumbling block comes from the fact that the code is not the only thing that is constantly changing; the levels also change, even after beta. When a level changes, the scripts underlying the level usually also change, leaving us with a problem: even if we can make the saved game robust enough to survive the level having changed since the game was saved, what do you do with objects whose scripts have changed? Where in the script should they continue if the instructions they are currently running are removed?

WHAT DO WE NEED TO SAVE?

The simplest of all full save systems would be to just save the entire contents of memory to disk. However, in practice this is neither possible nor desirable. We cannot save the areas of memory belonging to the operating system or any other program, and even if we could, we certainly should not attempt to load them. This leaves us with saving all of the memory areas that belong to our game. Even this is not simple; when reloading a saved game, it is not guaranteed (or even likely) that each memory allocation will occur in the same place, meaning that any pointers within the saved data immediately become invalid.

Although this method could be made to work, it is not a desirable method to use, for the simple reason that we would be saving a lot of data that is easily reproduced. Most of the memory that a game uses is taken up by invariant resources: the textures, models, sounds, and scripts that make up the current level. Saving these to disk is not necessary, since they can be trivially retrieved from the files making up the level.

What we really want to save is the dynamic data that represents the current state of the game. This includes the current state of anything that can dynamically change over the course of the level. Usually, this simply means all of the currently instantiated game objects.

SAVABLE DATA TYPES

Each of the objects that we want to save is composed of a collection of various data types, some of which are:

1. Integers (8-, 16-, and 32-bit)
2. Floating-point numbers (32-, 64-bit)
3. SIMD values (128-bit)
4. Pointers to other objects
5. Pointers to resources
6. Pointers to arbitrary object data members
7. Pointers into resource memory
8. Pointers to arbitrary data

As you can see, a lot of different types of data must be saved. Luckily, though, these can be collapsed into just three general types of data:

a. Data that must be restored to exactly the same value it had at save-time (items 1–3).
b. Data that must assume a value that is at the same relative position to a value that changes between save- and load-time (items 4–7).
c. Data that cannot be saved without more information (item 8).

Passive Data

Data of type (a), which must be restored to the save value it held when it was saved, is what we will call *passive* data. If we assume that the saved game will only be used on the same hardware platform (i.e., we can ignore any endian issues), then saving passive data is simple; we just write the specified number of bytes directly to the file. Conversely, loading data of this type is also trivial; simply read the correct number of bytes from the save file.

Two or more pieces of passive data that are contiguous in memory can be concatenated and saved as a single, larger piece of passive data. This means that arrays of passive data and structures containing only passive data can be saved in a single operation, simplifying the process. However, if an array or structure contains anything other than passive data, it must be broken into parts that must be saved separately.

Pointers and Blocks

Things become more complicated when we look at data of type (b): the pointers. Each pointer must be converted to a value that is inside a known block of memory prior to saving. When loading data of this type, we must first locate the new position of the relevant block and then add the offset stored in the file to it to restore the pointer. It follows, then, that each pointer written to the file must be written as two values; the first is an identifier that lets us uniquely identify correct memory block, and the second is the (positive) offset from the base of this block the we want to point to.

Figure 8.1 shows three memory blocks and four pointers. The shaded areas of memory have not been declared to the save system. Pointers 1 through 3 are savable, since they point into known memory blocks. Pointer 4, however, cannot be saved because it points into memory that we do not know how to locate relative to our known blocks. Figure 8.2 shows the same three memory blocks after loading. Notice that although the layout of the blocks is different, the pointers still point to the correct place inside each block.

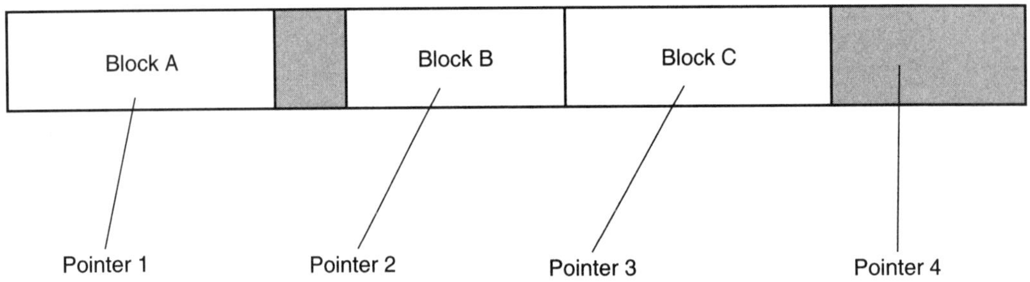

FIGURE 8.1 An example set of memory blocks and pointers.

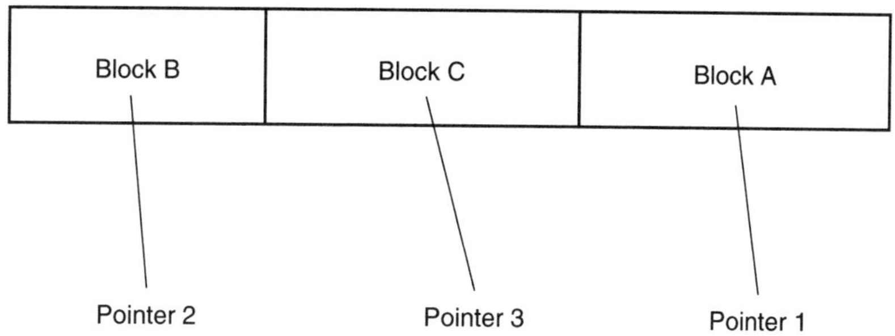

FIGURE 8.2 The same memory blocks after loading.

The simplest way to assign a unique identifier to each block is to declare all of the possible blocks to the save system prior to both saving and loading. These are then incorporated into a list, and the index of a given block in this list becomes the identifier for that block. When using this method, it is very important that the blocks be declared in the same order for both saving and loading; failure to do so will result in incorrect restoration of the pointers, and a probable crash. Luckily, it is possible to verify that the blocks are declared correctly prior to loading a game. We can do this by making a single hash value representing the lengths of each block and the order in which they are declared and saving it into the file. At load time, if the hash calculated does not match the one in the file, then our blocks have been declared differently, and the save file is therefore invalid.

Which areas of memory are actually declared as blocks varies by game, but usually includes all of the allocations for the data that we do not need to save (i.e., the resource definitions). Depending on the game, it can also be useful to declare each object as a block. This allows pointers to arbitrary data members within each object to be saved with no additional work.

DECLARING AN OBJECT'S SAVE TEMPLATE

If we can automate the saving of each of these types of data, then we can save any object in the game given only a list describing its contents. Each entry in this list would contain the offset from the starting address of the object of the savable element, its length in bytes, and the type of data that the element contains. It would then be a simple matter to iterate through this list and save or load each of the elements in the game object. This list of savable elements for an object is called the object's *save template.*

```
typedef enum
{
    ST_EndOfTemplate,
    ST_Passive,
    ST_Pointer

} SAVETYPE;

typedef struct
{
    SAVETYPE    type;
    u32         offset;
    u32         length;
} SAVERECORD;
```

The preceding code is a preliminary definition of an entry in an object's save template. Using this definition, we can describe any class of object as an array of SAVERECORDs. However, the act of authoring the array is very cumbersome, repetitive, and prone to error. If we create every single SAVERECORD by hand, storing the offsets and lengths of each item as actual numbers, the resulting template would be very fragile, since any change to the object's structure would invalidate some of the offsets in the template. Luckily, we can use the `offsetof` macro and `sizeof` operator to ease some of the burden here.

The `offsetof` macro takes two parameters: the name of the class that the element is in, and the name of the element that we want the offset of. This macro works by casting a `null` address as a pointer to an object of the correct type. It then dereferences the required element from this pointer and takes its address. Finally, the address is converted to an unsigned integer as the offset of the element. An example implementation of this macro is given here:

```
#define offsetof(structName,memberName)\
    ((u32)(&((structName*)0)->memberName))
```

The `sizeof` operator is a standard operator in C++. It returns the size of its parameter, in bytes. If passed a structure, it returns the size of the structure. If passed a pointer to a structure, it returns the size of a pointer.

Declaring a save template for an object is made a little easier by using these features, but it is still far from painless. There is also another pitfall with this method: if we want to increase the amount of data stored in each `SAVERECORD`, we would need to alter every record in every template so far constructed. Obviously, we need a better way to declare a template. Let's look at a simple example:

```
class ExObj1
{
public:
    const static SAVERECORD ExObj1_saveTemplate[];

private:
    Object      *nextObject;
    u32         objID;
    const char  *objName;
    f32         matrix[4][4];
};

const SAVERECORD ExObj1::ExObj1_saveTemplate[] =
{
    {
        ST_Pointer,
        offsetof(ExObj1,nextObject),
        sizeof(ExObj1::nextObject)
    }, {
        ST_Passive,
        offsetof(ExObj1,objID),
```

```
            sizeof(ExObj1::objID)
        }, {
            ST_Pointer,
            offsetof(ExObj1,objName),
            sizeof(ExObj1::objName)
        }, {
            ST_Passive,
            offsetof(ExObj1,matrix),
            sizeof(ExObj1::matrix)
        }, {
            ST_EndOfTemplate, 0, 0
        }
    };
```

The first part of this example declares a class of object called `ExObj1`, which has four private member variables. Notice that we declare the save template for this class as part of the class. Doing this allows us to access the private and protected data members of the class inside the template definition. If the template were not part of the class, we would get a compiler error for the template entries that refer to nonpublic data members. Notice also that the save template is declared as both `const` and `static` to protect it against overwriting and to ensure that there is only one instantiation of the template data for each class.

Examining the template definition, we can easily see that there is a lot of repetition involved in the declaration. Each entry in the template varies only by type and class and member variable name. This kind of thing has macro written all over it. We could write a single macro with three parameters—the data type, class name, and member variable name—but the `SAVETYPE` enum values are rather longwinded to be typing multiple times. Instead, we'll make two macros taking two parameters each—one macro for each type of data. Additionally, we will declare a macro for the end of template entry to make it just as easy to use.

```
#define SAVEDATA(obj,member)\
    { ST_Passive, offsetof(obj,member), sizeof(obj::member) }
```

```
#define SAVEPTR(obj,member)\
    { ST_Pointer, offsetof(obj,member), sizeof(obj::member) }

#define SAVEEND()\
    { ST_EndOfTemplate, 0, 0 }
```

Using these macros makes the definition of the template easier and less error-prone, and makes the template a lot easier on the eyes. Take a look for yourself:

```
const SAVERECORD ExObj1::ExObj1_saveTemplate[] =
{
    SAVEPTR  (ExObj1,nextObject),
    SAVEDATA (ExObj1,objID),
    SAVEPTR  (ExObj1,objName),
    SAVEDATA (ExObj1,matrix),
    SAVEEND  ()
};
```

Although an object's member variables can be declared in any order in the save template, it is often a good idea to keep them in the order in which they are declared in the class definition. This helps us to more easily compare the two when we find that there are one or more elements missing that need to be saved. Note also that we only need to declare member variables that we need to save in an object's save template; anything whose value never changes from the default, or that is recalculated every frame does not need to be saved and so should not be defined in the template.

Dealing with Inheritance

So far, we've defined a way to create a save template for a class of object. This template can refer to any variable within that object without worrying about its accessibility due to it being private or protected. However, what happens when the class we want to declare the template for is derived from another class that contains private member variables? The template for the new class cannot access the private members of its parent class, so we can't just declare the template as before.

However, there is no such restriction on the parent class; it can access its own private members with impunity. One solution, therefore, is to use the parent class's name in the macros when accessing its members in the derived class's save template. This presumes that a pointer to the derived class can be safely cast to a pointer to the parent class, but this is usually the case for a simple hierarchy of classes.

This method seems like a good one until we realize that, more probably than not, we will have to declare a complete save template for the parent class elsewhere in the code. This is repetition at its worst: if any data members are added or removed from the parent class, they must be inserted or deleted in multiple save templates. Obviously, we must find another way if the save system is to be at all practical to maintain.

Luckily, we already have the solution in hand, since we have already declared a full save template for the parent class elsewhere. We'll simply add an entry to the SAVETYPE enum (ST_Class) to direct the save system to use another template before continuing in the current one. Doing this requires also that we add another parameter to the SAVERECORD structure to hold the pointer to the save template to use, but this is trivial now that we define all of our SAVERECORD entries via macros. We define the following two macros to save the base class for the current class and an arbitrary member variable that is a class or structure, respectively:

```
#define SAVEBASE(baseClassName,baseClassTemplate)\
    {   ST_Class, 0,\
        sizeof(baseClassName), baseClassName::baseClassTemplate }

#define SAVESTRUCT(objName,structName,structTemplate)\
    {   ST_Class, offsetof(objName,structName),\
        sizeof(objName::structName), structName::structTemplate }
```

These macros are basically the same; the only real difference is that the base class is presumed to be at offset zero from the derived class. Notice also the use of the new fourth element that we added to the SAVERECORD structure. The previously defined macros should also be altered to include this element, but they should all use 0 for its value.

Now that we can tell the save system about a parent class, let's look at another example. This time, we'll declare a class, ExObj2, which is derived from our previously defined ExObj1.

```
Class ExObj2 : public ExObj1
{
public:
    const static SAVERECORD ExObj2_saveTemplate[];

private:
    float   velocity[4];
    u32     health;
    u32     maxHealth;
};

const SAVERECORD ExObj2::ExObj2_saveTemplate[] =
{
    SAVEBASE (ExObj1,ExObj1_saveTemplate),
    SAVEDATA (ExObj2,velocity),
    SAVEDATA (ExObj2,health),
    SAVEDATA (ExObj2,maxHealth),
    SAVEEND  ()
};
```

Looking at the save template for this class, the first thing we see is the SAVEBASE macro. This tells the parsing function that it should save the data at offset 0 from the current object using the ExObj1_saveTemplate template before continuing with the current template. This allows us to quickly construct a complete set of save templates for our entire class hierarchy without any duplication of template definitions.

Unfortunately, now that we have a little inheritance thrown in the works, it is not a simple task to retrieve the save template for a given object. To solve this, we'll add a little inheritance of our own.

THE SAVEOBJECT CLASS

Each object that we want to save needs to support a certain set of functionality. This implies that every savable object should be derived from a class that defines this functionality. We will call this class the SAVEOBJECT class, since it is the base class for all objects that can be saved. The first thing we need to do is to define the functionality that we require from the SAVEOBJECT class.

At the simplest level, we need to be able to retrieve an object's save template without knowing its exact type. This can be achieved through a simple virtual query function. Since every object needs to define a template for itself, we will declare this function as pure virtual, forcing at least the first level of derived objects to implement it. This function could be written for our ExObj2 class like this:

```
const SAVERECORD *ExObj2::GetSaveTemplate()
{
    return ExObj2_saveTemplate;
}
```

During loading, we need to recreate each object and load its data into the correct member variables. We already know how to load the object's data using the save template, but before we can do this we must first create an object of the correct type. Unfortunately, this is not as simple as reserving an area of memory that is the correct size for the object. Each object also needs a virtual function table to be initialized for it, and the easiest way to do this is to use the new operator with the correct object type. Therefore, we need some way to declare which type of object should be created for a given template. The simplest way to do this is to define an ID for each class of object, and to implement a large switch statement to create an object of the correct type for the given ID. In order to implement this, each class of savable objects must be able to return this ID so that we can save it out. Again, for the base SAVEOBJECT class, this ID would have no meaning, so we declare it as a pure virtual function.

Although conceptually there should be a single ID for each type of class in your game, there is certainly nothing stopping us from imparting extra information in this ID. Since this ID is simply a 32-bit number, we could encode other things in it that would allow us to instantiate the object with more than just the default parameters.

Finally, we need the class to provide the basic functionality for saving and loading itself. Each derived class can then override this as necessary to store any additional data that cannot be easily represented by the template. These functions should have a default implementation that is sufficient for most basic object types, allowing us to get away with the minimum of work when defining a new savable class.

```
class SAVEOBJECT
{
public:
    virtual const SAVERECORD *GetSaveTemplate() = 0;
    virtual u32               GetSaveID() = 0;

    virtual void              PreSave( SAVEFILE *pFile );
    virtual void              Save( SAVEFILE *pFile );
    virtual void              PreLoad( SAVEFILE *pFile );
    virtual void              Load( SAVEFILE *pFile );
};
```

From the preceding preliminary definition of the SAVEOBJECT class, we can see that the PreSave, Save, PreLoad, and Load functions take as a parameter a pointer to an as-yet undefined SAVEFILE class. This class represents the file that the game state is being streamed to, and is responsible for providing the functionality to process a saved game template, and to read and write data to the file. Given that the SAVEFILE class implements functions for saving and loading a template, then a possible implementation for SAVEOBJECT::Save can be written as:

```
void SAVEOBJECT::Save( SAVEFILE *pFile )
{
    assert(pFile!=0);
    pFile->SaveTemplate(this,GetSaveTemplate());
}
```

The default PreSave, PreLoad, and Load functions are implemented in a similar manner. When overriding these functions, it is important that the new implementation call the parent class's implementation as the first thing it does. This allows any functionality for the parent class's saving functions to still be properly executed. Additionally, by creating a complete call chain that goes all the way back to the SAVEOBJECT base class's implementation of these functions, we never need to worry about saving the template for each derived object; it just happens automatically.

The Save and Load functions are called by the save system when it wants to save or load an object, respectively. The PreSave and PreLoad functions, which will be described in more detail later, give each object a chance to declare any memory blocks that it owns prior to being saved or loaded.

SAVING AND LOADING A GAME

Now that we have defined how we are going to save the data for our objects, we need to decide how to collate these sets of data into a single file. We already introduced the concept of a SAVEFILE class in the previous section, and in this section we will expand upon its duties and responsibilities.

In addition to the data for each savable object, every saved game file needs to include certain other types of data. The first, and probably the most important, extra piece of data is an identifier representing the version number of the save system. This should be the first thing in the save file, and is used to make sure the save system can actually load the file before attempting to do so. Ideally, this identifier should be derived not only from a simple version number, but also from all of the object templates that contribute to the system. If an object's template changes, we will probably throw the file reads out of alignment when we read one item too few or too many for a given object, causing a probable crash.

The save file also needs a game-specific header. The contents of this header varies by game, but generally includes the name of the level that the game is saved on and an identifier of some sort for the level so we can see if it has changed since the game was saved. Many games also include a thumbnail-sized screenshot of the game at the point it was saved in this header and a summary of the game state. The header should be located as early as possible within the file so that its contents can be read and displayed as a summary for the user when selecting a saved game to load.

The process of saving a game can then be broken down into the following steps:

1. Open the file for writing.
2. Write the save game version identifier.
3. Allow the client program to write any arbitrary data (i.e., the header).
4. Declare all of the memory blocks that can be pointed into.
5. Declare all of the savable objects.
6. Use these objects' save templates to write them to the file.
7. Close the file.

Steps 1, 2, 6, and 7 can all be handled within the saved game system, since they remain the same across all iterations, whereas steps 3, 4, and 5 are the responsibility of the client program because they involve in-depth knowledge of the client game. Similarly, the process of loading a game can be broken down like so:

1. Open the file for reading.
2. Check the save game version against the one in the file.
3. Read and validate the header and any other game-specific data.

4. Load the relevant level, suppressing the creation of objects (since we will soon be loading them).
5. Declare all of the memory blocks that can be pointed into.
6. Read all of the objects from the file and create them.
7. Close the file.

Notice that when loading we have an extra step before we declare the accessible memory blocks: we must load the level that the game was saved on. This must be done before declaring the accessible memory blocks, since many of the memory blocks that we need to declare will probably be part of the level data. When loading the level, we must refrain from instantiating any objects that would have been saved in the save file. If we accidentally create an object while loading the level that is later defined in the save file, we will probably end up with two copies of the same object when gameplay resumes.

File Management

The first duty for the save game system that we must define is that of managing access to the saved game file. The functions for saving data to and loading data from the save file must be exposed so that the client game can use them to write its game-specific data. Although we could let the game supply a file pointer and make the saved game class direct all its file accesses through this, we retain more control and gain flexibility by letting the save game class abstract the file access.

Declaring Memory Blocks

When declaring the memory blocks during the loading of a game, care must be taken to make sure that the memory blocks are declared in the same order in which they were saved. Failure to do this will result in incorrectly restored pointers, as described earlier. This is such an important point that we will take measures to ensure that the memory blocks are declared correctly when loading the game. As memory blocks are added, we can construct a hash based on the size of each memory block and its index. This hash can be saved out before writing the object data, and then on loading we can compare the newly calculated hash with the one in the file. If the two hashes are not identical, then there is a problem in the code somewhere because the memory blocks have been defined differently between saving and loading, and we can refuse to load the file.

Since each savable object can be pointed to, they must each appear in the memory block list for the save file. We can take some of the burden off of the game by making the save system automatically add a memory block for each savable object as it is added. However, when loading the game we do not have immediate access to the list of objects to create the memory blocks for them, but we need the list of memory blocks to be completed before we load the objects. How can we solve this chicken-and-egg dilemma?

The simplest way is to separate the information needed to create each object from the information needed to restore its state. That's a fancy way of saying that we save each object's type into a single list before we save the data for any of them. This allows us to create all of the objects during loading and declare the memory blocks for them *before* we need to use those memory blocks to restore any pointers. This adds a limitation to our declaration of memory blocks: all of the memory blocks that do not correspond to savable objects (and that are not declared inside a savable object) must be declared before the memory blocks for any of the savable objects. To see why this is so, let's look at a revised version of the steps required to load a game:

1. Open the file for reading.
2. Check the save game version against the one in the file.
3. Read and validate the header and any other game-specific data.
4. Load the relevant level, suppressing the creation of objects.
5. Declare all of the memory blocks that can be pointed into.
6. Read all of the object types from the file and create the objects.
7. Compare the memory block hash against the one in the file.
8. Read the data for each object created from the file according to its template.
9. Close the file.

Notice that the object creation has now been split into three stages. The first of these is to read the object types from the file and to create a series of objects of the correct type. These objects will just contain the default values for the relevant object type. While doing this, we also add the memory blocks for each of the objects, completing the memory block list that we started in step 5. Next, we check the hash representing the memory block order with the hash stored in the file to make sure we have the memory blocks in the correct order. Once we have determined that everything is in order, we can load the state of each of the objects we created according to their respective save templates.

Failure to declare all of the nonobject memory blocks before adding any objects during the save process breaks the separation in memory block types that is enforced during the loading process, causing the game to restore incorrectly.

Declaring Savable Objects

After declaring all of the memory blocks to the save game system during the save process, we must then declare the savable objects. This is simply a matter of iterating through all of the objects in the game and making a function call for each object that needs to be saved. As stated earlier, each savable object needs to also be declared as a memory block so that any pointers pointing into it can be saved and restored properly, but this is automatically handled when a savable object is declared to the system. However, even without the burden of declaring each object as a memory block in addition to declaring it as a savable object, this can be a rather large and onerous task. Luckily, it is also one that we can automate away.

Games generally store objects in linked lists of some description. This means that, more often than not, the objects of a game form a single interconnected graph. We already know where all the pointers are in each of the objects, since we have to restore them later. If we can declare these pointers in the each object's save template as pointers to savable objects, rather than just pointers to data, then we can make the template handler automatically add the target of these pointers as a new savable object. Using this method, we can add every object that needs to be saved by adding a single object!

To accomplish this, we need to declare a new `SAVETYPE` (`ST_SaveObject`) and a new macro so that we can define pointers that specifically point to savable objects. The following macro accomplishes this task:

```
#define SAVEPOBJ(obj,member)\
```

```
{ ST_SaveObject, offsetof(obj,member), sizeof(obj::member), 0 }
```

Using this new macro, the save template for our first example object then becomes:

```
const SAVERECORD ExObj1::ExObj1_saveTemplate[] =
{
    SAVEPOBJ (ExObj1,nextObject),
    SAVEDATA (ExObj1,objID),
    SAVEPTR  (ExObj1,objName),
    SAVEDATA (ExObj1,matrix),
    SAVEEND  ()
};
```

Notice that in the preceding template, only the first pointer is declared using the new macro. This is because only the first pointer points to an object that is derived from the `SAVEOBJECT` class.

To successfully process these new macros, the save system must do additional work before starting to save or load the game. For every `SAVEOBJECT` declared to it, the save system must call either the `SAVEOBJECT`'s `PreSave` (if saving the game) or `PreLoad` (if loading the game) functions. These in turn call back into the save system to process their save templates. While saving, this can cause new objects to be declared; these will be appended to the list of savable objects and will in turn be processed before the pre-save finishes. Object dependant memory blocks can also be declared during this process, however, these memory blocks *must* be declared independent of the state of the object. This is because, during the pre-load sequence when the memory blocks are declared, all of the newly created savable objects will still be in their default states.

THE `SAVEFILE` CLASS

Now that we have defined the main responsibilities of the save system, we can design a class to meet them. The responsibilities that we have defined for the system so far are:

- Open and close the saved game file.
- Manage all reading and writing to the saved game file.
- Maintain a list of client-defined memory blocks.
- Maintain a list of client-defined savable objects.
- Verify that the memory blocks have been declared correctly (loading only).
- Process the list of savable objects using their save templates.
- Use knowledge of the save template to automatically declare linked savable objects (saving only).

The responsibilities of the client game in this instance are:

- Create the saved game header (saving only).
- Read and write the saved game header.
- Verify that the saved game header is valid (loading only).
- Load the correct level (loading only).
- Declare the required memory blocks in order.
- Declare enough savable objects that the save system can find every savable object (saving only).

Given this division of responsibilities, we can define the interface to the SAVEFILE class like this:

```
class SAVEFILE
{
public:
    SAVEFILE();
    virtual ~SAVEFILE();

    // opening and closing the file
    SAVEERROR   Begin( const char *filename, bool loading=false );
    SAVEERROR   End( SAVEERROR returnThisError=SAVEERR_OK );

    // reading and writing data to the file
    SAVEERROR   GetData( void *pData, u32 length );
```

```
    SAVEERROR   PutData( const void *pData, u32 length );

    // declaring memory blocks
    u32         DeclareMemoryBlock( const void *pBlock, u32 length );

    // declaring savable objects
    u32         DeclareSaveObject( SAVEOBJECT *pObj );

    // process the declared objects
    SAVEERROR   ProcessObjects();

    // manipulate templates
    void        PreSaveTemplate( const void *base,
                                 const SAVERECORD *pTemplate );

    void        SaveTemplate(    const void *base,
                                 const SAVERECORD *pTemplate );

    void        PreLoadTemplate( void *base,
                                 const SAVERECORD *pTemplate );

    void        LoadTemplate(    void *base,
                                 const SAVERECORD *pTemplate );

    // Create an object from a given saveID.
    // This must be implemented on a per-game basis.
    virtual SAVEOBJECT *CreateObject( u32 saveID ) = 0;
};
```

Notice that this class does not define simple functions for saving and loading a game, or loading the header from a saved game file. This is because the implementation of these functions is heavily game-dependant; the SAVEFILE class cannot be expected to know where your game's memory blocks are located, or how to find even one object that must be saved.

Game-Specific Implementation

A typical game that used this save system would derive a class from `SAVEFILE` and implement the save and load game functions within this class. Such a derived class is shown here:

```
class MYSAVEFILE : public SAVEFILE
{
public:
    SAVEERROR  SaveGame( const char *filename );
    SAVEERROR  LoadGame( const char *filename );
    SAVEERROR  LoadHeader( const char *filename, SAVEGAMEHEADER *out );

    // We must implement the CreateObject member.
    SAVEOBJECT *CreateObject( u32 saveID );
};
```

The implementation of these functions, although game dependent, generally goes through the same steps. A sample implementation for the `SaveGame` function could be written like this:

```
SAVEERROR MYSAVEFILE::SaveGame( const char *filename )
{
    SAVEERROR retval;

    // the first thing to do is Begin a SAVEFILE saving session
    retval = Begin(filename,false);
    if( retval==SAVEERR_OK )
    {
        // TODO: fill out a game-specific saved game header structure
        SAVEGAMEHEADER header;

        // write the header to the file
        PutData(&header,sizeof(header));
```

```
        // TODO: write any extra header data needed here

        // TODO: declare any memory blocks that may be used
        DeclareMemoryBlock(pLevelData,levelDataSize);

        // TODO: declare enough objects so that every object
        //       that you want to save can be found by following
        //       links within previous objects
        DeclareSaveObject(rootGameObject);

        // now process the objects
        // This calls PreSave for all objects to declare their memory
        // It then calls Save for all objects to write their data
        retval = ProcessObjects();
    }
    return End(retval);
}
```

After opening a saved game file via the `SAVEFILE::Begin` member function, the first thing that the `SaveGame` function does is create a header containing a summary of the game in progress. This header should include, at the very least, enough information to be able to reload the level that the game was saved on. After writing this header to the save file, we can then write any other data that we might want to appear in the save file, such as a thumbnail screen shot of the point where the game was saved.

Next, we declare all of the memory blocks that might be the destination of a pointer in an object that we want to save. In the given example implementation, a single memory block is defined; typically, a game will declare many more blocks than this. After the memory blocks have been declared, we need to declare the objects that we want saved. Although we do not have to declare every object currently instantiated in the game, we need to declare enough of them that the system can find every savable object by following object pointers declared in the templates.

Once all of the memory blocks and savable objects have been declared, the `SaveGame` function calls the `SAVEFILE::ProcessObjects` function, which causes all of the declared objects to be written to disk. Finally, we call `SAVEFILE::End` to close the saved game file.

Similarly, the implementation of `LoadGame` could be written like this:

```
SAVEERROR MYSAVEFILE::LoadGame( const char *filename )
{
    SAVEERROR retval;

    // the first thing to do is Begin a SAVEFILE loading session
    retval = Begin(filename,true);
    while( retval==SAVEERR_OK )
    {
        SAVEGAMEHEADER header;

        // Load the saved game header
        GetData(&header,sizeof(header));

        // TODO: check that the level has not changed
        if( GetLevelVersion(header.levelName)!=header.levelVersion )
        {
            retval = SAVEERR_LEVELCHANGED;
            break;
        }

        // TODO: read any extra header data needed here

        // TODO: load the level
        LoadLevel(header.levelName);

        // TODO: declare any memory blocks that may be used
        DeclareMemoryBlock(pLevelData,levelDataSize);

        // process the game objects: this loads them from the file.
```

```
            retval = ProcessObjects();
            break;
        }
        return End(retval);
    }
```

After opening the saved game file for reading, the LoadGame function first reads the saved game header. It then compares the version identifier of the level stored in the header with the version identifier of the same level on the hard drive. If these versions are different, then the level has changed and the game cannot be loaded. After reading the header and verifying the level version, we can then load (or skip) any other header data that we stored in the file.

The next step is to load the level that is indicated by the saved game header. Remember that, when loading this level, we must not instantiate any objects in it; these will be loaded and restored later. After successfully loading the level, we then declare any memory blocks that can be referenced by pointers. Care must be taken to ensure that these are declared in the same order in which they were declared during saving.

Once all of the memory blocks have been declared, we then call the ProcessObjects function to instantiate all of the saved objects (via our CreateObject function) and then restore their data. If we declared our memory blocks in a different order than the order in the saved game file, then ProcessObjects will return an error. Finally, calling the End function closes the saved game file.

Inside ProcessObjects

The bulk of the save system functionality occurs inside the SAVEFILE::ProcessObjects function, the behavior of which changes depending on whether the system is currently saving a game or loading one.

When saving a game, the first thing that this function does is iterate through all of the objects that have been declared to the system, declaring memory blocks for them and calling their PreSave functions. This causes each object to call back to the PreSaveTemplate function with a pointer to its template. Additionally, each object can at this point declare any additional memory blocks that it owns, as described earlier. The `PreSaveTemplate` function iterates through the object's save template and declares savable objects for the destination of any pointers declared with `ST_SaveObject`. Doing this appends the new savable objects to the end of the list, causing them to be pre-saved in turn. During the pre-save step, file writes are disabled; you cannot call `PutData` from within an object's `PreSave` function.

Once all of the objects have been pre-saved, we must then write all of their save IDs to the save file, preceded by the total number of savable objects. This allows the load system to recreate objects of the correct type prior to restoring their data. After all of the object save IDs have been written out, a hash is calculated based on the size and index of each declared memory block. This hash is then written to the save file. The hash allows the load system to ensure that the memory blocks declared to it are the same size and in the same order as they were during the save process.

Finally, the save system again iterates through all of the savable objects, this time calling their `Save` functions. This function calls back to the `SaveTemplate` function, causing the object to be saved according to its template. Additionally, any object can also write arbitrary data into the save file during its `Save` function. This allows the object to save any data that cannot be described by the template (e.g., any data for a third-party library, such as a physics system, that is not mirrored inside the object and so must be queried at save-time). Care must be taken during loading to read back all of the additional data in the correct sequence. Failure to do so can misalign any future data reads, causing objects to have their state restored incorrectly.

When loading a game, however, the `ProcessObjects` function behaves slightly differently. The pre-load sequence first reads the number of savable objects from the file—this is the first thing that the save path wrote to disk. Then, for each savable object, a save ID is read from the file, and the game-implemented `CreateObject` function is called, causing a new object of the correct type to be instantiated. This object first has a memory block declared for it and then has its `PreLoad` function invoked, which in turn calls the `SAVEFILE::PreLoadTemplate` function. The default implementation for this function is empty, since there is no work that needs to be done during pre-load for the default save element types. At this time, objects should also declare any memory blocks that they declared in their `PreSave` function. It should be noted that at this point the object has had none of its state restored; all of its variables will be in their default states. This means that any memory blocks declared here must be independent of the object's state.

Once all of the objects have been instantiated, all of the required memory blocks should finally have been declared. To check that they have been declared in the correct order, the save system now creates a hash for the declared memory blocks in the same way as during saving. This is then compared against the one stored in the file; if these are different, then the memory blocks have been declared wrongly and the load cannot continue.

Provided that the memory blocks have been declared correctly, the `ProcessObjects` function can now begin to restore the data for each of the savable objects. To do this, it iterates through all of the declared savable objects, calling their `Load` functions. This function in turn calls the `SAVEFILE::LoadTemplate` function, which restores the data members declared in the object's save template. An object's `Load` function must also read back from the file any data that it stored manually.

Once all of the objects have been processed, the final thing that the save system has to do is to clear the lists of memory blocks and savable objects. This is done regardless of whether the game is being saved or loaded. This allows multiple sets of memory blocks and savable objects to be saved in a single file, with user-defined data in between.

PROCESSING A SAVE TEMPLATE

In the preceding sections, we referred to the automatic processing of an object's save template many times, but never described how this is achieved. Although there are four basic functions for processing templates, they all operate in a similar fashion. They each take as parameters a pointer to the base address of an object and a pointer to that object's save template. They each iterate through the entirety of the save template and locate the correct member variables in the same way. The only real difference between these functions is how they process the individual member variables.

Let's start with what each of the template processing functions has in common: the location of the savable member variables. Actually, this is relatively simple; we just add the offset member of the save record to the base address of the object; voilà, we have a pointer to the member variable. For example, the `SaveTemplate` function could be partially implemented like this:

```
void SAVEFILE::SaveTemplate( const void *base,
                             const SAVERECORD *pTemplate )
{
    void *pVar;

    // iterate through the template entries
    for( ;pTemplate->type!=ST_EndOfTemplate;pTemplate++ )
    {
        // locate the current variable
        pVar = (void*)(((char*)base)+pTemplate->offset);

        // now do something with this
        switch( pTemplate->type )
        {
        }
    }
}
```

The two simplest types of data to process are `ST_Passive` and `ST_Class`, respectively. Passive data need only be processed in the `SaveTemplate` and `LoadTemplate` functions, and all that needs to be done in these cases is to read or write the appropriate amount of data (defined in `pTemplate->length`) to the save file. To process an item of type `ST_Class`, we simply recursively call the same function with the given template and the newly calculated base address.

It should be noted here that the `pVar` variable points to the address of the variable. This should be taken into account when de-referencing it. If `pVar` were to point at a floating-point number, we would cast it to a `(float*)` before reading the value. Similarly, if `pVar` points to a pointer to a floating-point number, we would need to cast it to a `(float**)` before using it.

When processing an item of type `ST_SaveObject`, the `SaveTemplate` function simply finds the index of the save object in the list of declared savable objects and writes this out in place of the actual pointer (these indices start at 1, with 0 being reserved to represent a `null` pointer). If the object pointer is non-`null` but does not occur in the list of savable objects then the given pointer cannot be saved. The `LoadTemplate` function then reads this index from the file and uses it to locate the correct object pointer. Finally, the `PreSaveTemplate` function declares a new savable object using this pointer; in this way, the save system can find all linked savable objects.

Finally, when saving items of type `ST_Pointer`, we must locate the memory block that the pointer points into, and write out both the index of this memory block and the offset of the destination of the pointer within it. Again, an index of 0 is used to represent `null`-pointers (we can omit saving the offset in this case). When loading a pointer, we must first locate the correct memory block using the saved index, and then use the saved offset to find the correct address.

AUTO-DETECTING OBJECT CHANGES

Although we have created a robust and automated saved game system, we have still not addressed any of the issues that we started with. Our biggest problem occurs when the member variables change inside our savable objects, causing the templates to become out of date. Unless the save templates are meticulously updated each time a member variable is added to a savable object (removing a saved variable will cause a compile error), our save templates will quickly become horribly out of date.

Wouldn't it be great if the save system could see a *hole* appear in a save template where a newly added member variable appears? It could then report that hole via a debug output channel to the programming team. The programming team could then find the missing variable and add it to the correct save template, and everything would be right with the world again. This is not as far-fetched as it would first appear. The save templates for each savable object already contain an entry for every member variable whose value we need to save. The only problem is that because some variables that we do not have to save are missing, the template already has holes in it. However, addressing this is as simple as defining another macro to use for variables that we don't want to save, like so:

```
#define DONTSAVE(objname,member)\
    {   ST_Skip, offsetof(objname,member),\
        sizeof(objname::member), 0 }
```

By using this macro to declare all of the member variables that we would otherwise omit, we create a template with no holes in it. Then, when a new member variable is added to a savable object but not to its template, the save system will see a hole in the template, and can report it as a missing variable. However, how do we detect a hole in the save template? There is no requirement that the member variables be declared in a specific order, so we cannot simply check that there is no gap between consecutive SAVERECORDS. Even if there were such a requirement, how would we detect that a variable has been added to the *end* of an object's memory?

The answer to these questions is surprisingly simple and low-tech. If we can find the size of the object to which the template applies, we can allocate an area of memory that is the same size as this object and set every byte of it to zero. We can then parse through the save template, setting the bytes in this memory corresponding to each variable with 1. Once the template has ended, we can then scan through this memory; any zeros remaining correspond to variables that have not been declared and need to be reported as such. To implement this, we need to define yet another macro to describe a single SAVERECORD. This macro, which *must* be the first thing declared in every save template, defines the size of the class.

```
#define SAVEDEF(className)\
    { ST_ClassName, 0, sizeof(className), 0 }
```

Although this is a nice feature, the available information about the missing variable leaves something to be desired. All we can report back to the programmers is the class that the variable has been added to, the offset in bytes of the variable from the start of the class, and the size of the variable. This increases the time required to locate the missing variable. There must be some way that we can provide extra information about the missing variable.

Actually, we can easily locate the variable declared in the template that is nearest to the hole. The macro declaring this variable already contains the variable's name and the class's name. If we simply change the definition of the SAVERECORD to also include a text string describing the variable, we can use the description of the nearest variable in our error message. This allows the programmers to more easily locate the missing variable and add it to the template. A new version of the SAVEDATA macro that defines this string would look like this:

```
#define SAVEDATA(obj,member)\
    {   ST_Passive, offsetof(obj,member),\
        sizeof(obj::member), 0, #member }
```

If we alter all of our macros in a similar way, we can construct an informative message every time we find a hole in a save template. An example error message constructed in this way could be "Missing 4 bytes in class ExObj1 after matrix." As you can see, this is much more informative than "Missing 4 bytes at offset 32."

The only question left to answer is when we actually do this check. We could do it at save time, but then we would only check the save templates for objects that occur in the saved game. Even worse, we could check each template multiple times, depending on how many objects there are of each savable class. What we really want to do is check every template just once, right when the save system is created. To do this, the save system needs to know about every save template ahead of time. The simplest way to do this is to declare all of the templates in a static list that the save system can iterate through. The declaration of this list for our example classes would look something like this:

```
const SAVERECORD **SAVEFILE::templateList[] =
{
    ExObj1::Exobj1_saveTemplate,
    ExObj2::Exobj2_saveTemplate,
    0    // the 0 signifies the end of the list.
};
```

IMPLEMENTATION

ON THE CD

A sample implementation of the `SAVEFILE` *class can be found on the companion CD-ROM, in the common/savegame folder. This implementation uses the previously defined* `XFile` *class (see Chapter 5) to handle its file operations, resulting in a compressed saved game file.*

Although this is a complete implementation of the save system, extra code is needed to actually use it in a given game. A simple example using a couple of different savable classes is also provided, in the chapter8/simpleGame folder.

FURTHER READING

An earlier iteration of this save game system can be found in:

[GEMS3] Treglia, Dante, *Game Programming Gems 3*, Charles River Media, 2002.

9 Optimization

In This Chapter

- Rule #9: "Measure Twice, Cut Once"
- First Measure: Where
- Second Measure: Why
- Making the Cut
- Final Measure: Results

Since the very beginning, computer games have not just been about fun; the most prestigious games were also about amazing the players with what their computers could do. With each new game that came out, the programmers had found new ways to push the computer to its limits, pulling off feats that were previously considered impossible.

A good example of this was achieved on the Atari ST, with its lowly 16-color, low-resolution TV-bound display. The accessible portion of the display was surrounded by a large and inaccessible border, ensuring that every pixel in the display would be visible on even the poorest TV set. Programmers found that by changing the refresh rate of the video hardware at *exactly* the right moment, they could enlarge the accessible area of the screen, producing an overscan effect. The first implementations of this technique merely extended the top and bottom of the screen to the edges of the display, but as the technique was refined, they soon learned how to increase the accessible area to encompass the left and right edges of the screen also.

To accomplish this, the programmers of the day had to know the timings of the instructions that they used down to the cycle level. This allowed them to change hardware register values at exactly the right time to achieve the desired effect. A cycle off to either side would produce a gap in the display or cause the entire effect to break down. This is optimization to a ridiculous degree, encompassing every line of the code to get the timings exactly right.

Modern games, though, have become much larger. It is not uncommon for the compiled code for a game to be over 2MB in size, encompassing hundreds of source files, each of which is hundreds of lines in length. Optimizing every single function in this mass of code would be a sisyphean task. Instead, our optimization efforts must be focused where they really matter.

RULE #9: "MEASURE TWICE, CUT ONCE"

Carpenters have been using this saying for hundreds of years. When mistakes cannot be rectified—an incorrectly cut piece of wood cannot be re-joined seamlessly—it is best to be certain that you are about to cut in the right place. It is therefore important that the noncritical step be performed multiple times to ensure that the step that cannot be undone is correct. A single cut in the wrong place wastes time (you have to go and find a new piece of wood), material, and money.

In the realm of computer programming, there is rarely a step that cannot be undone. However, with a slight modification, this maxim still applies. Although as programmers we do not consume material, we do consume time, and hence, money. Optimizing a module or function can be a very time-consuming task, much more so than determining which module requires optimization. The act of optimization, then, becomes our cut; optimizing the wrong piece of code consumes time and money without giving us the results we need.

FIRST MEASURE: WHERE

With the size of a modern game, and the sheer amount of source code that comprises it, we need a way to focus our optimizations where they will really matter. It does us no good to blindly optimize a section of code that hardly takes any time to execute; even if we optimize it so well that it takes no time at all, the net improvement in the overall speed of the game will be negligible. Instead, we must concentrate our efforts on sections of code that the CPU spends longer executing. It is in these sections of code that our optimization efforts will provide the largest improvements in the overall speed of the game.

The first measure that we must make, therefore, determines where our program spends the bulk of its time. The results of this measurement must obviously change based on the things happening in the game at the time that the measure is taken. Because of this, it is a good idea to arrange some sort of test that stresses the areas of the game code that you want to concentrate on. These areas can either be selected through previous measures or instinct (e.g., you might know that the collision routines are going to need some optimization work before you start measuring). However the areas to concentrate on are decided, the test should be repeatable more or less exactly so that any results can be verified and the efficacy of any optimizations made can be measured.

Units of Measurement

Before we look at ways to take our first measurement, we must first understand how we are going to present any measurements taken. In simpler times, before the advent of the PC as we know it, computers of the same type were identical. Assembly language instructions always took the same amount of time to execute. In short, things were predictable. This predictability allowed us to count cycles and compare results from two different machines with impunity.

The modern PC changed all that. Now, two similar machines can have very different specifications and performance characteristics. Even two PCs with the same speed CPU can differ in performance depending on the speed of the attached memory and how much cache it has. Additionally, modern CPU architecture—with its micro-code, instruction schedulers, and branch prediction—makes cycle-level timings impossible to take; the speed that a function executes at depends on the context that it is run in.

In short, then, although we can measure the time taken by each function, these measurements cannot be compared *as is* when taken on two different machines (in some cases, even two sets of measurements taken on one machine are incomparable). We need a more reliable measurement of the time taken by a function—one that is not so prone to fluctuation.

The answer is simple: instead of using the time taken for each function, we will use the ratio of the time taken to the total time measured, expressed as a percentage. Any fluctuations based on the speed of the processor will express themselves across all of the timings, leaving the fractions essentially unchanged. Other fluctuations, based on changes in branch prediction or instruction scheduling, are more problematic, but *should* be distributed more or less equally across all of the timings, again leaving the fractions essentially unchanged.

The total time measured can be defined in two distinct ways (more ways are possible, but are unlikely to prove useful), producing differing results. The first is simply the total time taken by the run. This spans multiple frames and also possibly multiple different modes of behavior for the game. Any fluctuations in function duration based on the changing game situation during the run will be smoothed out, rendering the method of measurement less effective for reducing periodic bottlenecks.

The second (and most useful) way to measure the total time is to simply use the total time taken for each frame. As each frame begins, each function's timings are cleared, and as it ends, the fractional timings are calculated. This method allows us to track local fluctuations in the time taken for a function as the game state changes. It also allows us to track minimum, maximum, and average percentage times for each of the functions called.

External Profilers

The first measure can be taken in several ways. The easiest is to use an external profiler—for example, Intel's VTune software—to pinpoint where the CPU spends its time. This technique requires no extra programming work to set up, and returns good results very quickly. Unfortunately, external profilers are generally limited to sampling an entire run of the game (although sometimes the start time of the sample taking can be delayed), with all of the pitfalls that this entails. Depending on the length of the run, a localized anomaly in the time taken by a function can be completely smoothed out by averaging, limiting the usefulness of the profiler.

Programs such as VTune work by frequently interrupting the application to be tested and recording the program counter register at the time of each interruption. While the program is running, VTune works happily in the background, recording these samples. When the program finally exits (either by user input or via VTune ending the program), VTune takes each of the recorded samples and uses the program's .map file (or other debug information) to find which function it belongs in. The result is an approximate map of where the program spent the bulk of its time, at the *function* level—the greater the number of samples that occur inside a given function, the longer the CPU must have spent in that function.

The accuracy of the results of such a program will always be slightly suspect. They rely on a delicate balance between the frequency of the samples and the speed at which the program runs. Although a faster sampling frequency will obviously return better results, catching more of the functions that execute quickly, the act of sampling the program counter is not instantaneous. This means that as the sampling frequency increases, the amount of time left for the sampled program to run between samples *decreases*, slowing the program being sampled. When the sampled program is running slower than usual, any frame rate compensation code present will kick in, possibly causing an atypical running situation as functions are called more often than usual or with larger time periods.

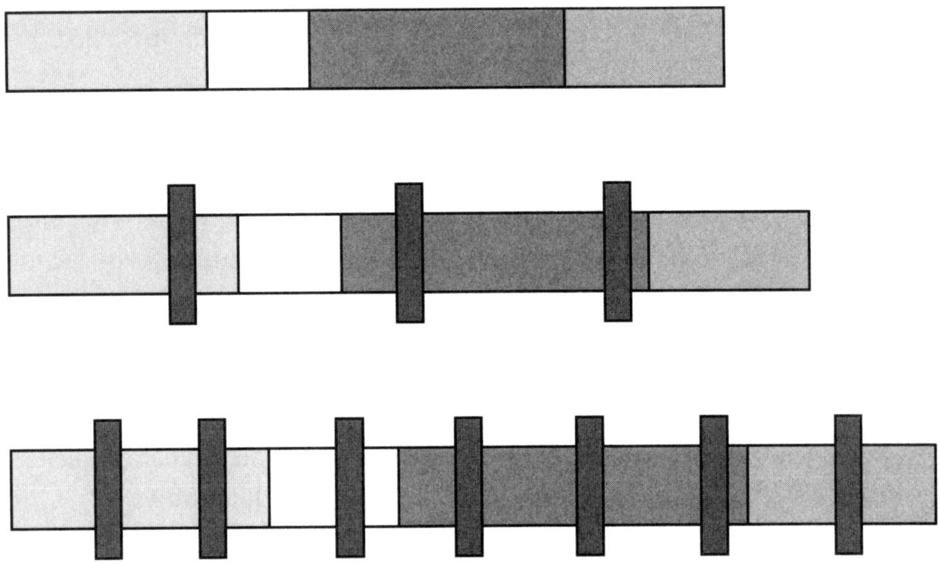

FIGURE 9.1 The effects of choosing different sampling frequencies.

Figure 9.1 illustrates this relationship. The topmost bar represents a run of a section of the game with no profiler present. Differently colored bar sections represent different functions in the code. The middle bar shows the effect of running the profiler with an initial value for the sampling frequency. A black bar inserted in the image represents each sample taken. Notice that each sample takes a discrete amount of time away from the main process, resulting in this run taking longer than the first one (represented by the second bar being longer). It should also be noted that the initial value chosen for the sampling frequency is too low, causing the white function to be completely missed by the profiler. The final bar shows the effect of increasing the sampling frequency enough to ensure that every function is sampled. This run takes significantly longer than the first, due to the additional time spent taking samples.

The result of an external profile run is generally a sorted list of functions and the number of times a sample occurred inside each one. Oftentimes, the profiler counts the total number of samples taken and uses this to calculate the percentage of the total running time spent inside each listed function. Sometimes the GUI for the profiler will allow us to look inside the functions to the source code and assembly levels and see which lines of code the individual samples were taken on.

However the results are displayed, though, they are lacking one important ingredient: context. Although we can see how many samples were taken inside an individual function, we know nothing about the circumstances under which the function was called (or indeed where the function call originated). At the very least, it would be nice to know how often a given function was called during the run. It would also be good to know the values (average, maximum, and minimum) of certain parameters to each function, particularly those controlling the number of times that loops are executed.

To get this context, the profiler needs to know more information than an external profiler can easily gather. The game code must be able to talk to the profiler to provide it with the contextual data that it needs. The best way to accomplish this is to implement a custom profiling class inside the game.

Internal Profilers

Internal profilers exist inside the game and so can be better informed as to its current actions. For example, internal profilers can easily be notified about the start and end of a frame, allowing them to perform frame-based profiling. Using an internal profiler requires a certain amount of setup time, however, and so results are not obtained as quickly as when using an external profiler.

The first thing we must do when creating an internal profiler is to get a fast and accurate way to retrieve a high-resolution timestamp. The actual timing units of the timestamp are unimportant (since we are using a unitless system of measurement), but it must have a high enough frequency so that even the shortest function call can report a nonzero time value. Two good examples of methods to retrieve a timestamp are the `QueryPerformanceCounter` function (from the Windows API) and the `rdtsc` assembly language opcode on x86 machines.

The `QueryPerformanceCounter` function takes as a parameter a pointer to a `LARGE_INTEGER` structure that receives the current value of the timer. A `LARGE_INTEGER` in this case is simply a 64-bit signed integer. The frequency of the timer returned by this function is so high that it can overflow a 32-bit integer in just a few seconds. This function is made available through the Windows API, and should work on any machine running Microsoft® Windows®.

The `rdtsc` assembly language function is available on most x86 compatible chips of Pentium or higher class. The mnemonic for the instruction stands for "ReaD Time Stamp Counter," which neatly describes what this instruction does. When this instruction is invoked, it returns the number of clock cycles since the CPU was powered up or reset in the `EDX` and `EAX` registers, with `EAX` containing the lower 32 bits of the timestamp and `EDX` the higher. The result is returned in two registers because, again, the frequency of this timer is so high that it would overflow a 32-bit register in just a few seconds.

Either of these two methods works great on any modern PC (even the Xbox). For other architectures, similar methods should exist, but might take more time to set up. For example, the PlayStation 2 has a user-configurable interrupt-driven counter that can be used as a timer.

The next thing we need to do is determine how our profiler will get its information. Although it should be possible to set up our internal profiler to work like an external one, sampling the program counter at a set frequency and finding out where in the code each sample lies, doing so defeats the purpose of using an internal profiler; we lose the context information.

Instead, we should move to an event-based profiler, where we are responsible for informing the profiler of certain events that it needs to know about. These events include entering and exiting a function that we want to profile, and starting and ending a frame. The time taken by a function is then represented by the difference between its entry time and its exit time, and similarly the time taken by a frame is the difference between the frame start time and the frame end time. Since a given function can be called multiple times during a frame, the function time must be calculated each time the function is exited, and a running total kept for all the invocations of each function during a frame. A possible function definition for such a profiler is shown in the following code:

```
class PROFILER
{
public:
    static void BeginFrame();
    static void EndFrame();
    static void BeginFn( const char *name );
    static void EndFn( const char *name );
};
```

Since it is undesirable to have the profiler running in all of the possible build configurations of the game (seldom if ever do we want profiling code in a shipping game), we need to have a way to quickly strip out any and all profiling code from a build. The easiest way to do this is by using macros whose implementation varies based on a preprocessor definition. The following code shows a possible implementation for such a series of macros:

```
#ifdef ENABLE_PROFILING

    #define PROFILEFNSTART(name)       PROFILER::BeginFn(name);
    #define PROFILEFNEND(name)         PROFILER::EndFn(name);
    #define PROFILEFRAMESTART()        PROFILER::BeginFrame();
    #define PROFILEFRAMEEND()          PROFILER::EndFrame();

#else

    #define PROFILEFNSTART(name)
    #define PROFILEFNEND(name)
    #define PROFILEFRAMESTART()
    #define PROFILEFRAMEEND()

#endif
```

Using an event-based profiler such as this puts a burden on the rest of the code; any function that needs to be profiled must inform the profiler when it is entered and exited. There are two main ways to do this; either each profiled function can include this code, or each invocation of a profiled function can include it.

When each profiled function is responsible for updating the profiler, we can be sure that every invocation of these functions will be recorded. Implementation of this method might cause some functions to be restructured, however, since errant `return` commands can cause the exit profiling event to be missed. Using this method, every profiled function will look something like this:

```
void profiledFn()
{
    PROFILEFNSTART("profiledFn");

    // actual function code here,
    // containing no return statements

    PROFILEFNEND("profileFn");
}
```

Putting the burden of the profiler's updating on the invocation of a profiled function gives us more flexibility for the internal structure of a function, at the cost of possibly missing some invocations. The easiest way to implement this type of profiling is through the use of macros; we can define a macro that takes the function call as a parameter and invokes this function call during its expansion. This leads to code similar to the following:

```
void someFn()
{
    // irrelevant code here

    // call our profiled function here using a macro
    PROFILEFN(profiledFn(),"profiledFn");
```

```
    // more irrelevant code here
}
```

The PROFILEFN macro can be defined in the following way:

```
#define PROFILEFN(fncall,name)\
    {\
        PROFILEFNSTART(name);\
        fncall;\
        PROFILEFNEND(name);\
    }
```

Unfortunately, one downfall of this method is that any result returned from the profiled function is lost. However, this can be somewhat circumvented by using an assignment statement as the function call macro parameter, assigning the result of the profiled function to a variable that can be read back later. The following code illustrates this:

```
void someFn()
{
    u32 result;

    // irrelevant code here

    // call our profiled function here using a macro
    PROFILEFN(result=profiledFn(),"profiledFn");

    // we can test the value of result here
    if( result!=0 )
    {
    }

    // more irrelevant code here
}
```

Using an event-based profiler in this way allows us to capture more of the context of each of the profiled functions. For example, we can now count how many times per frame each of our profiled functions is called. This allows us to easily pinpoint any atypical behavior that results in a function being called more times than expected. By adding another function to our profiler class, we can also record one or more values specific to each profiled function's invocation. This is very useful, since we can now pinpoint not only how many times a function was called, but also the number of things it was called with or other such value. A good example of this is a function used to transform a block of vertices by a matrix. If most of the time this function is called with a single vertex, then we should consider replacing this function with an inline implementation to transform a single vertex.

We still have to address what happens when a profiled function invokes another profiled function. There are two ways to go about this. In the first method, the first function's timer carries on running while the second function is executed. This can lead to the total time spent in all profiled functions being greater than 100 percent of the frame time and can be confusing. The second method relies on stopping the timer for the first function while the second function is running, and then restarting it after it exits. Luckily, this functionality can be included invisibly in the `PROFILER` class implementation.

SECOND MEASURE: WHY

The first measure determines where in the code the CPU spends most of its time. However, this measurement by itself can be misleading. Unless we understand *why* the CPU is spending the time it does in each section of code, we might end up making an unneeded optimization, or optimizing in the wrong way. To better understand why a given function takes longer than necessary, we must learn more about the context it was called in.

In the first measure, we can already count the number of times a function was invoked during a frame and certain values it was invoked with. We have seen how this data can be used to pinpoint some cases where a function is not used as intended. Although this in itself is useful, it would be more useful to know where the atypical function calls originate. Such data allows us to examine the code that produces the atypical function calls, which in turn allows us to examine the circumstances surrounding their invocation.

Luckily, we already have almost all the tools we need to accomplish this. As we saw in the first measure, we had to be careful how we treated the circumstances where a profiled function invoked another profiled function. The two solutions proposed in that measure lost an important piece of context: the fact that the second function was called from within the first. If we can preserve this information, we can better understand the cause of where a function's invocations are coming from.

The easiest way to capture the calling context of a function is by implementing the profiler as a tree. Each node in the tree corresponds to a profiled function, and its position in the tree shows the context in which it was called. Each profiled function can then be represented by more than one node, depending on how many places it was called from. Figure 9.2 shows an example of a profiled function hierarchy. In this figure, the frame consists of two profiled function calls, function A and function B. Functions A and B both call function C, causing function C to be represented by two different nodes.

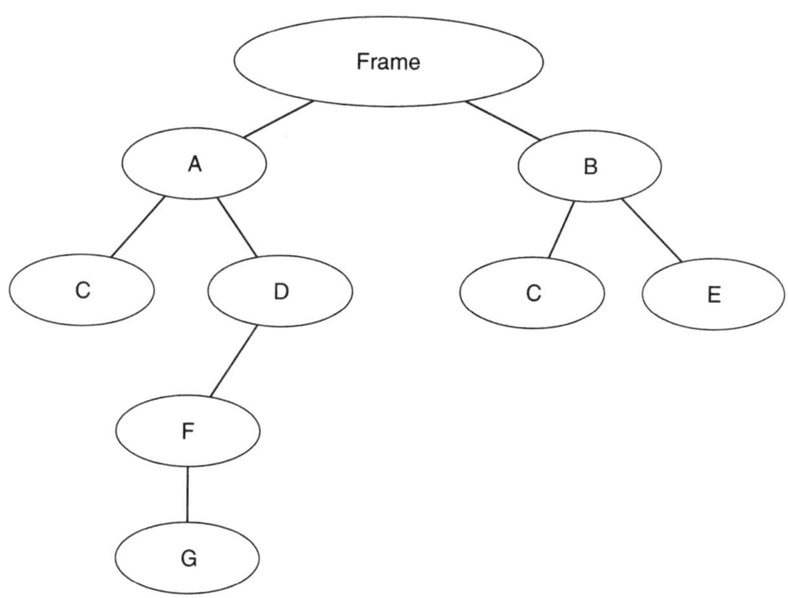

FIGURE 9.2 A profile hierarchy.

When using this method, there is no need to stop the timer for a function when it invokes another profiled function. Since we have a record of all the profiled functions invoked by a given function, we can easily calculate the time spent inside the first function's body by simply subtracting the time spent in any child functions in the tree. However, such an operation is usually not necessary, due to the way the results are presented.

Although Figure 9.2 is a valid profile hierarchy tree, in practice, a game contains many more profiled functions and its tree is much more complicated. The sheer amount of information available in a single profiled frame can be overwhelming, as illustrated by Table 9.1, and so we must find ways to limit the amount of information initially presented to the user.

TABLE 9.1 Example Hierarchical Timings for Figure 9.2

Function Name	***Time Spent***
Frame	100%
+ A	+ 70%
+ C	+ 30%
+ D	+ 39%
+ F	+ 25%
+ G	+ 15%
+ B	+ 25%
+ C	+12%
+ E	+ 11%

One of the simplest ways is to present the tree in a similar way to a Windows-style tree view. That is, initially present the user with just the first level nodes of the tree and allow him to expand and contract nodes as desired. This greatly reduces the amount of information presented initially, and allows the user to perform gross comparisons of the time spent in major sections of the game before diving into the individual functions.

MAKING THE CUT

Now that we understand where the CPU spends its time, and why, we are ready to finally make any optimizations needed. The types of optimizations that we can make are many and varied. Perhaps counterintuitively, the worst optimizations that we can make are those that simply speed up the code. These optimizations, including making functions inline and converting entire functions to assembly language, tend to obfuscate the original purpose of the code, making it harder to read and maintain. In cases where this is unavoidable, however, it is often good practice to keep the original code around, either in a comment block, or conditionally compiled in a debug build. This allows us to check the continued good behavior of the code, and to have the original code to refer to in case the optimized code must be altered.

The best optimizations that we can make are those that change for the better the order of complexity of any algorithms that we use, causing child functions to be called less often. After all, the fastest code is that which is never run. A large spike in the time taken for a given function under certain circumstances often indicates that a nonoptimal algorithm is being used.

For example, a quicksort algorithm used to sort transparent polygons will exhibit worst-case behavior when all of the transparent objects are already sorted. This situation can be easily remedied by using a structure such as a red-black tree to sort the transparent objects. Another good example of this is when a grid-based collision algorithm breaks down due to too many entities being present in a single grid cell. Moving to a dynamically updated collision structure such as a quadtree or octree can improve this by automatically changing the size of the cells to limit the maximum number of entities within each cell.

Although not strictly an optimization, bug fixes also play a large part in the optimization process. Oftentimes, a hierarchical profile shows that a function is called many more times than is expected for a given place. This more often than not indicates that some assumed condition in the code is not being met. For example, we might see that the path-finding code is being called far more often than is necessary when the player moves to a section of the map that an enemy cannot create a valid path to. Investigating further, we might find that the code for the enemy presumes that it has a valid path, causing it to try to move, which causes it try to make a path every single frame. Simply putting in a check for whether or not the enemy has a valid path before attempting to move him is a much better optimization than simply leaping directly into rewriting the pathfinder in assembly language.

FINAL MEASURE: RESULTS

Once the optimizations have been made, we need to measure their effectiveness: how much less time does the recently optimized code take? The easiest way to do this is to repeat the second measure with the new code and compare the results with the old. This final measure must be performed with the same test conditions (or as similar conditions as we can make them) as the second measure for the results to be comparable. For example, comparing results from a run with a heavy path-finding load against those from a run with a heavy collision load is meaningless; the perceived improvement in the path-finding routines occurs simply because it is called less frequently in the measured frame.

One of the most important things to remember when looking at the results of your optimizations is that the results won't be what you expect. Halving the execution time of a function rarely, if ever, halves the result that we see. This occurs because we deal with our timings as a percentage of the total time taken by a frame.

For example, a function that takes 32 percent of the frame takes 32 out of 100 parts of the frame, while a function that takes 23 percent of the frame takes 23 out of 100. If we then halve the time taken by the first function, what we have effectively done is remove 16 parts of the frame from the timings. This affects *all* of the results when they are measured again. Our optimized function does not take 16 out of 100 parts of the frame, but in fact actually takes 16 out of 84 parts of the frame, or around 19 percent. The second function in our example should now take 23 out of 84 parts of the frame, or around 27 percent.

Table 9.2 shows the results for multiple functions in this situation. Notice that although the `SortTransparency` function has been optimized and is now twice as fast as it was, this is not reflected intuitively in the measured times, which only show a 41-percent improvement. It should also be noted that the timings for every other function have apparently *increased*, although in actuality these functions still take the same amount of time that they did before. This is because the frame as a whole takes less time to process due to our optimizations, resulting in higher percentage timings for each of the nonoptimized functions.

TABLE 9.2 Results Might Not Match Expectations

Function	*% Before*	*Improvement*	*% After*
SortTransparency()	32%	50%	19%
Draw()	23%		27%
TestCollision()	15%		18%
Object::Run()	10%		12%
FindPath()	3%		4%
Animate()	2%		2%

Unless you have trained yourself in advance to expect this kind of result, this can be disheartening. After all, you've just optimized a function, making it in theory twice as fast as it was before (no mean feat in itself). However, the measured results show that the optimizations weren't as good as you thought, and you actually made everything else in the game slower . . .

APPENDIX About the CD-ROM

The CD-ROM that accompanies this book contains all of the example programs referenced in the text, in both binary and source form. Many of the example programs make use of the Windows programming API, and so are only usable on a Windows-compatible PC. The programs on the CD-ROM were developed using Microsoft® Visual Studio® and Microsoft Visual C++ 6, and project files for this compiler are provided for maximum ease of use. Although the source code supplied should compile with any compiler, it is recommended that you use the Visual C++ compiler to ensure correct operation of the example programs.

Additionally, the CD-ROM includes a full distribution of the most current (at time of printing) version of the Zlib compression library. The files for the distribution can be found in the `common/compression/zlib` directory. Although the Zlib library is free to use, you should read the license agreement at the top of the main header file, `zlib.h`, before using it in your own project. More information about the Zlib library can be found on the Zlib Web site at *www.gzip.org/zlib/*. All book figures are also included.

Before attempting to compile any of the source code, we recommend that you copy the files to your PC's hard drive, maintaining the relative paths of the directories. This allows the compiler to generate the intermediate files and the final output files.

The minimum requirements for compilation and use of the example code on the CD-ROM are as follows (although some of the example programs do not require DirectX):

- Windows-compatible PC
- Microsoft Visual C++
- DirectX 9.0 (or more recent) SDK

The CD-ROM is laid out in a simple manner. The root directory contains a directory for each chapter that is accompanied by one or more example programs, and two directories called `common` and `bin`. The example programs for a given chapter are located in their own directories within the folder for the relevant chapter. The `common` directory contains any source code that is referenced in a chapter, but is either not a stand-alone program or is referenced in multiple chapters. Finally, the `bin` directory contains the precompiled binary images for all of the example programs and their data, each of which can be found in a separate directory.

Index